Norbert Blei
DOOR TO DOOR

Door to Door

by

Norbert Blei

Ellis Press
1985

FIRST EDITION

"Wintering Near Death's Door" originally appeared in slightly different form as "Winter Makes Me Wonder If This Is Home" in the *Washington Post*. "A Death in the Village" appeared first in the *Milwaukee Journal*, Wisconsin. "In the Clearing" and "St. Pat—the End of the Rainbow" first appeared in slightly different form in the *Door County Advocate*. The author is grateful to these publications for permission to reprint them here.

Painting on the dustjacket cover, end paper pencil drawing, painting reproduced on page 7, and interior pencil drawings by Charles Peterson, Ephriam, WI, used with the artist's permission. Painting on back of dust jacket and uncredited interior drawings and photographs by Norb Blei, used with permission. Photograph on page 33 by Richard Klein, used with permission. Silverpoint and watercolor reproduced on pages 112 and 118 by Flora Langlois, used with the artist's permission. Envelopes reproduced on pages 145, 148, 150, and 152 by Howard Orr, used with the artist's permission. Paintings on pages 160 and 164 by Arlene LewAllen, used with the artist's permission. Drawings on pages 171 and 190 and photograph on page 193 by Ross LewAllen, reproduced with the artist's permission.

The poems in "Lost in Elburn" copyright (C) Dave Etter, from his books *Alliance, Illinois* (Spoon River Poetry Press, 1983) and *Home State* (Spoon River Poetry Press, 1985), used with the permission of Mr. Etter. Poems in "Crow Lady: Maggie Perry" copyright (C) Maggie Perry, used with the permission of the poet. Poems in "The Poet as Midwife: Sue Peterson" copyright (C) Sue Peterson, used with the permission of the poet. Poems in "The Summer I Was a Horse" copyright (C) Frances May, from *Night Letters, Tell Me About the People* and author's manuscripts, used with the poet's permission.

Published by The Ellis Press, P. O. Box 1443, Peoria, Illinois 61655, David R. Pichaske, editor.
Typesetting by *The West Bluff Word*, Peoria, Illinois.
Printing by D J Graphics, Peoria, and M & D Printers, Henry, Illinois.

ISBN 0-933180-73-X

Door To Door

DEDICATION

To Whom It May Concern:

The writer is not against fire numbers, volunteer firemen, paramedics, the county sheriff and police, the local post office and rural letter carrier, the highway department, etc. These are good people who give of themselves. Lord knows we need them. The writer's comments regarding the local fascination with fire numbers was merely an attempt to be facetious. His point was: Be wary in God's Country of all signs of big city life—especially numbers. People becoming numbers, places mapped out, cut up, names, everything made too accessible for too many. Life reduced to statistics.

If you like being #369521863210439991; if you would like the world to know you live at 489 S. Woodpecker Lane, Limelight, Door County, Wis. 3425678903261; if you prefer all the county roads marked with steel posts and quaint signs proclaiming Birch Bark Drive, or Sunset Lane; if it is to your advantage to have every road blacktopped and widened (two-lane roads giving way to four-lane highways), and every dirt road in the county paved; if you like trees removed or trimmed at anybody's whim; if you're acceptable to scenic and shoreline views lost to more condo and commercial development; if you like to see more of the peaceful interior of the county (farms, fields, the last stronghold of open acres) reduced to little lots filled with suburban-type boxes (which they are supposed to represent) called ranchettes or Retirement Heaven, The C.W. Pearsons; if you're willing to see small farmers abandon their livelihood and orchards bulldozed because development is more profitable than farming or raising cherries; if you like the idea of nameless, faceless big time investors involving their money in commercial enterprises hoping to fail—for tax write-off purposes (and sticking the county with yet another blight of a building or business on the landscape); if you yearn for more shopping malls, more conglomerations of gift shops, more traffic congestion, more water problems . . . you're going to love streetlights, increased police protection, parental watchdog committees, houses fenced in, locked up, lit 24 hours a day . . . Welcome to the good life. It's time to put the pink flamingoes in the front yard.

Just look around to see what has already been lost. Eventually all the numbers add up. And the total leaves all of us who love this place, short changed.

It's not a case of "Move back to Chicago if you don't like it here." It's a case of there eventually being no difference between a city's ugly urban sprawl and Door County. Then we'll all be "natives"; all our names and houses will be the same. And this place might just as well be called nowhere because it will have lost all those indefinable qualities of a natural landscape that made it unique.

Lest I the writer be accused of a conflict of interest, just another of hustler of Door County books, be assured that the writer's underlying theme has always been: This place is very special. Come see for yourself. Stay a while. Let it work its wonders upon your spirit. But don't screw it up.

You can't stop progress. Okay. But you can think about it. You can witness its after-effects. You can be thankful there are individuals and organizations who put the best interests of the county at heart for the good of others, the good of all, years and years down the road.

Mostly people complain only when their own toes are stepped upon. When "their" scenic view has been lost, when "their" business is in jeopardy, when "their" land speculation deals are in danger, when "their" peace and quiet is threatened by yet another roadside attraction. It's only human nature, of course. But it might be beneficial to listen to the other guy for a change, and both consider: Am I adding to the quality of life here, or am I diminishing the real value of the landscape for those who come after me, and have a need for such a place?

Just let it be known before they raise the huge sign above the Sturgeon Bay Bridge: THE DOOR COUNTY AMUSEMENT PENINSULA (formerly God's Country), that there were some here who could see what was coming. Some who did or said something. Many more who didn't give a damn.

The writer (and his Door trilogy: DOOR WAY, DOOR STEPS, DOOR TO DOOR) is for the native who digs in his heels and says: "No Sale;" for the outsider who holds the line; for all those in environmental organizations and government working for strict zoning; for anyone who in whatever small way forgoes the profit motive at the expense of the land and the quality of life in this county.

Preface

Notes At The Door

In my time here I have been many men: City man, country man, outsider, insider, husband, father, son, lover, hater, friend, recluse, traveler, believer, iconoclast, poet, painter, teacher, writer . . . door man.

*

Who stands there, poised, real and illusory, to be of service to someone. Gatekeeper, doorkeeper, porter, caretaker. Witness to arrivals and departures. The many personal journeys, others and his own, to many places. He offers directions. Provides access. The writer's way: to serve, to explain, to imagine, to enter other lives in other landscapes, to transform oneself in the process. To preserve.

> For the door is an entire cosmos of the Half-open . . . the temptation to open up the ultimate depths of being, and the desire to conquer all reticent beings . . . On May nights, when so many doors are closed, there is one that is just barely ajar. We have only to give it a very slight push! The hinges have been well oiled. And our fate becomes visible. And how many doors were doors of hesitation! . . . And what of all the doors of mere curiosity, that have tempted being for nothing, for emptiness, for an unknown that is not even imagined?
> —Gaston Bachelard, *The Poetics of Space*

To be the door itself . . .

> . . . "Now and again, however, an individual is called upon (called upon by *whom,* only the theologians claim to know, and by *what,* only bad psychologists) to lift his individual patienthood to the level of a universal one and try to solve for all what he could not solve for himself alone . . . " Erik Erikson speaking in *Young Man Luther* . . . The key word for me, of course, is "patienthood," for this is exactly who is involved for the poet or artist of either sex. Coles himself says elsewhere in the piece, "Not everyone can or will do that—give his specific fears and desires a chance to be of universal significance." To do this takes a curious combination of humility, excruciating honesty, and (there's the rub) a sense of destiny or of identity. One must believe that private dilemmas are, if deeply examined, universal, and so , if expressed, have a human value beyond the private, and one must also believe in the vehicle for expressing them, in the talent.
> —May Sarton, *Journal of a Solitude*

1

With the completion of *Door Way,* in June, 1981, the writer began to die again. The death of the writer's spirit.

Amidst the calm of *"Do I write again? What do I write next?"* appeared comments/criticism consigning *Door Way* to that literary limbo known as "regional" literature. "Regional" . . . meaning, life is elsewhere. Midwestern writers who stay here, write here, know this and must live with it all their lives, often with little recognition, little remuneration.

Though a writer's life is filled with its own rewards, it should be noted that a 1979 survey found the average author pulling in a staggering $4,775—or $4.90 an hour— annually, which included book royalties, freelance writing, movies and TV.

What is a writer worth? Really? Of what value is he? And to whom?

So this "writer-in-residence in Door County" had been living and dying for some time. The way it was and is. Now, suddenly faced with a "regional" bestseller in *Door Way,* he realized that basically it amounted to a shake of the hand and a kick in the ass at the same time. It's a foolish business, of course. And it takes a fool to persist in writing seriously. Especially a "regional" fool.

In the midst of the first phase of death and despair after *Door Way,* the writer received a letter from friend, poet, and fellow starving Midwestern "regional" author, Dave Etter: MORE GOLDEN GOSPEL FROM THE CORNFIELDS, he headed it—

> I'm just about ready to make a public (in print) blast at the people who keep using "regional" as if it meant something. It means nothing. It is only used as a putdown by slobs. A writer writes a book; it naturally takes place somewhere—and that's the end of it—period. A book takes place in South Dakota; another takes place in New York City—period. Neither one is regional. I'm really fed up with the stupidity I see and hear—and from people who should be thinking now and then. The first regional book will be about people who are living on Mars, but not until then. People are people, and they of course can't all live in New York City or Chicago. The word regional is for the telephone company and the fucking insurance companies; it is not for literature and the arts. It is only because Grant Wood painted Iowans that he is labeled "regional"—if he painted the fucking assholes in Brooklyn, he would never have heard the term. How's that, Norb? . . . The article "Can Writers Afford to Write Books?" damn near had me in tears. Christ, what an age we live in now. The way to fix these bastards is for every writer to boycott New York and Boston publishers and publish only with small presses. As the man said, " . . . They [the writers] are in effect subsidizing the publishing industry." . . . Booze? I'm nursing a bottle of Tia Maria through the month . . . How can we run away from home? On what? No place to go. I would be glad to stay here [Elburn, Illinois] the rest of my life if I could find a job . . . Met a guy from Chicago at Woodstock, who says that Chicago is a mean town full of mean people. They will get their kicks throwing slime on anyone lucky enough to be living somewhere else. They are also at each other's throats too. That's the way I see it . . . [a] Chicago guy, walking around with downers all day and night, hearing nothing but downer talk,

seeing only 20th century horseshit American manmade shit everywhere he looks. He's a product of the lousy environment; he's got nothing to uplift him when the dark angel brushes her wings across his beery face. There are no birch trees in his life, no County ZZ, no AC Tap, no box of potatoes to put in the trunk of the car, no walks to Europe Lake—not even any prairie Elburn to buoy his spirits . . . Am looking around for an excuse to drive up to Door . . . Then we will iron out all this shit and get ourselves a new philosophy so we can get through the goddamn eighties. We must keep down our rage and not do anything to hurt OURSELVES—nothing stupid, nothing childish, nothing suicidal . . . Hoping the phone will ring and someone will offer me a free-lance job to tide me over till November, when I depart for parts west to play the poet at various universities . . . and local taverns featuring go-go girls who take it all off two feet from my face. Want to raise a little hell with the boys out there and love up a girl or two. Wanna get real drunk and see the sun come up over a cornfield . . . Write soon . . . Thanks again for clippings . . . We're doing all right. You know why? Cause I say so, that's why. We're the BEST. I'll never doubt it. It's our role that we are playing—and it's the RIGHT role. It connects us with Kafka and Van Gogh and all those beautiful goddamn people.

*

A writer needs writer friends. Men friends, women friends. He needs their letters, their phone calls, their presence, their lives. He needs the love of strangers too, He needs the work of other writers and artists. He needs his own family, though too often they experience the worst of the writer—what's left—the dregs, the fears, the insecurities, the broken pieces, the uncommunicative parts, which often the family alone, unknowingly, in a love unspoken, serves to give the writer back to himself, in one piece . . . alive again.

*

What could be more "regional" than the *Door County Advocate?* Suddenly that door closed on the writer also:

The Door County Advocate—Tuesday, July 21, 1981
Our Point of View . . .

He Doesn't Agree

Things are looking up. It's only Friday and we're doing the editorial already. First, orders from Door County's No. 1 writer, Norb Blei. He wants it known that his profiles and Notes Along The Way will no longer appear because he disagrees with our new editorial policy.

We wrote to him and to several other contributors saying that

3

we were cutting down on the creative and non-Door material. This included Notes Along The Way, which are personal essays. Norb did a beautiful piece upon the death of William Saroyan. We set it in type but it was long and never managed to get in. Now you won't see it unless it appears in a book, which is a possibility since Norb is thinking about such a volume.

At our editorial conference we had to decide what we were. Does an article on Saroyan belong in the *Door County Advocate*? What are the limitations of our role? How big do we want to try to become? What is our market? We decided to retrench since there is more than enough local material to fill the paper. We would love to continue to run Norb's profiles of Door County people but he chooses not to submit at all any more and we respect his decision.

Norb also wants it known that he appreciates the support from readers in the past in the form of letters, phone calls, words on the street and that he will miss those readers immensely. Done, Norb, and we will miss your work too.

My intention was to write for the *Advocate* while continuing to publish short stories, novels, poetry, articles and books. To grow in place with the local paper. To grow as a writer with a particular vision of just what could be said within the confines of a local paper with an ever-increasing audience made up of not only locals but outsiders as well. People with summer homes and condos here, but permanent residences in Milwaukee, Madison, Chicago, Florida and elsewhere. Vacationers from the city who subscribe to the *Advocate* to keep in touch with the county. City people moving here permanently. The audience, as I saw it, would continue to expand and grow more diverse. And I had hoped the *Advocate* would recognize these changes and address them.

The local color aspects of the paper gave it heart and humor, and made it distinct. But there was still a need, I felt, to attend to other ideas, other readers as well.

My heart's desire was to see a local paper remain a local paper of news and announcements yet still reach. Reach in the way of solid profiles on locals and outsiders as well, written by the staff and freelancers. To reach with excellent photography—newsworthy and scenic. To reach with book reviews, movie reviews, restaurant critiques, columns from every little town and village, columns by those in the know (food, nature, politics, public services, etc.) and some hard-hitting editorials, especially in relation to a healthy environment and the growth of the county. I had hoped to see some space for serious poetry, historical articles, and even a little fiction—folk stories if nothing else. Occasionally some straight Q. & A. interviews with everyone from our local sheriff to our state representatives, just to find out exactly what's going on. Elected officials, especially, should be held accountable . . . explainable. We should not have to be subjected to the constant 'official' pap flowing from their offices.

To reach beyond the local because in this day and age nothing's local anymore, no matter how much we may desire to see ourselves separate from the mainland . . . no matter how much we may believe that living on a peninsula is old fashioned and quaint . . . and we're so far removed from the problems of the city or the rest of the world.

Preservation is a challenge. And if you're going to depend on the outside for your very existence (tourism, land development, the quality of individual life, etc.), then you better know what's out there, who these people are, what they're talking about, where they're coming from, to better understand what's going on within your own territory, especially within yourself.

Enter (and exit) this "local" writer. As long as I remained fenced in Door County, talking about Door County things, everything was hunky-dory. But if I crossed the border (literally and figuratively speaking) I was out-of-bounds, too far from home, a territory damn right strange. (So much for the world of ideas on Main Street.)

So in the summer of 1981, "Notes Along the Way" came to an end. The *Advocate* decided it had best pull back and concentrate on local news only, abandoning this writer and others as well.

One thing for certain: Any writer is expendable. The editor, Chan Harris, says he threw the ball back to me, and I took it and went home. I say I don't play games (though writers as a class are notorious whores). If, according to his rules, I was to write about Door County *only,* then it was all his game. Furthermore, in my neighborhood, no loaf is preferable to a patronizing half. And may you choke on the hunk you've kept.

*

What is the role of a writer? What is his value, especially in a place, a "region" like this? How does he, can he, should he attempt to rise above local journalism? Most importantly: Can he grow? Can he take his readers along with him to accompany this growth? How far should a writer reach? And aside from hard news and bad news, what of the good news of the human condition, wherever one finds it, in or out of Door?

> The writer is a creator of options. The writer enables people to discover new truths and new possibilities within themselves and to fashion new connections to human experience. Nothing is more vital for the creative artist than access to an audience . . . The writer properly insists on his right to express himself and to experiment as fully as he wishes. He does not believe he should be asked to explain what he means or to justify his belief that what he has produced deserves to be exhibited . . . An artist, like a philosopher, may draw energy from what he does not know; the deeper pursuit of the mysteries, the broader and more nourishing it becomes . . . The conditions of life are inseparable from the conditions of art.
> —Norman Cousins, *"Why Writers Matter"*

So the writer, faced with a closed door, looks at the materials at hand, the notes, the sketches, the notebooks, the pieces of conversation, the memories of people and place tucked deep inside, the plans for future books, and in his dying, laughs, cries and wonders: What the hell's to be done with all this?

> *Notes: —closing the door . . . summer women . . . the "thanks" of a box of red potatoes from Freddie Kodanko for including him in the book/"Did you see my baby picture hanging in the A.C. Tap?" he says./Freddie's going to Hollywood, he says, to be a movie star . . . or Ignacio Gonzales filling the back seat of my car with*

two-foot-long zucchinies, for a story of his own life he can't even read . . . under the apple tree at Charley's . . . waitress talk . . . the story of Winky bringing apples for the guy's coffin . . . the old man walking the road, waving at passing motorists, doing his little dance . . . Gust Klenke's night walks . . . the sun burning off the fog in an October field and the whole field suddenly woven in horizontal rainbows . . . Amos Rasmussen . . . Ossie Burstrom, machinist and rocking horse maker . . . Carl Carlson and his brother, John, both in their 80's, still logging the woods in winter . . . Dick Nelson, our environmental watch dog committee-of-one . . . Maggie, the poet, Crow Lady in the cornfields . . . Dusk and the final hours of another deer season, a few 'orange' men still in the woods as darkness approaches, a prayer, a meditation (a poem? a story?) I offer, something called "Putting Back the Deer," wanting a continued wildness of animals in my world . . . Overheard in Bley's grocery store in Jacksonport: "We've got a pig for you." "Oh, good!" "We're making sausage today . . . How do you want the bacon?" . . . the emptiness of Chicago streets at night . . . a line scrawled on a tavern wall in Chicago: "A closed heart can only be opened from the inside." What drunk could have put that there? And why? . . .

What's to be done with all this?

What's to be done about the death of Gust Klenke?

Requiem for Gust, January 31, 1981: Carol Newman saying to me in the Pioneer Store: "My mother is certain you're going to write a Gust eulogy. And maybe an obituary in the Tribune.*"*
My reply to her: "I almost wrote my own obituary this week" (rolling my car over on an icy backroad).
Thinking about Gust . . . were I writing for the Advocate, *I would have done something on Gust . . . the memory of Gust . . . Is this, then, the writer's role? To speak for these people? A spiritual mediator/medium not unlike a minister's role, a minister in the humanistic class of Phil Sweet? Yet the writer's role seems a different one entirely—to remember a man, a moment, in written words. (At Al's, too, this afternoon . . . the third or fourth comment: "How good that you had Gust in the book.")*

Gust's wake, February 1, 1982 . . . we go with the Tills . . . we're, perhaps, the only outsiders in the sea of local faces . . . I'm embarrassed (and pleased) by far too many acknowledgements for 'writing about Gus'. This, after all, is Gus' quiet celebration . . . How the man was loved! . . . a beautiful pine box coffin. To my dismay, I would have liked to see him laid out, honored in his work clothes . . .

The town seems diminished by his absence. I'll miss his bent form, bib-overalled Oskosh-by-Gosh body at the gas pumps, walking back and forth between the house and the garage, his dog hanging in his footsteps . . . Gust always carrying something in his hand, a tool, a part of something . . . while he was part of everything.

He'll be missed in the local coffee shops. He'll be missed by farmers, fishermen, townsmen, any stranger passing by who needed a hand and happened to luckily find him around to fix a car, a tractor, a lawn mower, anything in need of repair. Or lucky to just catch him to buy a bottle of honey and have old Gust pass that jar of golden light from his grease-worn, time-worn hand to yours . . . then maybe hear him breathe his special sigh, a long, distant, "Yeeeeeeeeeeeeeeeeep."

He'll be missed walking along the road's edge at night, heading toward the Ellison Bay swamp, flashlight in hand, broken zipper on his jacket, his waist gathered together in baling twine, tied in a neat bow. Where were you going, anyway, Gust? Why did you always seem to lose yourself with the dog toward the swamp at dusk?

And he'll be missed on the roads, slow driving that huge hunk-a-junk beige Buick of his with the trunk always partially open, lumber and tools and stuff sticking out. The backseat of the car filled with beehives.

He'll be missed, finally, in the fields, come spring . . . hives buzzing in sweet clover summer work . . . the splendor of fall . . . Gust in the fields insulating the hives for winter. What's to become of all you set out each day to do? Who will gather the honey, take care of the bees? And what of all of us, confused, seeking you out with things to be fixed?

There's talk in town, since Gust's death, of finding a fitting memorial to him. Some say a small park across from the Viking, in his name, would do just fine. Still others would like to raise a statue in honor of the man. (Which I think would cause Gust to smile, shake his head, center his cap more crookedly, and walk away.)

I think the painting by Chick Peterson honors the man perfectly.

The station itself is memorial enough. Long may it stand—in Gust's style, unpainted, broken windows, Standard sign at a tilt, abandoned cars, the dead school bus in the weeds, one pump, all the marvelous dark and greasy machinery inside, the faded red and white sign that says: GUS KLENKE'S GARAGE. And the HONEY sign too. Maybe a dog or two asleep in the sun and dust. Lilacs and vines crawling around the roof. Christmas lights strung each December. And the neon clock in the window to tell our way home at night. The shadow of Gust in there somewhere, mending machinery and hives.

*

What's to be done with all this? All this living and dying here? Beginnings of stories with no endings? Lives I may never come to know, to understand?.

To find other ways, other doors. To write other books.

To travel far beyond the door.

To provide access.

To be the door itself.

To be the writer . . . "to enable people to discover new truths and new possibilities within themselves and to fashion new connections to human experience."

8

Wintering Near Death's Door

> What does it all mean then? That you need a village, if only for the
> pleasure of leaving it. Your own village means that you are not
> alone, that you know there's something of you in the people and
> the plants and the soil, that even when you are not there it waits to
> welcome you. But it isn't easy to stay there quietly.
> —Cesare Pavese

In the dead of winter in the region where I live, the tip of Wisconsin's Door Peninsula, I like to think I see things more clearly.

Winter is both long and short. Though I walk thigh-high through drifted snow on a February morning, I am aware that the call of the chickadee has an air of spring to it. By midmorning, the sun (if it appears) casts softer shadows of birch, beech, and maple, reaching through my very window with a warmer light.

Yet I have journaled this place long enough to know the futility of hope. March and April snows are predictable. Blizzards arrive the same day you see the earth on your driveway for the first time since November. Ice storms lie in wait for the weekend in March you decide to drive across state, and you spin off the road a quarter of a mile from your own house, headed back in the direction you came. You are not going anywhere, yet.

It's a matter of settling in, in one's own head, till the young tomato plants (nurtured for weeks on the dining room windowsill) can be safely transplanted in the garden without the threat of a late frost—after the 4th of July. Or safely harvested (green with a touch of yellow) before the threat of an early frost—late August.

"Threat" intensifies the living here: threat of snow, wind, ice, fog, freezing rain, drifting snow, freezing temperatures, thin ice. Threat of receding lake waters, rising lake waters, electric storms, tornadoes. PCB's in our lake fish, alewives on our shores, contamination in our shallow wells because of fissures in the limestone Niagara escarpment upon which Door County is built.

An early frost, nipping the bud, threatens the cherry crop. So does a whipping wind in June or July, bruising the skins, turning the whole crop into juice cherries—unprofitable. Apples seem less susceptible to threats of all kinds—except for seasons of little rain, like last year, when the apples turn tiny, tough, and tasteless.

Stones are the real survivors in these parts. They crop up in our fields . . . mark the old fence lines, became part of the foundations of some of the oldest barns, and are fashionable in the fireplaces of the more lavish country homes and condos.

To "pick stone" in the fields at the end of winter is still a tradition and tribulation among local farmers lugging stone boats behind their tractors. Door County's legacy from the glacier age. There are buildings here built on bedrock. Soil depths of an inch or two.

Where *is* this place?

9

If you hold the palm of your right hand in front of you, you're looking, roughly, at the state of Wisconsin. The Door Peninsula is your thumb, with Green Bay tucked to the left of it, and Lake Michigan teasing the eastern shore. The lakeside is colder than the bay. But the bay freezes over in winter and the lake does not. To the north lies Washington Island, some 500 or so folk, some of Icelandic stock who, legend has it, keep passing the same $50 bill. You can get there year-round by ferry, though not as often or as quickly in winter.

Some 250 miles of peninsula shoreline. About 70 miles straight up to the "top of the thumb," where I live . . . just a prayer away from a mean passageway of crosscurrent waters called, appropriately, Porte des Morts, or Death's Door, where the remains of many an old ship still rest on the floor. Metaphysically, symbolically, what a better location for a writer to find himself? Ask not for whom the foghorn moans . . . though still I ponder: Did I choose this region of the heartland, or do I imagine it chose me?

I have lived here for almost 15 years now, but I am not at home. Once again, in the dead of winter, I rest uncomfortably in my burrow, shift to another vantage point, hoping to see things more clearly. I see that the connection to the mainland is actually a new bridge and an old bridge across the Sturgeon Bay Canal, and so the distinction between an island's separation and a peninsula's attachment rests in the imaginations of men.

Surrounding water is the true spirit of this place, though it is rarely honored as such. We have lost our myths here if, indeed, they ever existed. Except for a few names—Potawatomi State Park, Chief Oshkosh, etc.—our Indian lore is rather non-descript—Oneida bingo in the next county, occasional "troubles" on the Menominee reservation on the other side of Green Bay.

No traditions of Great Spirit enter our consciousness, affect our art, heighten the natural mysteries of living in these climes. We kill deer (1,482 last season) but don't dance to them or honor the hunting grounds. One of the sweet solaces of a solitary winter is getting to the bones of this. (Where, *truly,* is one's tribe?) To live within the interior and relish it . . . walk the roads alone, see every variation in light upon the snowy fields, from the faintest gold to the deepest violet. To ski the woods and read the language of each tree, the calligraphy of branches against an infinite white sky. To visit men huddled in ice shanties carrying on the work, the ancient dialogues beneath ice. To seek the old deities within the natural landscape and learn their restorative powers.

All this speaks of more than what is. More loudly in winter because of the nearness of vast space, the intensity of silence. And all this I have come to discover in 15 years as part of my mission here. A mission of one. The single, solitary writer who happens to find himself with no history of his own to speak of . . . no family, no traditions, no ancestral name on the plat map to call the land my own. But faced with a need to preserve and protect the sanctity of such a place upon occasion with words—words some of the natives, some of the business factions deem uncalled for.

They don't like to be called spoilers of their own nest. They resent the implication of greed—more of everything, more gift shops, more motels, more campgrounds, more condos, more shopping malls, more developments, more people dragging more of their urban blight over the new bridge which bypasses the old town of Sturgeon Bay. They don't like my choice of language. Who am I to be tossing stones?

I remain an outsider in their eyes. To many of the natives a "transplant." And to some of them a threat.

No history to speak of. So what do I know? In the middle of my life I want to continue what I began to do almost twenty years ago—living it, writing it within whatever form takes shape. Sometimes fiction, sometimes nonfiction. Here or elsewhere.

Neither facts nor history offer as much meaning as the seashell-colored sunrise over open water and ice this morning, the sound of one creaking birch tree in conversation with the wind, the smell of cedar, the ghostly movement of the deer all night under a sky raining stars upon tree tops. The only evidence in daylight: tracks in the snow leading far from the petty conflicts of civilized minds.

It's a precarious place, where a writer finds himself. Out of season. But a place worth keeping a watch on in spite of or because of past and present history.

From Indian tribes who once fished sturgeon from the bays; to the early French explorers, Jean Nicolet, in search of a passageway to the Orient; to the Scandinavian pioneers who found this landscape a mirror to their native land—woods, water, climate—to an area of the Midwest known for shipbuilding, cherry and apple orchards, quaint and quiet resorts in Egg Harbor, Fish Creek, and Ephraim offering village life, summer and autumn solace to those weary of city life; to its threat of destruction since the late 60's and the onslaught of tourism.

Over 2 million visitors the last summer season.

Over a 100 million dollars annually for the tourist industry.

Is it any wonder we'll need a wider or yet another new bridge soon?

Everyone wants his piece of the peninsula. Everything's up for sale.

In the dead of winter all of this can be seen in a starker light: the new suburban-type homes buried in the woods and fields of summer, now visible on a winter's day. The condos ringing the limestone cliffs, the shorelines, the backwoods of villages, remain forever (time-shared or privately owned) an unnatural presence upon the land. The survey stakes (painted red or beribboned) thrust above the snowcover, foreshadowing just what field will next be cut into little pieces.

What this place offered initially, essentially, was nothing. Nothing but clean air, fresh water, pristine beaches, cool summer nights, brisk bright autumns, woods, wildlife, acres of silence, nothing to do but find your place in the natural scheme of things and be still. Every road, it seemed, eventually led to water and all its forgiveness, all its mindlessness.

Nothing any man can hope to possess. Yet we've made an industry of it here. Selling illusions so much a foot, so much an acre, until only the realities we once fled surround us, blights upon a shrinking landscape. Dissatisfaction with our own lives. Our inability to read the waters. The spirits cannot be heard on an Arctic Cat. They do not ride in Winnebagos.

Which leaves me here in the midst of this, both in and out of place. God's Country, some still call it. While others, knowingly or not, seem hellbent in renaming it another Paradise Lost.

And all of us are to blame. I've come to see that too in winter.

As a writer of fiction, I bear no guilt. But as an author of some articles and books about the county, I rest uneasily with my words this winter. I'm ready to close the door on nonfiction. I've taken plenty to nourish my own spirit, and hopefully shared it with others in equal parts. But have I been good or bad for this place? Every word seems an invitation. Even to say "stay away" brings on the hordes. Yet to say nothing is to accept everything. And any attempt to air things in the open brings on the native's ire: "If you don't like it here, go back where you came from."

But what's a writer do who suddenly finds himself a "regionalist," a designation he never aspired to, much less understands? His writing, his life, locked in an area he escaped to for the sole purpose of living peacefully and frugally for a while, practicing the art of writing, imagining other settings, other lives?

11

I'm from an ethnic, Slavic, Chicago neighborhood. Much of my work still remains there. This is not my "place"; these are not my people. This was supposed to be the cabin-in-the-woods, the Thoreauvian retreat many writers aspire to. Merely a way station before moving on.

Yet here I remain (after *15* years?), faced with a Crusoe consciousness, surrounded by water, too far north to suit my taste for sun, too distanced from my closest friends, doubly doomed in winter—I *can't get* out . . . I'll *never* get out— living a life I never expected to explain, let alone live. Loving and hating it.

Loving the wonder of each season, the old but constant surprises outside my door—be it fox, deer, pileated woodpeckers, or northern lights. Winter moons more immediate and illusive than any writer imagines; the unbearable beauty of snowfields that merge horizons into sky, extinguishing any man's desires, lifting him to a vision of the holy realm; relinquishing digital time and hour hands for the last autumn call of the whippoorwill, the return of evening grosbeaks, meadowlarks, the geese navigating directly over my writing place both departing and arriving. There are more "signs" here than any man can interpret in one lifetime.

Sounds, too: the foghorn in Death's Door is a comfort beyond church chimes (which can also be heard). The fishing tugs chugging out into the waters around dawn, puffing back into the harbors mid-afternoon with crates of whitefish. Snow falling . . . one becomes attuned in time to hearing even *that*. A freakish electric storm blossoming the skies on winter's edge . . . no weatherman can predict *anything* in these parts. They chalk it up to "the lake effect," a local brand of meteorological poetic license.

Then there's that unexpected clap? boom? explosion? coming sometimes in March or April, usually in the middle of the night. You lie there asleep, still another night of blue snow, and a sound both near and distant attacks the dreaming mind with a force you are sure has lifted the roof heavenward. But then you swallow your heart and remember it's probably the ice cracking in the bay, 20 to 30 inches of it, shifting, breaking up, following whatever ancient time and water table ice alone comprehends in this northern latitude.

Loving some of the people too, particularly the oldtimers, who pass too quickly from a writer's loving eyes, who made sense of this land—farmers, fishermen, orchardmen, handymen, rural folk—who made little or nothing of their lives, but lived deeply in place, holding the secrets of stones. No developers, condo occupants, Chambers of Commerce can replace their loss. Or what they gave to this place by leaving it essentially alone.

Men like my late neighbor Charley Root whose very name bespoke his entire life: a poor farmer, a maker of fish boxes. Chet Elquist, fisherman, cherry grower, all-around handyman who knew more truths to the water, the earth, the good quiet life than every minister in the county could hope to explain in a lifetime of Sunday sermons. Gust Klenke, garage man and beekeeper whose faith was the machinery of man and the mystery of bees . . . which he expressed simply by helping anyone in need. "How much do I owe you, Gust?" All of them now gone.

Men still around like Ignacio Gonzales (a transplant too), a migrant who followed the crops in 1969, picked cherries here, and never found his way back. He's still picking them. Still poor. Still witty and wise and looking for work this winter . . . age, 75. "You gotta a roof to shobel? I do anything [Big smile]. Jest lemme know." Still raising and eating rabbits.

And Freddie Kodanko, a simple truck farmer, still living alone with his dozens of cats, still holding court at the AC Tap, still relying on his old Ford tractor as his sole

means of transportation, having lost his driver's license years ago over a fondness for firewater. You don't need a license to drive a tractor. Farmer smarts. And should the day come . . . Freddie will no doubt find a horse.

And Uncle Tom Collis, the pancake man, an old Chicago Greek whose gift of love for man and country remain 100% genuine.

And Al Johnson of Sister Bay, famous for his Swedish restaurant with the goats on the grass roof. A place where some of us hang out, especially winter mornings, exercising our sanity over cups of coffee, world news, point spreads, bad jokes, gossip, and the Green Bay Packers.

Al, along with his wife Ingert, seem the man and the woman of the hour who best understand the balance between business and beauty, growth and destruction, who put as much into the county—encouraging the old world ties, Scandinavian arts and crafts, festivals, authentic buildings and landscape, nothing shoddy, appealing to a tourist's highest tastes—as they take out.

Loving the place for many of these people and others who often unknowingly provide hope to a writer's heart who, in the darkest hours, just before the annual summer tourist rush, fears the whole county is lost.

Still, the writer's territory . . . wherever . . . the human heart. The "material" is all around me—paradise lost or found. I suspect I would find myself fiddling with words, watching it all go up in flames. And how can a writer but sit up and take notice if he considers no more than the ads in the local *Door Reminder*:

"Hi There! Friends and neighbors of Freddie Kodanko. You are invited to my 70th birthday party at the AC Tap on the 6th. Hear my albums and dance and have a beer with me."

"Paying up to 28¢ lb. for disabled or problem cows, bulls, heifers, steers. Must be able to walk."

"REWARD OFFERED For the name and proof of the persons who started two very nasty and slanderous stories about me . . ."

Stories indeed. And then what happened? Who? Where? Can you imagine that?

—Delicious gossip—re-imagining our lives. Any writer's home turf.

Still loving and hating it all.

Hating the *Winesburg, Ohio* and *Main Street* consciousness which still exists here. The people of *Spoon River* live just down the road, bitter and stifled lives resurrected in my time and place.

The Christian self-righteousness which is neither Christian nor right. Hypocrisy heightened to a sameness of niceness that it damn well better snow another ten inches tonight because I want something *real* to vent my energies upon tomorrow. Even though, eventually, a writer must do what writers do: turn it all into themselves and see what can be made of it.

Hating a culture so insular that despite the panoramas from the highest limestone bluffs, the purest air begins to suffocate. I need more room to breathe! I want *out*!

And I don't want a month of Florida sunshine, or a 3-day package tour to Vegas.

I want a couple of nights in Nicaragua, a week in El Salvador, a peek at Poland. A shot at Angola, South Africa, and Afghanistan. I want the view from the other side of the door, the other end of the bridge, though I can't make change this morning for a five dollar bill, and I know damn well I'm not going anywhere now but Al's for a cup of coffee and the local news.

No one seems to feel deeply about anything or anyone anymore. I feel a numbness, beyond winter's cold, entering me: It doesn't matter who's president; let them work for a living like everybody else; nobody ever helped me; there's a lot of that going around; nice weather we're having, huh?

My sense of spirit grows dull to a degree that I begin to share Max Brod's feelings about Kafka: " . . . nine elements of despair and one of hope." I need a Graham Greene priest to confess my confused compassions to concerning the spirit of lost souls, and acts of good faith toward the human race.

Yet here I remain. Stuck in place. Spinning my wheels on ice. Hating a condition of selfish interests at the expense of a landscape and way of life we all need for the good of our souls, but being neither willing nor able to do more about it than bitch and work it out with words.

A passionate condition, nevertheless. A writer's home brew. It keeps me alive.

Alive enough to witness an animal crossing a field the other 15-degree-below-zero-morning, suddenly leap from the blinding snow cover and disappear into thin air.

Alive enough to recall a winter past when I lost the car on an icy backroad, turned it over into a field, and after pondering my predicament for a moment—no one saw me, no one lived nearby, no one would be coming to rescue me—I rolled down a window and crawled into and out of the snow. Then turned in my tracks, saw how ridiculous the car looked up-ended, and began to laugh. "Dead in Door County"—I began to write my own obituary. No . . . not me . . . not here . . . not yet.

To live to tell about it. That's all a man can do.

Continuing to imagine the metaphysical, geographical, ecological, philosophical dimensions of this place, caught in the middle of the Midwest, in the middle of my life. Planting my feet in deeper, dreaming my escape—which door next? But always mindful of one of Wisconsin's own writers, Glenway Wescott, who made it out of here: "There is no Middle West. It is a certain climate, a certain landscape; and beyond that, a state of mind of people born where they do not like to live . . . How much sweeter to come and go than to stay; that by way of judgment upon Wisconsin."

Though his most compelling book of short stories, by title alone, gives a writer pause to consider carefully the boundaries of his life and art—*Good-bye Wisconsin*.

14

The Coop

It sits, huddled in the woods, its cedar shingles blending with the trees, just far enough from the house to appear separate, distant, though it is connected by a dirt path, and an underground electrical line to provide communication and light.

For a long time it stood there, an abandoned chicken coop, a relic of the rural past, like a story told or waiting to be refashioned for another vision, another voice. I imagined William Carlos Williams' poem of white chickens and a red wheelbarrow set amidst these woods in summer rain. So much depends upon . . . seeing twice.

I must have opened the door to the white-washed interior more than a few times in those years when it stood there through the seasons, sometimes in view, relegated to an abandoned storage shed, a hiding place for kids to play and reimagine.

The previous owner, a sailor, a wheelman on the Great Lakes, had pretty much allowed it to become that when his wife died, the woman who lived alone and raised chickens while he was away. Upon his retirement and her death, he slowly filled the small building with broken tools, old furniture, rusty cans, a bed spring, a large tin to store grain, a cracked dresser mirror, a bird cage, a broken box of lime, a roll of chicken wire, and his battered sea trunks filled with mildewed magazines, newspapers, books, and an assortment of rocks—treasures from voyages on the Great Lakes. Objects of little use. Things men find hard to throw away. A legacy of an old sailor's life and the egg lady who minded the land in his absence.

I honored his preservation of the coop for years, peeking through the barn-sash windows at times in revery, always spotting something I had not seen before—a coil of rope, milk-colored glass eggs to give the chickens a start—expecting the loneliness of objects to explain a man's life, undisturbed. Hoping someday the white chickens might return.

At times alone, or introducing city friends to my new homestead, I would open the door of the coop and enter the musty darkness, never taking more than a few steps, intruding on a family of red squirrels who had taken occupancy, scattering everything in their frenzied lives. The women would scream. The men, shake their heads. Life in the country, I'd smile.

My children deemed it haunted, somewhat off-limits, out of bounds. Though inviting enough for Halloween pranks and scavenger hunts . . . tacking messages inside the door.

The roof had begun to leak near the lower end of the shed roof. The cedar boards inside were deteriorating and a smell of rotting wood merged with the smell of mildew, the partially earth floor hard with old chicken droppings, the sun's warmth upon skeins of spider webs, the glow of the white walls (not unlike the gritty, dull sheen of fresh country eggs), the smell of rain, the coziness of snow, and the cool air of the surrounding woods—birch, maple, and pine.

The outside was slowly working its way in. Under washes of moonlight, the layering of blue snow and rain-dark shingles, I would stare at its transformations from

15

a distance. Awaiting a time when perhaps the only evidence remaining might be the pulpy particles of a fallen branch left to disintegrate to earth undisturbed on the forest floor. Some small plant life, dead leaves, and a mushroom or two.

*

For almost eight years I worked in a small, upstairs bedroom of the house facing the road. The room had a gabled roof, and as I sat at the center of the desk, the ceiling swept down upon each shoulder lending me the strange comfort of being nestled between wings.

Stacked orange crates served as bookcases. The walls radiated with my water-colors, art reproductions, photographs, newspaper clippings, etc. . . . anything that made me think, smile, or desire and could be taped or tacked to the wall.

An old army cot occupied the back wall. Beneath it were stacked still more paintings, manuscripts, carbons of published work, boxes of old letters. An army footlocker, which held much of the same, sat at the foot of the cot. The back wall itself I gradually transformed into a watercolor-mural, alive with graffiti. I urged others as well to write or paint upon it.

I remember painting a sun (which usually manifests itself in many of my watercolors) in the upper left-hand corner. The largest sun I had ever painted. While allowing it time to dry, I turned my back and resumed working at the desk. Sometime later, glancing over my shoulder, I noticed a rim of watercolor had gathered along the lower arc of the sun—vibrant reds, oranges, yellows—and in that instant, begun to trickle down the wall. Grabbing a paint brush, I attempted to both stem the tide of the trickle and redefine it, adding, for some unexplainable reason, a dash of yellow, and turning the whole accident (vertical stroke after vertical stroke) into an old fashioned birdcage.

I sat and pondered the sun and the birdcage for some time till I recalled an incident from Nikos Kazantzakis' autobiography, *Report To Greco*. He relates how at the age of four his father gave him a canary and a revolving globe, and how, closing the doors and windows, young Nikos would open the cage and let the canary fly free in his room. The bird, when it came to rest, would perch on top of the globe and sing for hours.

Suddenly I moved to the wall again, grabbed a brush, wet the colors, painted an open door to the cage, a bird perched on top of the cage, singing, and a man's head (unruly hair, bushy mustache), which vaguely began to resemble me. A man with an open birdcage on his head, a bird singing from the top of the cage, and a luscious sun looking on.

I turned again to the passage in Kazantzakis and copied his words directly on the wall: "Wandering insatiably over the earth for years, greeting and taking leave of everything, I felt that my head was the globe and that a canary sat perched on the top of my mind, singing."

As I look back now, that painting helped set the tone of what I felt in that room.

The room became my obsession: writing, reading, painting watercolors, adding more and more to the wall.

Later a large white bird appeared on the very center of the wall, painted in watercolor and acrylic (white on white), its presence mysteriously visible and invisible. The wall was also heightened in places (at various times) with occasional shots of spray enamel: blue, green, white, yellow.

A cloud or two developed. Also some stars . . . green, violet, blue. And a large, lemon-slice of a moon, which I watercolored on the upper right-hand corner.

16

All of this happened gradually. And served as a break . . . yet another inspiration to write. I would sit at my desk sideways, facing east, reading, thinking, daydreaming, my feet propped high upon a stool . . . the road, the woods, the birch trees, all of nature in my peripheral vision to the right, while on my left would be the wall, beckoning: paint or say something else.

I had put a small hook-and-eye latch at the top of the door to lock myself in. No visitors. No interruptions. Please leave me alone.

A man could lose himself in such a room. I wandered in it insatiably for years. Locking the door behind me, I was immediately changed. It was *my* room. It was the room of a writer determined to wrestle with all the usual assortment of demons and angels. It was a room where I could smoke, drink, tell myself and the world what I felt in words and paintings. I had a phone. I could hear the movement of the family downstairs. I was in touch with everything.

The light was extraordinary up there, above it all, especially in winter. And so was the view. The room glowed in a February sun, warming the desk, bouncing off the snowdrifted roof outside the front windows and onto the white painted walls. There were times I was certain I held it in my hands. I lived in the tops of birch and maple. I moved with the wind. Read the elements from rain to ice. Told time by the arrival of swallows, the silence of the last whippoorwill's call. I learned there are only two seasons, and one's work was all beginnings and endings. All else was the balance of grace. A high-wire act.

On the wall behind me I recorded more graffiti to remind me of the way:

TO BE ON THE WIRE IS LIFE; ALL THE REST IS WAITING
        —Tightrope walker Karl Wallenda
        shortly before he fell to his death

I TRUST ALL JOY
    —Roethke

        THERE US A DANGER THAT ONLY
          OUR MISTAKES ARE NEW
            —Ball

TO SEE AND TO TRANSFORM
    —Alan Watts   REPETITION KILLS THE SOUL
                                  —Mailer

      NOW WHEN I GET BACK
      I EXPECT TO FIND ALL OF YOU
      RUNNING THROUGH THE STREETS
      HOLDING GREAT BUNCHES OF WILDFLOWERS
          —Kenneth Patchen

I wrote *The Second Novel (Becoming A Writer)* in that room. Such a joy. I never touched the earth. I wrote a number of short stories, a play, poetry, magazine articles and book reviews. I began what would become my first collection of short stories, *The Hour of the Sunshine Now,* and my first nonfiction book, *Door Way.* I painted watercolors galore, sending them off to friends and strangers as letters, my words penned or typed in the clear spaces.

I envisioned much more: poems, stories, paintings, books. I merely entered the room, closed the door behind me, and felt the fire: feelings, words, forms, color, and light. The room never failed me. Such was my faith in place.

IT TAKES A MAN TO MAKE A ROOM SILENT
—John Cage

*

There are times, especially the early dark hours of winter mornings, when I leave the warmth and light of the house behind me, trudge knee-deep in snow toward the coop, pull the door open into a white arc at my feet, and step into the darkness with a vague trepidation, fully expecting to find myself seated at the typewriter with the flip of the light switch.

Spectres of animals too, birds, snakes, ancient voices, inhabit and imagine my darkness.

It is a fear to be met only by fire.

It is a fear I wish to explore in words and paintings, in journeys in this immediate landscape or a long distance from here.

Sometimes I light a candle. Extinguish the electric light. Remain in the darkness, awaiting the sun.

EVERYTHING IS THERE BEFORE YOU DISCOVER IT
—Bill Stipe

I carried that thought with me from the wall of the upstairs room to the chicken coop, much further away.

The children were getting older. They needed separate rooms. My daughter would occupy the room where I felt most free, most alive, most in touch with the natural world outside and the family, downstairs, living within.

The possibility of building an extra room was considered but quickly dismissed as too costly.

I could work in our bedroom, but that was too small.

I could work in the corner of the living room, but that was too distracting.

There was always the garage—impossible.

The cellar—too dark and damp.

Then I discovered the coop. Which was always there.

*

On September 28, 1976, the work began: the clearing, renovating, and gradual transformation of the coop. Somewhere in the drawer of this desk is a small notebook containing a record of daily progress and impressions.

Thumbling through its pages I read some of the entries, relive that time:

> September 28, 1976
> I begin emptying the coop of old junk—furniture, rags, an old love seat, 4 broken pieces of luggage belonging to Elmer Daubner [former owner], the old seaman. Windows, doors, a canister of lime, a broken shovel . . . a box of old books, all from a ship's library. One of the books contains a love story, hand-written upon

the printed pages, running in sequence. A seaman's old love affair? More interesting than the book.

September 30, 1976
I tear out what remains of the floor over the bare earth. Crowbars, hammers, etc. The terrible dust. Rotting wood in the back wall and lower roof. Johnny Gonzales comes by, helps me rip out the floor. Mike Till comes in the late afternoon, helps me lift a huge rock from the earth floor, checks on the progress of the building. His knowledge of construction, material, design, is an invaluable resource.

Pa [Mr. Carl Carlson, a neighbor across the road] and Uncle John [Pa's brother] arrive about 2 P.M., lend a hand, and begin to jack-up the coop so a concrete floor can be poured. Pa wants to do it his way . . . not willing to listen to Mike Till's ideas. "You don't have to be an architect to do this," says Pa of the old school of native builders, plumbers, all around handymen. Watching Pa and Uncle John work . . . like an oldtime comic movie. Laurel and Hardy, Ben Turpin, Buster Keaton, the whole lot of them. "Now how will we do this?" asks Pa. Uncle John stares, holds his head with his crippled hand. Through trial and error the coop is raised. Common sense and hard work reveal much of the meaning to their daily lives.
John Gonzales stops by. Too much joking and conversation at one point. Pa saying to all at hand: "Sometimes one man can do more than eight of them."
"Oh, then I'll leave," says Gonzales, winking.
"Oh, I don't mean you," says Pa. (He means *all* of us.)

October 6, 1976
Time Capsule: Buried in the sand (a day before pouring the concrete) at approximately the place where my desk and chair will rest (the 3rd window, east) the following: 1 glass egg (which Bridget saved from the junk in the coop); 1 note (left from a scavenger hunt during Christo's 10th birthday party), the note reading: *Go to the Painting of the Crow;* 1 old pipe.

October 7, 1976
While Pa is finishing the concrete he is asked about the new Lutheran minister. "Well, I really don't know what to say about him," says Pa. "He's one of these young guys does things a little different. But they're all headed the same way. They just go around the corner a little different." Pa and Uncle John come back and forth all day checking on the concrete.
When they finally leave I tell Pa to send me a bill or drop it off when he goes past the house in the morning. "That can wait for a rainy day," he smiles.

After pouring the floor, most of the work that remains is mine, except for Bruce

Schaufer's help with the windows. The rest of October and into November finds me cutting studs for the windows, replacing cedar shingles outside, cutting headers, and insulating the walls.

The weather is changing. I am fighting the approach of winter. I am so far behind in my own writing as a result of the coop, I rarely think of myself as a writer anymore.

Late in the afternoon of November 3rd, 1976, Don Peot completes the installation of the electrical line. Darkness sets in early. Snow begins to fall. I connect an extension line to a socket and for the first time electric light fills the coop. I move the light around in my hand for a long time, from corner to corner, wall to wall, familiarizing myself with all the possibilities of shadow and illumination within this habitat.

November 4th, the final entry for 1976. Winter has set in. I cannot proceed with the completion of the coop till next year. I both delight and despair in my defeat. I will go back to the upstairs room and write for one last time.

In June, 1977, I begin the final push: insulating the ceiling, nailing cedar boards (cut by Pa from his woods) to the walls and ceiling, laying a wooden floor over the concrete, varnishing it, making window casings (inspired by the Santa Fe artistry of Jerry West and Charley Southard, who shape and carve casings in a New Mexican/Spanish style, two wizards in wood, metal, adobe, and the fine arts).

There are hundreds of small jobs to be done. I have sworn off writing one word till I can occupy my new place.

Every day seems the same. I rise early each morning, walk to the coop, and pick up where I have left off. Though I experience a joy in building something physical with my own hands, I grow weary and anxious. When the hell will I ever be done? I vow never again to take on a project like this. I want to close the door and begin writing again.

August 8, 1977: The coop is finished. I have moved in. It is occupied. I write some letters to loosen my fingers, to tell others I'm here now, in the coop, writing again. I begin to write a profile in memory of Bill Beckstrom, which will one day become a chapter in *Door Way*.

(A few years later I go upstairs to my daughter's bedroom and begin to cover the wall with coat after coat of white paint. The words disappear rather quickly. The sun persists for weeks. And then it is gone.)

*

I open the door, draw it tightly behind me till I feel the latch click, and flip the light switch by the entrance which illuminates only the lamp over the typewriter, bathing that corner in warm light. The rest of the coop remains dark—a deliberate plan on my part, the comfort of shadows around my back.

I may burn some incense. I may stare out the east window a while, adjusting my sight to the season's light. I may focus a single eye through a small crystal hanging in the window, seeing the world out there in myriad: tree, rock, earth, sky, to the final power. I may hold one of the primitively fired pots of Spanovich in both hands, feeling comfortably complete, in touch with form, reaching to the very sun or moon outside that window. "I Wear the Morning Star" proclaims the poster on the wall to my left. Prayers come unexpectedly when we do not voice them.

On such a morning as this, I may pick up a brush and begin to paint.

It is good to be inside. Here. In touch with all this.

When the time demands it, I will sit at the desk, pour some coffee, light some tobacco, possibly rummage through the week's mail. I will answer some of it, for letters promise both a release and a delay, helping to orient the writer's spirit, redefine the hope in proceeding with the other work at hand. Every letter we write is to ourselves.

Or I may stare out the desk window a while, unconsciously seduced by the woods and all the elements: rain, snow, wind, sky, birds, animals, leaves, moon, light, and stars. Distractions, yes. But mesmerizing moments. The silence speaks. Images take shape. I write, unaware I began. Hours pass before I see anything clearly in the window again.

This is today, yesterday, and tomorrow.

I am sitting here in the midst of a winter storm.

The trees are in bud.

It is so hot and humid today my bare arms stick to the desk.

The harvest moon in a far field . . . the whippoorwill calls.

I am no longer in touch with sky and the tops of trees as I was in the upstairs bedroom. I inhabit the earth now, the space of chickens, eye-level with the trunks of trees, my feet joined to the roots of ferns and flowering plants. I share the composure of stones. The low shadows lengthening toward me. The still-life beyond glass.

This is a love affair with place.

I am beside myself with poems . . .

In winter
I have webs here
of no design,
spider sacs
of no exit,
sea shells
beached on windowsills;
a moth adhered
to death
upon a cedar wall,
a feather of a
golden flicker,
a wing of a
Monarch,
a package of
cactus seed,
a long strand
of hair
I pull apart in my hands.

                                        I don't want to
                                        speak the language
                                        anymore . . .
                                        am,
                                        loved,
                                        lost,
                                        be
                                        buried in
                                        back pockets . . .
                                        naming

22

is not knowing.
Hear me
far beyond the door,
speak to me
in branches,
question me
in stone,
command me
in creek water.
I'll say
the space
of spider web,
laugh the night
of whippoorwill,
love light
within ice.

There will be no winter.
There will be no spring.
Instead,
a time here
called winsprin.
Days of only moonlight.
Nights of nothing.
The temperature hovering cold.
Mornings will either begin fogbound
and end in hesitant, freezing rain
or vice versa.
All the villagers will remain damp inside,
uncertain of each other,
unhappy.
As now.
Nights will be the color of rainy tombstones.
Clocks will be buried in old medicine cabinets
smelling of iodine.
You will know it is morning
by the distortion of trees
trembling into crosses
on wet windowpanes.
And you will bow your head.
Your hands will become strangers.
And you will not dance.

*

My intention was to keep the coop uncluttered. Every room I have worked in has
eventually gotten away from me.

The space within the coop seemed serene.

Rural. Country. Woodsy. The common touch. From the aroma of freshly
sawed cedar upon the walls and ceiling, to the seasons naming themselves within their
particular light, the glow of the lamp upon the wooden desk, the view of the natural

world's beauty from each window. The promise of new beginnings within a framework of the past.

This same wooden desk that I have lugged with me for years from my father's basement in Chicago. The native and new labors of all those who helped put this coop in place. The painting table which I refashioned with barnwood from my neighbor, Charley Root, soon after his death; the carved window casements echoing another landscape but at home here; the same orange crates of books; a few paintings and assorted artwork on the walls, beginnning with Ross LewAllen, Jerry West, Arlene LewAllen, and Virginia Tibbetts. (To be followed by Henry Miller, Kenneth Patchen, Howard Orr, Charley Southerd, Bill Tate, JoAnn Hoppe, Gil Eaton, Mildred Armato, John Hogan, Earl Linderman, John Nichols, Chris Spanovich, and others, in every way, shape, and form.)

It keeps on coming. Objects of art from many friends. Most of it eventually finding a home here on my walls, windowsills, shelves, this very desk. All of it bespeaking the sender. All of it affecting me and the aura of the coop. The coop crammed now with color, shape, form: paintings, prints, postcards, weavings, sculpture, pottery, glass, plants, stones, shells, clippings, graffiti, carvings, photographs, candle holders, crystals, stained glass, masks, kites, calendars, buttons, milagros from Mexico, Navaho rugs, Guatemalan trouble dolls, Greek icons, Indian fetishes, bones, books and more books.

All of which I need and love. All of which reflect the spirit of the makers and givers, who in turn transform me and the space within.

I began with a desk, a chair, a painting table, an army cot, a footlocker and some files. And at the moment every space is filled but the ceiling and the narrow passageway between the door and my desk.

Wonderful clutter. Wonderful habitat to look into and find oneself in the beginning and end of each day.

Glorious objects of art and otherwise to hold one's attention, center one's desire, lead a writer into his own imaginings. And then to bring something back, wholly new, yet graced unconsciously with energies mysterious, miraculous, and ancient.

This is what comes to me . . . this morning . . . this evening . . . this long night . . . *here* . . .

And about this time I find the natural structure of this piece I am writing in and about the coop begin to break apart in my hands, fall into fragments . . . perhaps because of the very nature of the coop itself.

I too feel fragmented this moment. It is winter outside the window. I want to be elsewhere. In it or beyond it. I want to be writing or doing something else.

I wanted to end this piece the way I began, merging it in good form. But the coop fills me with fragmentary flashes, and I listen.

I see myself this movement making more notes about the coop. Things to include which might better reveal me in this place. What was it Roethke said? "The desire to leave many poems in the state of partial completeness: to write nothing but, fragments."

Visitors to the coop (invited and uninvited) . . . what about them? Strangers and friends. They steal my time yet add to it immensely. I am happy to be with them, happy they have left. (For those who come to call and do not know the coop, I remain hidden, hoping they will go away.)

Visitors who enter the coop and feel uncomfortable, feel they do not belong. It is too cluttered, too dark, too strange. Other overly sensitive types may fear they are invading another man's privacy (fantasy?) and beat a hasty retreat. And then there are those who will find the odd chair, or sit on the edge of the cot, and feel immediately at home. The coop indentifies each visitor. I can see in their faces if they are of my tribe.

The woman writer (also a student of human potential and consciousness raising) who stepped inside the coop, perceived the very essence of it in one slow sweep, then whispered, "This place is filled with spirit. I feel it. Everywhere." Watching her, I became an observer myself for the first time and felt like a stranger visiting a wayside chapel in some foreign clime.

The visitors from New Mexico seeing all the familiar names of artwork done by mutual friends from there . . . smiling, quietly observing: "Strange, to see these works here . . . here in Wisconsin. Like they belong out there . . . but they fit here." My Wisconsin chicken coop adobe. ("You ought to put it on wheels and move it out here to the mountains," says another friend.) "It even smells like the Southwest," said the same visitors. The burning of pinon incense has permanently settled into the woodwork.

The coop slowly assimilates all the various energies and spiritual invocations till it becomes a blessing in itself, affecting its inhabitant(s) in redeeming, unconscious ways.

You leave yesterday's anxieties, today's obligations . . . you begin to gently rub a pebble from the windowsill in your hand . . . You come to a space where nothing matters but what you will make today . . . how you will reimagine yourself and the world . . . the place to tell tales.

How the desk area becomes a nest to be made over and over again . . . feathered in books, manuscripts, letters, notes, pipes, ash trays, mugs, pens, pencils, tobacco, writing paper, carbons, matches, stamps, paperclips, dust, crumbs, bits of tape, the phone, the typewriter, and the ever-burning light. How the mess increases with clutter as the writing grows more intense. A clear desk signifies emptiness, false starts, incomplete acts, or the writer in the throes of depression.

Any sound but the natural is a distraction to the writer. (Music, only when he paints.) A love of wind, birdsong, rain on the roof, turbulent waters on the distant yet near lake . . . the mournful moan of fog in Death's Door . . . the wind clacker of tin, wood, wire, and stone which I made to hang outside the coop's door, signaling a north wind, a sound wind . . . winter . . . religious rites in pueblos and the mountains of the Southwest. All this is as right as breath.

Though much of the coop remains constant, periodically I find myself reshuffling paintings, postcards, artworks for greater effect. I seem to need *everything* near me which might enhance the spirit of my work. Objects that no longer affect me are removed. Some, perhaps, never quite possessed what I felt they held. Still other things given to me but not belonging (either for lack of spirit, though lately for lack of space) either never become part of the coop, or must await their time.

But for the practical existence of the chicken coop itself, its past and present history upon this land, there is little inside the coop that speaks Wisconsin except for some stones, the glass egg, and a few weeds. No paintings or artifacts. No subconscious dialogue. This has not been deliberate, but its absence within my framework of instinct, need, and design must say something. The spirit within the coop speaks mostly Southwest Indian, the Far East, Eastern European, ethnic Chicago, and rituals of old Catholicism which linger like pennance, a hundred Our Father's and Hail Mary's, intent upon answered prayers and final salvation. Suffering, too, knows its place here, whatever good comes of it. Wisconsin, within these boundaries, seems bloodless, bereft. A separateness persists. Neither rituals nor talismans to guide the wanderer's way. Only the world outside these windows— fields, woods, water, birds, animal, sky—without myth to enlarge a man's life. Nature itself, which at times is almost enough, yet fails inevitably to fully engage one's passions with a life force divine, in love with the dark and the light, in touch with the art of daily life.

Mornings, afternoons, evenings, I may clear a space on the cot and lie down. I may read for a while. I may nap for no more than a few minutes. Through half-closed eyes, I see my legs stretching into the far walls, my arms entangling themselves through paintings, books, manuscripts, windows, and plants, my shoulders rising toward the ceiling till I am in this coop absorbed, absolved, abandoned in a higher world, dimensions beyond reason. I may move with the light in the east window, see it burst in rainbows through the crystal hanging there. On a late afternoon in summer, the door of the coop open, I may stretch again, my arms folded beneath my head, glancing through the screen door into the depth of green woods, the whiteness of birch bark, the sun filtering through branches, filtering me in the widest expanse of sleep. Some harvest moon nights I may light a single candle, lie again upon the cot, watch the candle's play of light upon the cedar walls, and sometimes track the moon's rise, fused with firelight, darkness, stars, experiencing an ancientness of rites, communion in the universe. I will go then to the road, sometimes, and in the darkness seek the light of the coop between trees. Wondering . . . Who lives there? What goes on? Relishing the stranger's vantage point. Mystery without, within.

The room upstairs in the house was a poem. The coop is a short story. Whatever shelter awaits my future occupancy will be a novel. The whole work will consume me. And I it.

Rituals prevail in this place. Seasons honored. Offerings made. Certain cups I will drink from at certain times. The words, the art, the power, come only in this way. It can't be helped. Or explained. Given who I am, what I do here, and all the coop contains. Certain measures must be taken, the darker recesses made light. To open *Door Steps,* read the day's entry, and find my place. To burn the incense, light the candle, sip the wine, hold the fetish, explore the form, find the breath, close the eyes, open the way . . . Tao, Zen, Buddha, Christ, Great Spirit. The priest of love inside ourselves. The silent language in nature to be transcribed. The coop of the communicant. The writer's priestly way. When we know nothing—in the passion of physical, natural, sexual, artistic, mindless union—our godliness becomes us. The sacredness of being in our place.

A Prayer of the Navaho Night Chant

Tse'gihi.
House made of dawn.
House made of evening light.
House made of the dark cloud.
House made of male rain.
House made of dark mist.
House made of female rain.
House made of pollen.
House made of grasshoppers.
Dark cloud is at the door.
The trail out of it is dark cloud.
The zigzag lightning stands high upon it.
Male deity!
Your offering I make.
I have prepared a smoke for you.
Restore my feet for me.
Restore my legs for me.
Restore my body for me.
Restore my mind for me.
Impervious to pain, may I walk.
With lively feelings may I walk.
As it used to be long ago, may I walk.
Happily may I walk.
Happily, with abundant dark clouds, may I walk.
Happily, with abundant showers, may I walk.
Happily, with abundant plants, may I walk.
Happily may I walk.
Being as it used to be long ago, may I walk.
May it be beautiful before me.
May it be beautiful behind me.
May it be beautiful below me.
May it be beautiful above me.
May it be beautiful all around me.
In beauty it is finished.

27

In The Clearing

I have taught at The Clearing in Ellison Bay, Wisconsin for over ten years, and each year as my time approaches (usually mid June) I dread the thought of returning.

That's a hell of a confession to make. Especially for a writer who loves to teach. I see my former students beginning to smile; I see the Friends of The Clearing excommunicating me; I see the resident managers, Don and Louise Buchholz crossing me off their list; I see Jens Jensen,the founder, turning over in his grave.

The Clearing is always in danger of becoming an institution. Institutions are death to the creative process. How does the writer (this writer) keep The Clearing alive for himself and hopefully for others?

By fighting his "call" there each year. By turning the place into a virtual writer's camp for one solid week, day and night. By inciting others to the rebellious act of trying to write.

The trouble with trying to describe The Clearing is that everybody who has ever attended a class there tells about it, photographs it, paints it, poeticizes it, films it, documents it in scholary pieces, writes articles, letters, reports and books about it. Goes home a convert. Returns next'year a disciple. And returns again and again. And becomes, in his or her small way, a spiritual part of the place. Which is OK. And what is supposed to happen, the way its teacher, founder, legend, Jens Jensen, envisioned it.

The problem is: Almost everything to be said about The Clearing has been said. Almost any halfway decent article, research paper, book will do. And if you're looking for that, then don't read any further. Because I'm not going to tell you about that. I'm going to tell you why I hate to teach at The Clearing each year.

Trying to write about The Clearing is like trying to write about the Grand Canyon. The problem, therefore, is to make the poem, the story, the article, the book *yours*. And if you can't make it yours, make it as different as who you are, then it really doesn't matter who writes it, and you should stick to writing recipes, obituaries, weather reports, or go into computers. And you should not take a writing course from me unless you are prepared to be introduced to yourself.

I return so as not to disappoint myself. Each year I must re-learn this lesson. A lesson perhaps so simple as: You must go back there and teach because it's good for you. And which doesn't begin to sink in till the first or second day of teaching when I suddenly *know* why I am there. By the end of the week, I don't want to go home.

Ironically, I find myself preparing for the event throughout the year. I am reading newspapers, magazines, literary quarteries, poetry, novels short stories, books of all kinds. And I am marking passages, inserting bookmarks, making notes, discovering some phenomenal piece of writing which I would like to use in class. I try to set these things aside, but usually lose track of them. I keep a folder handy for notes and clippings, yet inevitably find it empty when I open it in June. The notes are in my mind or elsewhere.

The notes may read: Use Isaac Babel's story "In the Basement"; check Ray Carver's "Cathedral"; that line from Takahashi's poem, "My woman is like an orange"; Royko's column on the Viet vet; Ann Beattie, Eudora Welty, Edna O'Brien; Chekhov's "A Day in the Country"; Sydney J. Harris' essay on the egg; Silko's poems; Joan Didion on keeping a notebook. What did John Haines say about writers and place?

But the conflict continues. I would almost always rather be writing than preparing to teach at The Clearing. I really fight it. Especially the week just prior to my classes (when the mania to get organized begins to take hold), right up to and including the moment of meeting with the students for the first time on Sunday, in the lodge, and assembling for dinner at 6. I usually slide into my spot (the same table and chair each year) at precisely the time Don and Louise invite everyone to sit down and eat.

Unless some of my former students have returned for independent study or an advanced writing course (I discourage anyone from taking the same course twice. I discourage anyone from taking more than one writing course in his life), I remain relatively inconspicuous for the time being, just one of the gang. The one who refuses to wear his plastic nametag.

Without fail my cover is blown halfway through the meal. Maybe a student has asked Don or Louise who/where is Mr. Blei? Maybe others have detected that the guy at the other end of the table, the guy with the long hair, the guy who is staring into his plate of second or third helpings, that guy seems out of place, even for a bunch of writers. Here and there I feel eyes turning upon me then. It's first impression time. (Was that the phone that just rang, Don? Is it for me? Some editor maybe wanting to send me to Mozambique?) I feel people passing judgments:

"Him? *That's* the teacher? You mean, *he's* Blei?

I feel I must be an awful disappointment to some of them. I am too young for the old and too old for the young. I detect people rolling their eyes. I detect little old ladies feeling instantly crushed because I do not look like the type of nice writer who will let them wax nostalgic over kitty cats, bluebirds, or hepaticas. They would like to catch the next bus home. I detect suburban housewives, uncertain, anxious, afraid, but perhaps willing to give me the benefit of the doubt. I detect both arrogance and fear on the part of the young and the overly educated.

Much of this is my imagining, but maybe some of it is true. Occasionally, should the conversation grow more relaxed, even deafening around the table that first evening, I may glance around the room and find a Born Writer. Just like that. I haven't met or read one word the person's written, but I feel it. Just a hunch. It's happened perhaps a half a dozen times. And only four of the six proved to be true. And they've gone on to do everything else but write. While the others, who were only blank faces that first night, went on to become the writers they wanted to be. *Because* they wanted to be.

I play no favorites. And wonder about them all occasionally, years after the class. But it's mainly the ones who really want to write, who make the personal sacrifices, that I remain closest to. I see their names appearing in newspapers, magazines, and on the covers of books. We came together first, though, at The Clearing, under these very same circumstances, and we created a mutual respect for words, forms, ideas, each other, that might even be defined as love. And it doesn't happen to everyone, or overnight. But you'll know when it does.

Soon after dinner I meet with the students in the lounge. It is evident to all, by now (including myself) who I am: I am the teacher of writing for the week. We all feel a little relieved but still wary. I go over their names on the class list, try to make them feel comfortable, answer their questions, and carefully ease them into a writing assignment due tomorrow, the very first day, even though we haven't yet met as a class.

By the end of that first night I am feeling a little more comfortable about them and me and The Clearing . . . once again.I've resigned myself to Thomas Wolfe's delimma: You can't go home again, Blei. At least not until next Saturday. Even though home is only a few miles down the road, a few miles from this simple room of Jens Jensen, bed, desk, dresser, incredible view of woods, clearing, water, I will occupy during my stay. I can't help lying awake that first night, thinking of him and The Clearing.

There's a reverence about the place, immediately felt, which goes beyond mere physical description. The particulars have been explained hundreds of times with minor variations: The Clearing is an adult education school, located in Ellison Bay, founded by Jens Jensen, a landscape architect, in 1935 on 125 acres, including woods, meadows, native stone and log buildings, all situated on a limestone bluff overlooking the calming waters of Green bay. It's a setting, once experienced, where even the most enthusiastic lover of cities feels quite naturally at home, at rest. Which was Jensen's intention from the outset: only in nature will man find the peace within himself. And this lesson, none of us here as teachers, need teach.

Jensen himself was a simple man, quiet, reflective, complicated perhaps only in those ways a man does live his visions (the Chicago park system, the Lincoln Memorial Garden in Springfield, Ill., many private commissions, and his school, The Clearing) then leaves only the visible evidence of his faith in plants and trees and nature's ways for us to ponder and appreciate the heart's desire in man. Not unlike an artist or teacher. He was all that too.

In an early Declaration of Fundamentals which he addressed to potential students of The Clearing some 40 years ago, he stated: "Profound in its teaching, the school is a way of life. Here the student receives a penetrating reasoning which follows him in whatever field he chooses for his life work. There are no grades, degrees, medals, not any other method of ranking the individual. Each student must feel that the joy his own accomplishments give is full reward for work well done . . . "

The truth of that statement and this: "It is the urge to do things that is found here . . . to do things worthwhile . . . not for oneself but for others. In that way only, life has not been wasted," is the openness of the approach. Both student and teacher can breathe easily, function imaginatively, sometimes significantly, within those boundaries as interdependent as nature's own. Even the teaching of writing roots well here, though likely it will flower and spread in clearings of mind far away from here.

Though The Clearing has grown and undergone many changes, the influence of Jens Jensen remains evident, whether it be the traditional bowl of oatmeal served at breakfast, or the need for both fellowship and private meditation: "There is merry making, there is music, there is dancing, there is dramatic expressions in the wood-land player's green. The bay has crystal clear water for those that love the water. There are hidden nooks in the cliffs of the bay for the thinker, for those that want to be alone."

I am confident he would recognize The Clearing as his own this very day: the entrance, the road, the landscape, the lodge, the cliff house (his meditation place), his room, his root cellar, even his beautiful schoolhouse, now rebuilt after the fire of June 12, 1981.

All those particulars remain. Even the classes as well, though the yearly schedule (April through November, including winter for those of us living here) and the broad range of subjects offered reflect, perhaps, a different time.

In Jensen's day one might study botany, horticulture, landscape architecture, woodcarving, weaving, poetry, painting, along with plenty of physical labor in the forests, fields, and garden. These days classes might include everything from Navaho Rug Weaving to Chinese, French, Spanish, Chamber Music, Writing, Zen, Dance, Painting, Shakespeare, Photography, Nature Study, Beowulf, Woodcarving, Selfawareness, Independent Study, and more. New courses for the year might include the Dulcimer, Wellness (the holistic approach), Bavarian Folk Art, and others.

Each year, usually in January, The Clearing prints a new brochure (The Clearing, P.O. Box 65, Ellison Bay, Wis. 54210) describing the course offerings, schedule, and registration form. The classes tend to fill quickly. There is room for only 28 students, two classes each week.

The particulars of this private place are unending. Further history and lore can be found in various books such as: *The Story of The Clearing* by Mertha Fulkerson and Ada Corson, *The Jens Jensen I Knew* by Sid Telfer Sr., and Jensen's own writings, *The Clearing,* and *Siftings.* Visitors too are welcome on Saturdays and Sundays, 1-4 p.m., June through October.

Yet none of the above quite explain The Clearing, as well as experiencing the place first hand, as student or teacher. And it's the teaching that involves me. In that relationship do I come to know and love The Clearing once again and see Jensen's vision, each year, in a new way.

Don Buchholz, the resident manager, will tell you that the teachers come from all backgrounds."From very professional to those who are just interested in whatever they're doing. I think the wonderful thing is that they teach for the love of teaching. They certainly don't do it for the monetary reward. We've not had any who really didn't work out. We've had some who are more interested in doing their own thing.

"I think one of the nicest things is the close student/teacher relationship, and the close fellowship and friendships that are built . . . part of Jensen's idea of eating together around the table.

"I am always amazed at how much the teachers give of themselves. They certainly don't watch the clock. If anything, they probably go deeper and further than they intended to originally.

"I think one thing Jensen might take a difference with us is that we spend too much time in the classroom, and not enough getting to know nature in the woods and things. And that's true of all our classes. Yet how do we stimulate this and not turn them off to the class?

"Each teacher is so unique in his own way. Each looks at The Clearing in a different light and relates to it in a different way."

The carefree preparation months and months prior to my scheduled week is nothing compared to the final countdown of days and hours before the first class.

I never want to repeat myself, for that leads to stale teaching, as uninspiring to me as the students. Certain experiences bear repeating (the image of the poem, the moment of the story, the narrative design of an article for lasting effect), but never, *never* to teach anything precisely the same way twice. It's got to be a new discovery for me as well as them. And there must always, *always* be enough time/room/space within each class session for the surprise, the sudden inspiration, the accident. Something that may turn me and the whole class upside down instantly (forsaking

all assignments, lessons, plans), whether it come from something I just thought of, or spring from the ideas, questions, writing of the students themselves. Improvisational teaching, perhaps. I'm for anything that works.

By Sunday morning (of the Sunday night I am about to begin) I have packed bags and boxes of books; I have accumulated a stack of pages resembling a loose outline of a lesson plan; I have stuffed all the notes and pages in a manila folder; and on the cover of that folder, in a final burst of inspiration, I have painted a wild watercolor for good luck, labeling it THE CLEARING 19__.

Now I am ready . . . to face the Sunday night dinner . . . to face the students for the first time . . . to begin one class each morning, one each afternoon . . . to come to know the students around the table at breakfast, lunch and dinner . . . to get something going a few hours in the evening by inviting other writers (usually close friends) to come in and read and talk and meet with the students . . . to fill almost every hour of every day (nights included, we keep a dream journal) with writing, writing, writing. Total saturation.

When one class meets, the other writes. And vice versa. And in between times I read assignments, make comments, give personal conferences and direction, and encourage, encourage, encourage. There are no non-writers in my classes (except for those who came expecting a vacation, and I try to weed them out before registration), only people who came to The Clearing to write. And I can only deal with their desire. If the desire is a mere flirtation with "wanting-to-write" but not willing to make the commitment, they will realize their own illusion soon enough. And I will not take the blame or feel guilty for their failure. Only bring an honest willingness to my class, and I will bleed for you the entire week—and often beyond.

For these reasons, then, I do teach, I do return to The Clearing each year for my own self-realization—not unlike the students who came to experience theirs. It consumes me entirely. I lose an entire week in preparation, a week in teaching, and another week or more trying to touch earth again after it's all over, and I'm left with the solitariness of my own life again, staring at the typewriter, not sure where I left off or how to begin.

The incredible joy and satisfaction is not so much the result of what I have been able to give, but what I receive from serious students of writing. Watching them shape stories and poems and pieces. Goosebumps in a class while they're reading something of their own that has caught fire. Experiencing the give-and-take among people from all backgrounds, all ages, each digging into him or herself, trying to make meaning of their lives in words.

It's a heavy load—what they carry, what they desire to reach in a way of art, what they sometimes heap upon my shoulders. But I listen. I do my damndest to guide. "Why am I telling *you* these things?" said a student to me after an hour of baring her soul in a personal conference, "I'm the psychiatrist!" And she was. But nobody ever listened to her. She had no one to tell it to. Not even herself. Which is a perfect reason for a person to begin to write. Most of us start that way.

Put it on paper, I told her. What you're telling me. Put it all down on paper. You don't even have to show it to me. Keep them your secrets for now. We'll work on the form, the transformation process leading to art, later.

I might also advise, though the students soon come to realize themselves, that they utilize the setting, the peace, the age old themes of The Clearing as well. Trees, plants, rocks, water, birds, light, darkness, stars, peace . . . they all teach. Know and use that language too. Jensen's own lesson.

And in that spirit I enter my first class at The Clearing on Monday morning. And begin.

The Watercolor Way

I enter the coop some mornings, my mind cluttered with writing (a work-in-progress that is not progressing, a story to revise, a review to be typed, letters to be answered), or totally blank. I am hardly aware I am here.

In either case, I may take a fresh piece of typing paper (or any kind of paper within reach), turn from the desk to the small table behind with the little window facing north, reach for a brush, dip it in a goldfish bowl of murky water, hit the colors and paper, begin to paint.

Watercolors come to me as unexpectedly as that. Day or night, all seasons, throughout the year, I paint when I get the urge. I am always unprepared. No sketchbooks, no plans, no burning images. If I'm out of one color I'll use another. No one has ever accused me of being an accomplished artist, given me a one-man show, or asked me to teach a class in watercolor painting. No one really gives a damn—except me. Which is fine. I've come to accept that. And much more.

Obsessions intrigue me. Why anyone keeps doing what he does. For no reason.

I don't paint portraits or pretty pictures. I don't know gesso from egg tempra, and don't care to know. It's a challenge at times just to maintain one's ignorance—or innocence. Well-meaning people can lead a man astray.

There is almost no demand for my work—except for one or two friends. No encouragement—except for one or two friends. No one has attempted to analyze it—but me. Or offer any critical commentary. Most people (especially artists) who come across my work pretend they don't see it, or make light of it, or offer an enigmatic smile.

What all this means is I am free.

When someone finds my painting crudely hilarious, I join in the fun, even though it may hurt.

I mean, who the hell *really* knows what's good or bad? What moves some and leaves others cold? What holds value, and what seems worthless?

Who the hell has the right to tell anyone he can't paint?

I paint because it makes me feel good.

And anything I do that unconsciously, so all-consuming, with so much passion, has value to me. And perhaps others as well.

It's like making love.

Minutes to hours may pass. I may paint one or a dozen watercolors, I am that occupied. That ecstatic. When the time comes, I will lay the brushes down, let the painting dry, and turn to the typewriter. But all day and night, and into the next day, I will be aware of watercolors in the midst of me, feeling good about what I have done, peeking at them, making changes. Totally captivated by what I see.

I have painted since the 1960's, ever since I came upon the watercolors of Henry Miller: "One of the important things I learned in making watercolors was not to worry, not to care too much." My first book, *The Watercolored Word* (Quixote Press,

1968 o.p.) reflected the innocence of creative acts. Child's play.

Miller was and remains my inspiration, along with an artist friend, Ross LewAllen, whose advice to this day is "Just paint."

Which I've been doing, hundreds and hundreds of watercolors since . . . mostly untitled, undated . . . a couple framed, a few stashed here and there . . . most of them given or sent to strangers and friends. Lately, many of them stashed under the army cot, gathering dust.

In 1971 I wrote and illustrated a personal essay ("Me and My Watercolors") for the *Chicago Tribune Sunday Magazine,* which is as close as I've come to explaining it, till now. Everything I felt then still holds true.

I'm probably a little better at watercolors today than I was then. But not much. Yet as I look back upon my painting life these years in Door, where, when, why, how I now paint continues to intrigue me. I wonder what I've learned. And if I see things any differently.

I work more in cycles now. A tremendous output for days and weeks, then perhaps nothing for two or three months. I painted every day when I first began. I would like to get back to that.

I still can't paint with anyone watching me.

I still can't paint anywhere else but the room where I write.

I spend more time with each painting these days, continually returning to it. No painting is *ever* finished, I've come to learn.

I'm more in touch with the way of watercolor now, discovering little interior truths that seem self-sustaining. The joy is immediate, intense, often overwhelming.

More symbols appear in my work, more patterns, more mystery than I'll ever understand. Not that I want to understand a watercolor I've made. To have painted it is quite enough.

I seldom write on them as much as I used to. But I imagine I'll discover myself coming back to that one day.

My watercolors are still very small, seldom larger than a standard sheet of typing paper, and often smaller than that. Artists and friends have encouraged me to paint larger, given me beautiful blocks and full sheets of heavy watercolor paper, but it's rare I attempt something so large on paper of such quality. It intimidates me. I possess a vague feeling I *must* paint a masterpiece. I don't have enough to say, to want or need to fill all that space. I'm more comfortable working smaller, where more intimacy and privacy seem to prevail. I can still put whole worlds, relationships, mysteries, visions, in a painting no bigger than my hand. This too could someday change. If so, the watercolors themselves will tell me when.

I have never studied painting, and never intend to. I never took a single art course in all my education. I paint. I have never been able to read past the first page of a book on How to Paint. But I delight in the works of others, old masters and moderns, books, museums, galleries, and reproductions. I favor the strange ones like Odilon Redon, Emile Nolde, Klee, Hundertwasser . . . anything Japanese, Native American Indian, African, Mexican, South American, the self-taught Yugoslavians . . . the works of children and the insane. Everything primitive seems new, honest, and holy to me.

I am unable to 'talk shop" or "do business" when it comes to the color wheel, the characteristics of brushes, the qualities of paper, the value of my own work. I buy the colors I like. The brushes that feel good in my hand. Paper, one way or another, somehow comes to me. I give most of my paintings away—though "contributions" of all sorts are honored . . . food, drink, books, other art work, supplies, blank checks, whatever cold cash people send or put in my hand. Thank you all.

My drawing is hopeless. I've come to prefer it that way. I paint what I paint the way I paint.

I paint . . . everything. I paint one thing and it becomes another. I paint the sky, the trees, the grass, the flowers, the fields, the sun, the moon, the stars, the animals, the mountains, the desert, the sea, the man, the woman, the child . . . Sometimes all in one painting. Sometimes only one.

Color to me is like eating candy. Whatever satisfies my appetite for now. And I might try anything else as well: pencil, ink, chalk, crayola, acrylic, charcoal, watercolor crayons, markers, glue, spray-paint, block print, stamps, wax, etc. Usually just watercolor though—cakes and tubes—and maybe some ink. Sometimes I'll paint on white posterboard and spray it with a can of clear sealer to really heighten the color. I've painted with a roller . . . with *anything* that comes to me. Sometimes I'll write a word, a line, a poem on a painting. Possibilities. Everything's worth trying. The boundaries will define themselves—and you. Whatever wants to be expressed—I'll act. In love, some believe, nothing is wrong.

My "exhibits" have almost no history. One just has to believe in the mail . . . in himself. Someone asks me to submit a painting somewhere, and if I can, I will. Rarely do I hear anymore after that. My watercolors disappear. They never return to me.

One went to Africa once. Another to South America. *The Watercolored Word* was a big hit at the university in Warsaw, Poland. Once a watercolor went to Spain . . . a batch to Canada . . . a bunch to Bennington. One to a postcard/painting exhibit that toured the Midwest. About a dozen watercolors I loved dearly (actually, watercolor poems) were sent to a New York publisher and subsequently lost in the mails. After all these years, I'm still hoping they may show up someday. There were some beauties among them . . . or at least I thought so then. A few years ago, about ten watercolors were sent to a gallery in Chicago, and for all my inquiries (Please Return!) I have never heard from the owner since. (Were they sold? Lost? Thrown away?)

I will probably never see an exhibit of my work in my lifetime. I don't know how many paintings are out there, where they're at, or how good they are except in the eyes of a few beholders.

I amuse myself at times with a posthumous exhibit (maybe here in the coop, Chicago, or New Mexico). That might be the best time for them to surface. A dead man one-man show. Maybe 20 or 30 of them from way back when to the end, and everything under the sun. ("Hey, look. That was once him!")

There are three intimate joys to watercolors. Painting them. Coming back to them the next day. Losing them completely (selling them, trading them, forgetting them, giving them away) only to rediscover them, unexpectedly, framed and glowing on the wall of someone's living room. (Did I do that?)

Lately I've come to view my watercolors as talismans, charms, fetishes, meditations, icons, holy cards for those I love and others I have never met. At least I *feel* this way when I have painted one, and finally let go. They are not masterpieces and were not meant to be. But they come from deep within, are executed in joy, and bear witness to the dark and bright wonder we all share. If they affect the spirit of one person—to paint, to write, to feel a little more alive—the message has been received. A painting should stick. Inside. And keep working away at a person's psyche. Keep calling him back. Blessings in disguise.

I remain fond of writers who were also painters. I feel close to them: Henry Miller, Kenneth Patchen, Lawrence Durrell, D.H. Lawrence, e.e. cummings, etc. Words

were not enough. Writers who paint are seldom considered "great" painters, but remain in a class to themselves—often more unique and compelling than much of what passes as art in the marketplace these days.

I continue to paint what I paint the way I paint for my own good . . .

. . . The heart rushes . . . breathing becomes audible . . . the face feels warm . . . these hands catch fire. A stroke of blue, crimson . . . a spot of yellow, some green, more yellow . . . make a sun. There. Some more. Rounder . . . fill it in . . . more water, more color. Wed the deeper yellow over there. Add that to the red/yellow/orange/crimson sun . . . maybe outline it now in violet or vermillion . . . use a smaller brush. What do we have here? What's this taking shape? Follow the shape. Extend it with color . . . bring in some of the red from the sun. Bring in the blue . . . bluer than that. Green. Yes, green. That light green that looks like the plants in spring. A face emerging. Pencil it in lightly, lightly . . . no, that's enough. Go for the brown . . . an oval face . . . hmmmm . . . some yellow . . . Hello . . . a woman. Women live in my paintings. So does the sun. She's red and yellow and blue . . . and her form, if I find it, may be divine. Flowing hair . . . yellow hair . . . a touch of brown . . . more yellow, more golden . . . a little blue . . . yeah, yeah, yeah. The face . . . always a challenge. I'll leave it alone for now. Work that sky around the sun . . . lighten it . . . strengthen it . . . bring it all the way down to here . . . earth? Earth? Green? Yellow? Brown? No. Nothing too definite . . . let it all float. Try for the eyes . . . go back to her . . . just so much, no more. Damn . . . I lost them, lost them. Keep it wet, keep it wet . . . move in the hair. Move in the sky. Bring in the eyes with, with, with Burnt Sienna (is that the name of it?). Where the hell's the Sienna? This table's a mes. Not this, not this, not this one or this. Try a brown marking pen. Yeah . . . that'll do. More water. More hair. The sun is running . . . pick it up, pick it up . . . no! That's good. Let it run into there . . . merge, merge, merge you motha, and be beautiful . . . there in her eyes . . . I like that! She's beautiful! (Maybe) And the mouth . . . a dash of red . . . oh, shit! That's terrible . . . oh, no! It's in the eyes! Bring in the white, the mouth, the nose, the eyes . . . the FACE, always beyond me. I can work a face so much (minutes, hours, days) and suddenly catch it! Or wear a hole in the paper, throw the whole goddam painting away. White . . . my salvation . . . white and more wet white . . . let it dry. It may or may not suggest what still lies beneath (strength or weakness). And I can still do the face again. Keep it all flowing . . . don't let it dry, not yet. Too much technique, too much tension, too much thought, and it's wrong, all wrong. Don't think! Paint. Just paint. More color. Mix it up. Maybe paint a line or two of red/orange, yellow, right from the tube. AieeE! A slash right there. Excellent! Nice. Lightning afloat. She's afloat . . . rising. Another tapestry/weaving painting? Could be. How many have I done these past few months? Why does the image/form persist? Why does it suddenly then go away? Get the pen. Open the India ink. Outline this almost dry side . . . follow the forms of the color line . . . open the spaces . . . another line here . . . there . . . too much, too much . . . the ink's spreading out of control. But it may be all right later when it dries . . . This is something like that other one I once did. Jesus, that was great. Where did it go? Did I give it to Rausch? Ross? The Schweigers? John and Audrey Cibulka? the Tomses? The Kallals? Maybe it's still here somewhere. Bank this other blob with color . . . with pencil . . . with fingers. Draw it up quickly in a paper towel. There. Not bad. That can be left . . . or changed . . . later. Work more inside with the pen. Define and redefine other images coming to light. Yeah, another tapestry painting sure as hell. Rectangular. Weaving. Leave the loose threads, yarns . . . the Navaho way. Indian blanket. But what is she doing in there? A range of mountains above . . . above and outside the whole damn painting. Am I putting it there? Why? Work on the dry as well as the wet. A tiny black sun . . . Is that what I've made? A slice of a moon. Three suns . . . two moons . . . What the hell's the difference. This is *my* world, my universe, my blanket/tapestry/weaving/painting. Silver, silver ink. Maybe some gold.Use it all. Everything. This painting's coming alive! Stars. We must have stars . . . up there above the mountain range. Coyote, are you in here again? These will have to pass for stars . . . so crude. Who cares? The top of the painting seems too separate from where I began. Must tie the two together . . . the tapestry part and the mountains. Make it one with line. All of it . . . the color, the forms, the image of the faceless woman . . . the dull, the bright, the black and white . . . the suns, moons, mountains . . . wet/dry. Enter/interdependency of all things. Where's my favorite, worn, once-pointed brush? A puddle of color there . . . muddy . . . yuck! Pick it up with a sponge, paper towel. New . . . and blue. A blue sun in the lower color. And a wet touch of white in the center, floating, floating . . . wow . . . starburst! What now? Spread, spread, spread . . . beautiful. If only the goddam white will hold. It won't. It won't. I know white. Can't trust it. It dries and looks blah. I wish I understood white. How it makes or ruins a painting. The same as black. Everything's precarious now . . . on the edge. Walking the line again. You either find it or you lose it. Like a story, a poem. But if you don't risk it, you don't get it. If you lose it . . . try again. Color! More color. The woman is drying . . . floating free. I like her . . . what she's trying to say. She could be an angel. Give her some wings. Gray . . . white . . . yellow . . . a little blue. The mountains grow more mysterious. Get the black ink. Make some crosses there . . . one . . . two . . . three. Crosses? Why crosses again? That long ago dream of tiny black crosses all over some bed. I pulled back the blanket, more and more black crosses. They belong in these mountains . . . seem just about perfect there. The lady/angel/woman needs breasts . . . curve, form . . . a finished . . . underneath the drying layer of white, her face, her features suggest themselves again. There's still hope for her mouth. Now her body seems wrong. Turn it with line . . . ink and paint. Better. Arms? I can't draw. Give her wider wings instead. Blot the face a little . . . paint the face again. (Women and horses . . . the ultimate challenge.) For her to be no one yet a woman like no other. Paint. Pencil? Ink? Some brown ink, brown paint . . . bring it back slowly, slowly . . . bring it up . . . a little more . . . the eyebrows . . . the eyes . . . now, to make the mouth right . . . yeah . . . there she is. Put the brush down! Hide it! Leave her alone! Turn around, away. Look out the window. What's going on out there? Spring? Light a pipe. Burn some incense. Pour a cup of coffee with a slug of brandy. The typewriter seems abandoned. Answer a letter. Make it brief. NO! Don't look at the watercolor yet. Let it simmer. Let it bake. Consider it in the kiln. Write that letter . . . *Dear Friend, Things are a little crazy in the coop today* . . . Answer the damn phone. Make it short. Don't turn and gaze at the painting while you're talking, "Yeah, it's too cold . . ." (or too wet, too windy, too humid, too snowy). "No, I can't. Busy. See you maybe next week. Sure, whatever you say. So long." Get up . . . *don't look* . . . go for a walk. Leave it alone. Walk around the stone garden (ceremonial grounds?) in front of the coop. Find some peace there . . . these stone pilings: the totem of birds, the buddha, the shaman, the woman, the lovers, the medicine woman, the marriage, the mother lode. Where did they all come from? What do they say? They appear like watercolors . . . maybe put one of the forms in a painting sometime in there. Not consciously. Let them appear. Keep walking. Through the woods . . . along the stone fence . . . back through a field. Check the gravesite of Sadie, great spirit of a dog. More stone pilings. And a weathered wooden cross . . . shades of the oldest, poorest graveyards of New Mexico. Wooden cross. Humble dignity. Death . . . Pick a weed. Bring it in the coop . . .

throw it on the painting table. I looked! But it didn't register. Put the weed in paint . . . press it on the painting without looking at her face. Some music . . . classical? rock? jazz? Something Far Eastern . . . the floating world . . . meditation stuff . . . slow resonating strings (one string, plucked soulfully) . . . mournful winds (a singular strain) . . . put it in the painting, in the work. Music and painting mix. Music and writing do not. Remember the joy in doing the art for the

41

special editions of my books? Painting a 150 signed and numbered original watercolors for *Door Way*, right on the title page. Doing 150 signed and numbered original prints for *Door Steps*. Painting 100 covers of the novel, *Adventures In An American's Literature*. Days, afternoons, nights of a painter's craze within this coop. What to make next? And next, and next? To make each piece of artwork as satisfying as I can for those I know and for strangers as well who will open the book and find a surprise—something handmade, one of a kind . . . for him or her or them. Here, this is for you—from me. A talisman of sorts. May you know the joy I received in making it. The coop whirling in smoke—pipe, cigar, incense, candles. Mugs of coffee, slugs of booze, nips of wine. Music! Watercolored hands. No, I don't want to go in to eat (or sleep). Bring the food out here. The phone again? "Come on over. See what I've done so far. Maybe there's one here for you." I don't want to give *any* of these away. Or today's watercolor either . . . let me look at it again . . . hmmmm . . . the woman's face is questioning . . . which I rather like. I may leave it like that. I may find myself working on it again tomorrow, hoping to pull more magic from it. I may add some symbols: the bird, the cross, the whirl, the man, the tao . . . whatever calls . . . That may be the final blessing . . . the final lift . . . "To paint is to love again," says Henry Miller. That's it.

Notes Along The Watercolor Way:

Writing hard all day with the intention of rewarding myself with a watercolor to paint in the late afternoon, just before supper. And seeing it fresh the next morning, a welcome surprise.

What I paint at the moment is who I am.

Mystery, with a silent, secret sexuality—painting a woman's face.

Rain, winter, storms, gray skies—watercolor weather.

Often it transpires that the very ugliness of the painting (the woman?) becomes, in time, its (her?) most redeeming quality. A woman who, perhaps, can be ridiculed for what she is not, yet holds a raw attraction for what she is, becomes, in time.

I work backward, the primitive within, rather than outward toward more control. The painting is already there. The further I go in to find it, pull out the images necessary to my living, the more my own life takes shape. The more the painting takes on a "religious" air.

Almost any failure can be redeemed at any time once you reestablish, redirect interior connections.

"Any attempt to make a horse, if it is genuine and done with conviction and passion, must be successful—and must make a horse, what! I haven't yet struck the really sincere note in the watercolors, but it will come. I must become more humble still. I will. I am ready to get down on my knees before the fucking paper . . . "—Henry Miller

If a watercolor has been ruined, I will seldom throw away the whole painting anymore. Instead, I'll tear or cut pieces of it to be used as bookmarks, stationery, entirely new little paintings in themselves. Nothing dies when one gives all of himself.

From writing actual words, lines, poems on paintings, to extending the words beyond language . . . Chinese characters, petroglyphs, broken letters, illegible writing for the sole beauty of what the form suggests.

Frustration when visitors appear, unwrapping artwork, gifts, trinkets, hundreds of dollars spent at local galleries and shops . . . "Look at this." . . . I stand before them in the coop, dead broke, wishing they could see their way clear to buy one little watercolor. Then again, these paintings are not "souvenirs" in the vacationer's sense, nor great artworks of the county to hang in one's home. These are small joys, dreams, meditations, mystical journeys, adorations of the private sort, for the very few. It is not my "business" to paint. Just paint.

My paintings will never be anything till someone else says they may be something. Then no one will understand anything.

Occasionally a visitor will say, "Show me some of your paintings," and I will begin a frantic search, never coming up with enough, or ones I especially like. In my own mind I am always better than what I have to show. Most of the watercolors I like (or can remember) are in somebody else's hands.

I hope that after I'm gone, some of these watercolors might reappear and bring a small amount of joy, speculation, or inner journeying on the part of the owner or beholder. (For my own children: This was a crazy part of your old man. He had fun.)

I seem to forget "how" I painted something, "how" I surprised myself, "how" I achieved a certain effect, within hours after the painting is done. And it could be years later before I do something similar, rediscover a technique, fall in love with the beauty of such a watercolor again.

I am more and more convinced that a watercolor which seems so raw, so crude, so "bad," so undisciplined in its inception may/will take on a power and loveliness in time very near "art." A painting that is alive keeps changing, forever working its way into one's consciousness, unconsciousness . . . always moving . . . always different.

"But I notice another thing, that going at a thing in earnest, no matter how limited your knowledge, something good always develops. No man can do a really bad painting who is in desperate earnest and who does it with love or passion."—Henry Miller

I like my paintings best in candle light.

The great moments in painting are mindless.

The watercolor begun during my mother's final days of dying . . . still unfinished.

"Art is only a lesson—the real art must be one's life."—Henry Miller

Lost in Elburn

I'm on the East-West Illinois Tollway, outbound after an overnight at my father's in Cicero, fresh from Wisconsin the day before, and looking now for Illinois 47 and friend Dave Etter's town of Elburn, Illinois.

We've a dual autograph session to do (his book, *Alliance, Illinois* and my *Door Steps*) around noon at Town House Books in St. Charles.

I'm looking to see Dave again, whose presence this year has been mainly letters, poems, and a phone call in lieu of his annual visit to Door. I'm looking for Etter and a good time on his turf or a change. Usually we talk, laugh, drink, and commiserate on mine.

I glance at his last letter, dated November 14th, and study the quirky little map he's drawn in between the typewritten lines: Chicago . . . East-West Tollway . . . Aurora . . . Jog to left, no right—Sign that says Elburn Rte. 47 . . . Go North of #47 . . . Ill. #47 . . . Elburn . . . Go Through Business District And Turn Left On Reader St.—Go One Block and Turn Right on Gates—414 is Second House On Left—Up By Dead End Sign.

Mostly his map's a mystery. There ain't no sign that says "Elburn, Rte. 47." And I can appreciate that. I'm beyond the territory, confused, amused, and turning back (an illegal U), deadheading it to Dave's dead end, before I find the way. (Which is usually my way.)

A man should journey by intuition, mistakes, and the hope of good times at the end of the road. Mystery. It's no use going anywhere when you know the way and what awaits you.

I can't even *imagine* Elburn or Etter's real life there, but for his heartland poems of people, aglow in a kind of autumnal beauty . . . all the particulars of quiet, rural, midwestern life. The pungency of place. Like the quick bite of a hard apple. And only then first realizing you've sunk your teeth home again.

In The Middle Of A Long Summer Afternoon in Elburn, Illinois

> "Hey, Larry, what time is it in there?"
> she said, stretching in the hammmock.

> "The same time, Mary, it is out there,"
> he said, yawning on the daybed.

More promising than Etter's hand-drawn map is the last line of his letter: "You bet, I have some taverns ready for us to drink in! See you soon, my friend."

And when I pass the first graveyard approaching Elburn (pop. 1200), I know from his love of bone orchards, yeah, this is Etter's kind of place . . . "But I am at home

44

among the dead,/the deformed, the discolored."

It's a nondescript, small town-downtown Illinois place with a Main Street mostly unmemorable as most main streets are in their very nature to be main and the same. A bank, savings and loan, gas station, drug store, meat market, some doctors' offices, a restaurant, a farm equipment shop, some empty spaces, and some evidence of a bar. There's the office of the Elburn *Herald*—closed for the weekend for building renovation. The news is taking a nap.

It's a 1930's kind of town flirting with a facade of whatever it is some folks see as "modern," be it a packaged liquor store, a hair styling place, a pizza parlor, or the digital time in lights outside the local bank. But underneath it all, Elburn's *anywhere*. Etter's Our Town, Spoon River, and Alliance, Illinois. Real fiction.

Ned Swift: Downtown

Anything going on downtown, you ask?
You better believe it, my good friend.
The mail truck got in early
but went out late,
and a Funk's G-Hybrid seed salesman
and a retired pharmacist
from Prophetstown, Illinois,
were hammering out a new foreign policy
on the stone bench at the Courthouse.
But that's not all,
that's not the half of it.
Up at the Dairy Queen,
Jennifer Hornbeck told me
that she wouldn't speak to me again
unless I got rid of my shoes,
my jeans, and my T-shirt that says
IT TAKES LEATHER BALLS TO PLAY RUGBY.
Now, my question is:
Does she want me naked tonight
after the band concert in the Square?

I pull a left off Main on the outskirts of town and a right down Gates. There's a big old white house looming ahead . . . Dave's dead end. I reach behind the seat for a gift of Door County apples, some Wisconsin cheese, and a bottle of Early Times.

A car swings into the driveway behind me and out comes Dave's lovely wife, Peg, charming daughter, Emily, and in the front seat sits Dave's mother-in-law, whom I greet with a handshake. Nice woman.

There's some talk about this being a new used car Peg just bought, since Dave's Monza lost a door to a local garbage truck, and more talk about returning to town to shop for a refrigerator to replace the back-up one that just conked out. I don't understand any of this—and neither does Dave, who has just sauntered out of the house in amazement, pipe in hand, looking mildly confused.

"You boys will want to spend some time together," says Peg.

The house is wonderfully big, small town midwestern white, welcoming, and in some need of paint and repair—like most homes of creative-type people whose energy seems channeled in other pursuits of the heart.

I hand Dave the apples, the cheese, the booze, and follow him in, waving goodbye to the ladies. *Where did that car come from?* seems to be on his mind. But he tells me about his Monza minus a door and what life is like without a car. But a writer's life is always minus a door, I assure him. And two refrigerators don't make any sense at all. And think of all the poets in the world going to bed every night underfed! He understands the plight of the have–nots. And anyway, he's just returned from a trip by train and prefers that mode of transportation to all others. And whatever the state of the world or the USA today, his spirit inhabits another time zone entirely. The present is too unbelievable.

Warren Eggleston: Nostalgia

I live only in the past, boy.
The present is a flat beer
I poured down the kitchen sink,
and the future is a loaded shotgun,
locked in the toolshed
with the busted power mower.
Hooray for Lincoln Zephyrs
and interurban trolley cars.
Three cheers for Jack Armstrong.
The trumpet of Harry James
is sweeter to me now
than it was in high school.
I still carry a smiling picture
of Jeanne Crain in my billfold,
and I never miss a single movie
Errol Flynn ever made.
I dream of grammar school fun,
cherry Cokes, Dick Tracy Big Little Books,
and my collection of milk bottle caps.
Bee shit on all that's buzzing around
in this falling down world.
Don't come to me with your news events,
your insane babblings
about men blasting off to the moon

46

or teenage singers who can't sing.
I just wish I could write
President Roosevelt
and tell him he's doing just fine
and the war is going our way,
and that I got another date
with Marjorie Jo Kincaid
to dance to Tommy Dorsey tonight.
Go get 'em, Cardinals,
beat those damn Yankees.
Touchdown for Frankie Sinkwich!
Oh, there's no doubt about it.
I'm going to stay put
in the fabulous 1940's.
Close the door, children.
Daddy doesn't know you anymore.

Dave seems a little nervous in the presence of a visitor. *Just where do I go? What do I show him? Where do I put these apples? What do we talk about first?* Like there haven't been that many friends searching him out in Elburn, or certainly spending the night. And I'm talking a manic mile a minute as usual, in an up-beat, long-time-no-see friendly encounter between two writing friends. It will take a while to synchronize our patter.

The house is roomy, comfortable, woody and wallpapery, thick with nostalgic furnishing—Etter perfect. Nothing nonsense-modern to clutter an aura of time-gone-by. And old dog and some old cats too. And the sound of music: Etter's preference for good old jazz.

His study, right off the large dining room, right between the kitchen and the living room, appears a veritable way station in the home . . . his own heart of the house.

Built-in bookcases, two windows, two desks, and a plush old green easy chair with a floor lamp beside. Above his main working desk, some pictures of Abe Lincoln and a photo of Adlai E. Stevenson, sitting on a white fence. There's a love of Illinois history here. There's evidence of a poet hard at work on his desk. Plus the frustration of any serious midwestern writer who knows the odds of ever seeing any of his books on anyone's bestseller list. Dave's clipped the Chicago *Trib's* current list of Best Sellers and penned his feelings in the margin: All Shit. For a major poet and small press writer who's put some of the best years of his life in a classic book of American poetry, *Alliance, Illinois,* and has never received the national attention he deserves, he has the right to judge the bestseller list for what it is.

We're talking fast and loose about all sorts of things, covering all kinds of territory, catching up because we know our time is short. Our voices rise above Woody Herman coming in full blast from a record player above Dave's other desk. We're exchanging hellos, regards, bits of news from our respective places and recent journeys, mostly other writers, poets, and friends we both know or have heard of: Sue Peterson, Maggie Perry, John Judson, and Richard Boudreau . . . they all say hello.

"I brought a couple of copies of *Alliance,*" I tell him, "that Hal Grutzmacher would like you to sign. He said to remind you he meant it when he called you a major poet."

Etter nods, smiles, pulls down a bottle of wine from the shelf, takes a quick swig, and turns Woody up a little louder. "How's Dick Nelson?" he asks.

"Okay. I have coffee at Al's with him most every morning. He worries about you.

Wonders how you survive."

"Me too."

"Me too. Got any freelance work?"

"Naw. Nothing for over four months."

"I'll talk to my friend, Ralph Rausch. Maybe he can dig something up."

"Yeah. That would be great. Want something to drink? Some coffee? I got some Jack Daniel's somewhere."

His bookshelves are filled with midwest memorabilia, all the old writers of the heartland he so dearly loves. A lot of Sandburg on hand, including Dave's own Carl Sandburg award for poetry in 1982 in honor of his book, *West of Chicago.*

"I've been working on *Home State,"* he says, pouring the bottom of a bottle of Jack Daniel's in my coffee cup. "I'm kind of excited about it. I'm just throwing in all kinds of things. Mixing it all up."

"Good, good."

"I just keep working on my stuff all day here," he says, taking another swig from the shelf, part of him tuned into the jazz he keeps hearing, part of him anxious to talk. "I don't know what's going on out there," he laughs, pointing to the world beyond his door. "Used cars, refrigerators . . . I just turn on the music and stay a little juiced up all day. Christ, we got so much to talk about, we need a week."

I'm sitting on the edge of Dave's old easy chair looking at some new poems he's dropped in my lap."

"I don't know if you want to see any of this stuff or not . . . "

"Of course I do."

"Most of these are new, stuff I'm adding to *Home State,* I got stuff like this 'Real Farmers' . . ." and he begins to read a line or two:

Real farmers have sunburned faces and white foreheads.
Real farmers don't wear T-shirts that say *Kiss Me I'm Italian*

and then breaks out into that old Etter laughter, bringing me right along with him. Now a man laughing at his own words may seem a bit strange. But with Etter it's genuine, bottled inside of him, at least 100 proof. He so loves humor in the world, giving language to laughter, that though I've never actually seen Etter the poet-writer in the solitary act of composing his words on paper, my guess would be you'd find him hunched over, very carefully making lines, fitting words, then suddenly doubling over, just cracking himself up over what people say or how he imagines it might be said.

"*Real farmers,"* he continues, "*don't drink strawberry margaritas or eat crepe suzettes . . ."* and he breaks up again, letting me pull out the final line which I love: "*Real farmers know they are real farmers and know that you know they are real farmers."* So much for authentic people—of the Etter kind.

An Etter laugh begins somewhere around mid-gut, rises to the shoulders which begin quaking, setting off the neck and then the whole head in a nodding tempo which may climax with a hoot, the removal of his glasses, and the wiping away of tears. Only to begin again.

"Check this," he says:

Chicago

City of the bent shoulders, the bum ticker, the bad back.
City of the called third strike, the blocked punt. City
of the ever-deferred dream. City of the shattered windshield,
the loose wheel, the empty gas tank. City of I remember
when, of once upon a time. City of not "I will" but of
"I wish I could."

"The bent shoulders," he laughs.
"The bum ticker," I counter.
"The bad back," we break up, blow smoke, and drink in celebration of work-in-progress. "It's going to be a great book," I tell him. "You're moving right into Twain's territory with this one. Etter as local color humorist . . . it's in the American grain. How we doing for time?"

"Marilou, she's the owner, said something about noon. She wants to take us to lunch first."

"Oh, fine."

"Yeah, you'll like her. I wasn't so hot on doing this autograph gig unless you showed up," he says. "The last time I think I sold about five books."

"It could be a long afternoon."

"What do you think of this," as he begins to read another poem from *Home State:*

Looking for Work

So I said to the little man behind the gray steel desk,
"Look, I'll do anything, but I won't do everything." . . .

Which breaks Dave up again considerably . . . "I'll do anything, but I won't do everything," he repeats in a lower register of his voice, the equivalent of "Goddam," or "Too much."

And I'm already half on the floor realizing how Dave himself, 55 years old, a fulltime poet and out-of-work editor, is all too familiar with the predicament of unemployment. I remember him telling me how he finally went to register with an employment agency sometime ago, a fit of desperation, and when he got to the front door he discovered they were out of business. He found that mighty insightful, and damn right funny.

"A great line," I tell him. "I know the feeling," I say, while Dave reads the poem on to the end, repeating that second line to me again for one last laugh.

I think of two other poems from *Alliance, Illinois,* a little more sad and serious in tone, and wonder again how much of Dave Etter inhabits the interior lives of the people he imagines:

Crystal Gavis: Depressed After Being Fired from Another Job

The black ant drags a bread crumb
clear across the kitchen floor.

That's something else I can't do.

I'm thinking of how useless a writer sometimes feels.
I'm thinking of no longer being as young as one feels.

Estelle Etherege: Fifty

Today I am 50 years old. 50!

Coming up the hill from the meat market,
I can see that my house is in sad shape.
The front porch sags, a window is broken,
and the wind chips off flakes of paint.

51, 52, 53, 54, 55, 56 . . . 70!

I'm thinking young or old, past, present or future, rich or poor, known or unknown, Elburn or Ellison Bay, what matters most is this moment in the midst of Dave Etter, sharing his daily life and his words. While he looks for another shirt to wear, I shuffle through the new poems he's left in my lap and discover "Lust":

"Say something from the Bible," Doreen said, as we made ourselves comfortable in wicker chairs on the front porch and looked at three good-looking high school girls getting off the school bus down at the corner. "Okay," I said. "How about this: 'Let her be as the loving hind and pleasant roe; let her breasts satisfy thee at all times; and be thou ravished always with her love.' That's *Proverbs* 5, verse 19." "That's from the Bible?" she said. "Yes, it is," I said. "And so is this: "How beautiful are thy feet with shoes, O prince's daughter! The joints of they thighs are like jewels, the work of the hands of a cunning workman.' That's *the Song of Solomon* 7, verse 1." "Wow," she said, "the Bible is a lot more interesting than I thought." "You got that correct," I said, watching a pair of shapely sixteen-year-old legs walk up the driveway and disappear into the house across the street.

We're in my car next, heading out of Elburn for St. Charles. We're weighing the advantages of a hip flask on a rainy grey November day such as this. Dave's pointing out some forgettable landmarks. "What I like about this place is there's a cemetery at each end of town," he explains. "This old gas station we'll be coming to was in 'Harry and Tonto' with Art Carney, you remember? So was the bone orchard at the other end of town. That's about it for Elburn's claim to fame. But I like it here. Chicago's only 45 miles away, but who cares?" he laughs. "No, I like farm country. I love cornfields. I'd like it up in Door too, if I could find some work. But I suppose I'll stay here. If I lose the house, I'll find an apartment or something in St. Charles."

Coming into St. Charles, I like it immediately. The main drag is alive. There's an old movie house still thriving and a good feeling of people proud of their town. When Dave points out the bookstore, Town House Books, on the corner of 2nd Avenue, it's love at first sight—a wonderful old house with rooms full of books.

Approaching the entrance to the shop we spot copies of *Alliance, Illinois* and *Door Steps* in the window, a poster announcing an autograph signing, and an article for the *Chronicle* (St. Charles, Batavia, Geneva): "Bookstore Will Host Writers," with photographs of the authors.

"Know anything about these guys?" says Dave, nodding to the photos, puffing his pipe.

"Never heard of them before in my life."

"Let's catch their act."

We meet Rick, an employee, and Marilou Kelly, the owner, two folks who plainly love people and books. After a good lunch next door, we are guided to a table in the center of the store stacked with our books.

"You can sit there," smiles Marilou, "or stand up, or walk around. Whatever you feel like. I don't even care if we sell any books; it's just great to have the two of you here."

If there's any place I feel comfortable, it's a bookstore, though under these circumstances, I'm a little on edge. There's not exactly a line waiting to meet us. I recall Dave telling me about some reading he once gave in some church basement in Iowa or somewhere, and only one person showed up.

I don't know how Dave feels at the moment, but he's already wandering around looking at poetry books. I'm checking on all the wonderful fiction on the shelves and wishing I had a 100 bucks to blow. I take a copy of Ray Carver's *Cathedral* back to the table to read.

There are people milling around the store, but so far none of them seem the least interested in us.

But slowly it begins to happen: strangers, friends, friends of friends, readers you never knew you had. It's the perfect tonic for most writers who always feel locked out in the cold. There's even a phone message waiting for me at the desk—someone from my old Chicago neighborhood—and a note from a woman in St. Charles who vacations in Door and expresses her fondness for *Door Steps.*

"Hey, Dave," I whisper. "There are people out there. People who like us. And they're buying our books! Maybe we should declare residency in this store."

Dave is signing books, shaking hands, trying to keep his pipe lit, and being his usual mild-mannered self, occasionally bursting into a laugh. I'm talking to a lady who has bought three copies of the new book, a young man inquiring about winter in Door, and a wonderful Swedish woman, Ingrid, from St. Charles and Door, along with her lovely young lady companion from Sweden whom I'm trying to convince to spend the next summer waitressing at Al Johnson's Restaurant in Sister Bay. Dave seems a little envious at this point.

The people continue to appear all afternoon, some to talk and buy, some just to talk. At one point I hear Marilou joking with a customer over the relative wealth of writers. The customer seems to think we all winter in the south of France and drive Mercedes. I'd like to tell him about Etter barely hanging onto his house, his Monza minus a door, and his check from a poetry magazine the other day for fourteen dollars and forty-four cents. I'd like to take him out to the parking lot and show him a Honda with a 110,000 miles and a lighter-than-air body made of rust. I'd like him to know that whatever the percentage in sales Dave or I make on books sold today, neither of us will see it for at least another year, and I doubt it will amount to a full tank of gas. You've got to be desperate to write.

We depart the bookstore late that afternoon, giving Marilou a hug and a kiss goodbye. She is happy. Our publisher should be happy. Dave and I are happy. It's time for a drink.

We're expected back at the Etter house for dinner in an hour or so, but first we try to find a tavern he seems to remember.

We walk into a place that looks like a refuge for the unemployed, the Saturday afternoon barroom football fans, the "real farmers" who don't drink strawberry margaritas. The bartender is a is a laid-back lady in tight fitting, faded blue jeans. Dave warms to the atmosphere immediately.

He has a beer. I have some beer, some Scotch. And we're off. We begin with the journeys, real and imagined. I've been to Santa Fe twice since I last saw him, and just

51

recently returned from Florida where I visited my son at the university in Gainesville. "Made it to Key West," I tell him, "Sloppy Joe's, Hemingway's old house, stone crab, conch soup, Mallory Square, tropical breezes, the sun always rises, just about every damn day. You'd love it. A hide-out for writers, past and present. Even old Frost done time in that clime. And it's never snowed there. *Ever!*" Etter seems ready to head south just as soon as he finishes his beer.

"And what about Santa Fe?" he asks. And I do my usual hour routine on life in the desert Southwest.

"I gotta get out there," he says. "Maybe we can line up a reading. Can't you see me telling Peg: 'I'll be gone for a bit. I've got to do this reading way out west of Chicago'."

Talk of the Southwest reminds him of his younger days, living and loving and drinking in Tijuana. And there's nothing better than good old downhome Dave Etter, the king of the cornfields, talking Tijuana. How he was under the influence most of the time. What the houses of ill repute were like. How he could have been damn near killed in some of those places. Why he considers himself lucky to have escaped to the Midwest with his life. "I mean, I was drinking real heavy down there. Real bad. I mean it was like 'The End'."

The Last Show in Tijuana

She shimmys and rolls her hips to
a drum-heavy beat: gyrations
of artless sex. We've come to leer.

We stare at her thick thighs, shiny
copper belly, jelly breasts, and
drink bottles of Tecate beer.

This stripper, a girl not sixteen,
shakes her plump can in our faces.
We smile weakly, too drunk to cheer.

We're midway between our second or third refills. The woods are getting lonely, dark and deep, and we have dinner promises to keep . . . but we've still got a lot of ground to cover. We're talking about the things men usually talk about when they find the release. What turns some men into writers, early on, when there's no one else to tell it to.

We're talking all those things men desire but can't quite grasp. We're talking women, survival, and recognition. We're talking material rewards that will never visit our door, and all we could do with just a little bit more. We're talking friends who are either long gone, or lost it on the way. We're talking remembrance and desire, our most constant themes.

"What do you say we have one more drink?" we say, which is what men always say when they try to prolong the story at hand and avoid the inevitable ending.

I tell Dave my parrot joke, and he tells me about a piece of graffiti he saw: Oral Sex Sucks.

Just about everything sounds hilarious at this point. "I love parrot jokes," Dave says.

"Then you'll love the one about the woman who goes into a tattoo parlor and tells

52

the guy she wants a tattoo of Robert Redford on her thigh. The guy tattoos Redford and asks her, 'What do you think?' 'Okay,' she says. 'Now I want a tattoo of Paul Newman on the other thigh.' So the guy tattoos Newman for her. 'Well, what do you think?' 'Not bad,' she says. But the tattoo artist isn't so sure, so he calls for a third opinion, a drunk who happens to be passing by. 'Hey,' he says, 'Come in here. Help me out. Who does that look like?' he points to Redford on the woman's thigh. The drunk checks it out. 'I'm not sure,' he says, 'but it looks sort of like Robert Redford. 'And what about the face on the other side?' he asks the drunk. "Lemme see . . . I'd say maybe that's Paul Newman. But that guy ther ein the middle, no doubt about it. That's Willie Nelson'."

I buy a boilermaker to quiet him down, make my way to the men's room in the back, memorize some great graffiti on the wall, and forget it once I've returned to the bar.

"What happened to the parrot?" he says.

"What parrot?"

"It's time to go," somebody says.

Dave leaves a healthy tip for the barmaid, whose service he's grown fond of.

"That's for her blue jeans," I tell him.

"She works real well in them," he replies.

Outside it's cold and raining dark blue. We head the car down the road with visions of blue jeans dancing in our heads:

Lester Rasmussen: Jane's Blue Jeans

Hanging alone on a blue-rain clothesline,
hanging alone in a blue rain,
hanging alone:

a pair of torn blue jeans,
a pair of faded blue jeans,
a pair of Jane's blue jeans.

Blue jeans in the shape of Jane,
Jane now in another pair of blue jeans,
blue jeans that also take the shape of Jane.

Oh, Jane, my rainy blues blue-jeans girl,
blue jeans without you inside
is the saddest blue I've seen all day.

"There are parrots in Key West," I explain to Dave. "And Hemingway's cats, which all have at least six toes. I saw a parrot walking down the street. And another one in Sloppy Joe's."

"It must have been thirsty."

"It **was**, it **was**! I saw this guy on a bike with iguanas all over him . . . the Iguana Man."

"That figures."

"A lot of strange people down there, Dave. But you gotta do it, you know? You gotta just do it. I mean where are the iguanas of Elburn?"

"Or yesteryear."

"Right. And in the recorded history of mankind, it has never snowed in Key West. That's what's waiting for me up in Door: the Big Winter. From Iguana Men to Snow Men. Talk of future shock. I came from the desert Southwest to the north woods, to the tropics, and now back to the tundra. I mean, where am I?"

"Elburn, Illinois."

"Jesus."

"I've been to Nebraska."

"That's right next door to Minneota, Minnesota, where our buddy, Pichaske, lives, ain't it? Now you're talking desolation. I was out there to see him last year. I thought I landed on the moon in February."

"Yeah, it's pretty bleak."

"Where do we live? How do we live? What the hell good are we to any place if we're not good to ourselves? How much time we got? That's el question grande. Want to see everything. Be everything. Be everywhere. And it's either happening faster than I can make something of it, or it's not happening at all."

"Yeah. Right. Exactly. But Jesus, I don't know. Remember Twain talking about carrying all your eggs in one basket. Why can't you carry them all in one basket? Like Like Streisand said on TV the other night, people always saying, you can't have it all. Why not? Why not have it all?"

The lights are burning in the Etter house in Elburn. The dining room table is beautifully set. Dave's daughter, Emily, wife, Peg, and mother-in-law are sitting in the living room nibbling on crackers and Wisconsin cheese. Dave's son, George, is reportedly somewhere in the depths of the basement, pumping iron.

There seems to be some concern whether we'd make it back in time or make it back at all. "Actually, we're on our way to Key West," says Dave. "How did the autographing go?" somebody asks. "Oh, they were really pleased with us," says Dave. "We sold a lotta books." "I loved the people," I add. "We're thinking of taking the act on the road."

"We were worried you guys might not find your way back," says Emily, "but George says you're used to driving the Door County roads at night with a bottle of Jack Daniel's between your knees." "Somehow George has the wrong impression," I say. "How do you want your steak?" Peg asks. "What do you say we have a drink?" someone suggests. Dave's mother-in-law says she wouldn't mind a little bourbon but says, in an undertone toward me, Dave won't get it for her. Dave returns with drinks for all but neglects to fill his mother-in-law's request. "See, what did I tell you," she says to me. "I'll get you your drink, mother," says Peg, who is most accomodating.

It's wonderful dinner. The conversation is all over the place. Dave and I seem to be wondering: Who invited us to this excellent feast tonight? Dave cleans his plate and is looking for further contributions. "Oh, I won't eat this all," says Peg. "Here, Dave, take some of mine." Dave's mother-in-law is talking about big houses, big cars, and servants in the olden days. How once on a trip they made a whole roast on the running board of a touring car. Emily rolls her eyes and says she's waiting for her date to take her bowling. George, a health food nut, has decided to pass on the steak and remains somewhere in the basement still lifting weights. I feel we're all in a George S. Kaufman play, ready for whatever happens next.

Dave gets out some old photographs, and I'm looking at Etter as a young man, the Etters in New England, and the Etters in Door County. Dave stands up to announce, "I'm *really* disappointed we did not get to Door this year. We can't let that happen again." Peg says she's going to make reservations for next year just as soon as she can.

Dave hands me a copy of the *Elburn Herald,* 20 pages, 20 cents, and points to the announcement of the autograph party held today. The news in Elburn is mighty thin. But I can see Dave perusing every edition for any little bit of small town information that might be transformed into poem.

"Check this," he says to an ad he's circled on the last page: 'Interesting Facts Brought to You Every Week By Bucki Insurance Agency . . . Although the English language alphabet now has 26 letters, it had only 25 letters until the 17th century. The last letter to enter the alphabet was J.'

"Can you imagine spouting off with that choice bit at some cocktail party," he laughs. "How many people you suppose *know* that?"

In the Classifieds, under WANTED, there's only one ad: "Looking for tenant farmer for farm house," it reads. Slim pickin's for the unemployed.

"Look at this," I tell him: " 'FOR SALE, Two five month roosters—Show quality. Pencil stripped Wyandotte and Golden Polish, $5 each '."

"Golden Polish!" chuckles Etter. "Pencil stripped Wyandotte!" his shoulders begin to quake.

It could be a poem will come from this. I nurse a small sadness in my heart that I didn't see the ad earlier. That along with the apples, cheese, and Early Times, I had not handed Dave two roosters for his backyard.

"Five bucks a piece. How could you go wrong?" I tell him. "You could be the Roosterman of Elburn, Etter. Every man needs a myth. Myself, I find comfort in coyotes."

Later that night we literally walk the streets of Elburn, and Dave's love affair with the rural, small town Illinois life seems planted in every step. "I always walk on the street," he says. "I make this trip every day to the post office and back."

Most of the houses are dark at this time. Here and there a light in the window. The lawns are large, the fences few, and the style of the houses—midwest ordinary. "There are two churches," he says. "That's the funeral parlor. I've been there a few times."

Though Dave's work, it seems, will always echo the influence of Sandburg, Lindsay, and Edgar Lee Master's Spoon River, it's Thornton Wilder's *Our Town* that haunts me most on this late night walk through Elburn with Etter . . . *Well, I'd better show you how our town lies. Up here . . . is Main Street. Way back there is the railway station; tracks go that way . . .*

Down Main Street everything seems dead and gone. The pizza parlor is open and empty except for the cook sitting alone at a back table watching TV.

Crossing some tracks, I'm glad for Dave there's a railroad going through, and a shadow of a grain elevator in the distance. He's a man who so loves and needs those particular midwestern monuments and images (however ghostly they've become) to do a poet's work at home . . . to sing their praises. And for such a lover of the rails, I wish him an old depot near to hang around in, and a courthouse square with a clock, a cannon, a statue of Lincoln, some pigeons, and some benches filled with some real farmers for him to talk with and grow old.

Dave stands between the tracks facing an eastern sky clouded in darkness yet glowing in an eerie haze of pink. "Chicago's down there," he says.

We walk down the entire length of Main Street on one side, then back up the other, Dave pointing out the fairgrounds and other ordinary things. It's a common enough place no one would ever suspect a poet to be living in, which is probably why Etter is there.

The tavern we turn into doesn't even have a sign or a light in the window; it is *that* dead in Elburn on a Saturday night. Even Etter thinks the joint is closed. We sit at a dark bar with three customers (one of them the bartender), nursing a final drink, staring at dusty pennants on the wall, watching TV.

I steal a glance at Etter, lost in the lascivious antics of Benny Hill on the tube, and suddenly feel old. Etter looks old. The bar is past its prime. Elburn is on the road to nowhere, the Midwest is history, and we've even bequeathed our imaginations to places lost in time. But let no man write my epitaph . . . yet.

Late that night, lying on a cot in Dave's dining room, fighting the demons of darkness, desiring more spirit, light everywhere, I turn the lamp on and read an early Etter poem:

> *On Growing Old In A Quiet Town*
>
> The old codgers across the street
> at the Presbyterian rest home
> are sticking seeds on clammy cardboard.
>
> I want to run away to cornfields.
>
> Summer bathrobes are worn loosely,
> exposing the worn inner thighs
> of men gone fallow behind bricks.
>
> Night knocks in my head of harvests.
>
> Crows fly among the shrunken pine cones.

I arise in darkness hours later, the house fast asleep, and head for the car hoping to find my way out of Elburn the same way I came. But signs point me in other directions, and all the roads seem different in the dark.

With the coming of daylight, I seem to recognize the way.

St. Pat—and the End of the Rainbow

Ah, for the breath of some blarney in a confused world of too many serious people trying to make too much sense out of everything. And nobody serves it up better (straight or on the rocks) then St. Patrick (alias James Patrick Fagan), Door County's father to fallen souls, comforter (Southern or name you own nirvana) to troubled and untroubled hearts, Grand Marnier Master of Ceremonious Nights on the Door. (He tells of one forgettable night in his particular parish—the Top Deck of Gordon Lodge—when Grand Marnier flowed in such abundance that the Saint himself seemed baffled the next morning to find all the money slots of the cash drawer filled with it.) A man of many miracles. Wine to water was easy. But a cold cash drawer to Grand Marnier? Only an uncanonized Irish bartending saint could do.

Smile, Patrick! (Which is his winning way with the world.)

He's always smiling. (Or will be again, he promises, as soon as he gets his teeth fixed. He's made a deal at the bar with some dentist. And you can bet your own teeth that St. Pat will soon be smiling with his new ivories—high-tailing it to Chicago, to Florida, or back to Door—while the dentist will be wondering who took the big bite out of him.)

He's a rolling stone, a ramblin' man, the veritable "condition" our elders warned we might someday find ourselves in if we weren't thrifty and well-behaved: a man without a pot to piss in or a window to throw it out.

Smile, Paddy! Your horse is in the money.

There he goes, snapping those fingers in front of your face, brushing that long wisp of black hair over his balding pate, flashing that smile, giving you the Irish: "I'm tellin' ya! Listen to me!" Giving you his beautiful BS.

Dressed, always, partially in green, baggy pants hanging from his rather thin frame, his hands constantly fishing his front pockets for a cigarette lighter or cash. One of the biggest tippers of all time, he carries a crumpled wad of bills (his life savings) in his front pocket, pulling off fives and singles for the "help"—with whom he of course identifies. A single cup of coffee from a smiling waitress (say Denise Braun at Al's) will net her at least a three dollar tip. Maybe five. The last of the bigtime spenders. Definitely a city-type.

Much of his personal history he carries in his back pocket: brochures for Gordon Lodge, business cards of his customers, tickets to the up-and-coming Bartenders' Benefit Roast, crumpled copies of his column, "St. Pat Sez," letters of love and thanks, including this one from a kid: "Dear St. Patrick, Thank you for the pretty sweater. I love it. Love, Maria."

He loves children. Loves people. Loves charitable causes. More than a bit of the Irish in him. He's definitely the guy who would give you the shirt off his own back. "I will donate to anything, as long as it's a worthy cause." Rich or poor, he's been both. Sometimes in a matter of minutes.

Bless the fast horses, St. Patrick. And the long shots.

Of course there's a bit of the con-artist about him. (But aren't we all a little envious of the fast talker?) It's the language of the survivor who must live by his mouth. A hustling life doesn't come easy. And there are times the piper must be paid. Even moments of sadness around those black, beetle-brows and bright blue eyes of St. Pat. Bartender! Maybe just one more before I have another.

Let's hear it for the *good* St. Pat. Isn't there always a smile for the ladies, a joke for the men, an "occasional" drink on the Saint himself? Isn't he a Door County Chamber of Commerce of one? (Note to the Chamber: When you're passing out your annual awards, don't forget to pass the hat for St. Pat.) Hasn't he always drummed up the business for every establishment he's ever worked, collaring people on the street, in restaurants, wherever?

Doesn't he bang the drum loudly for any benefit that captures his attention, consummate ticket salesman, the softest touch? "It's for a good cause," he assures you with that devilish grin.

Wasn't he on the hustle again at Al's the other morning, snapping his fingers, ("Money in the bank!"), predicting he'd sell more tickets to the Roast than Wink Larson? "It's a sellout, man! A *sellout! The* social event of the year in Door County! For SCAND. For the old people. Gotta help 'em out, right?" He turns to a full table of tourists who are smiling into their Swedish pancakes. "Say," he says to an attractive lady smoker, "Weren't you at Gordon's the other night? The Top Deck? Would you have an extra cigarette? Thanks. Did I hear Chicago?" he swings around toward another table. "Isn't it beautiful here, this county? Stop by at the Deck for a drink." He begins passing out brochures from his back pocket. "By the way, we're roasting Al Johnson this year. Only $30 a person—proceeds to SCAND. A deal! A deal! I'm gonna be one of the m.c.'s. Yeah, Al. Only don't mention it to him. Shhhh. He's not supposed to know. He's madder than hell. He might be a no-show. Winky says he'll hang Al's picture up. The hell with him. It's *our* party! Listen, a $3,000 contribution to the Roast could possibly guarantee you a corner room of your own at SCAND—with cross ventilation!"

There are more than Irish eyes smiling when St. Pat's on a roll. He's seen good times and bad times—but he'd rather be on a roll. Quote (from his exclusive and unsyndicated column appearing irregulary in summers in the *Door Reminder*): "Even though your chips are low, there are some left for giving." Or, "A cocktail a day keeps the blues away."

Who *is* this guy?

I manage to hustle him off one morning to a quiet picnic bench along the Lake Michigan shore for a few hours—definitely a fish out of water. St. Pat without a crowd—without strangers, without a bar to sit at or set up—is a drinker, a smoker doing cold turkey.

"Sit down, St. Pat, goddamit! This is Mother Nature all around you. This is what you keep telling the tourists you love about Door County. Yes, I know, all it needs is a racetrack," I tell him.

What's worse, he's on his last Camel cigarette. (Not that it matters what kind of cigarette at this point.) Already his flickering eyes are scanning the horizon, the empty picnic benches, the empty beach. St. Pat in exile. Who's he gonna hit up for a smoke?

"Don't you have *one* cigarette on you?" he pleads. It's OK. I'm alright. I'm telling you . . ." And he does.

His father, Peter Fagan, from County Cork, a railroad man, died when Patrick was 10. His mother, Mary Lenehan, lived to the age of 93. Cleveland, Ohio is home—was home. He doesn't really have a home, except for summers in Door County, tending bar.

He lives in a suitcase, owns no car, no house, no bank account. Nothing. Zero. Zilch. Zip. A man on the run.

"I travel with a deck of cards, ten pairs of socks, five pairs of shorts, and a rosary," he laughs. "I'm not afraid to go into any city without a dime in my pocket. I've never missed a meal. Willing to do anything. I'm at ease with the Vanderbilts and the bums on the street because I speak the international language—friendship. Money is nothing to me. Money is a kernel of corn the Indians used to trade. I've seen wealth in action—many, many unhappy people screaming over a few measly dollars."

Like many a good Irish lad, Jimmie Fagan seemed destined for the priesthood. That was his mother's wish. "And there I was, on my way to Sacred Heart Seminary in Detroit. I left Holy Name High at the age of 14. I worked nights on the railroad as a switchman. But I loved horses too. I worked days at the racetrack—Ascot Park in Akron, galloping the horses. Exercise boy. And then the family threw this party for me, sending me off to the seminary to be a priest. I had the black suit and the sheets and everything. And I was on the bus, talking to the driver, and we passed a racetrack in Maumee, Ohio . . . 1945. And the driver knew! He knew! Let me out of here! And I was off to the races. Because of my Irish mother, I didn't go home for three years. Nor did I talk to her.

"I knocked around racetracks all over the country, and I noticed how dressed-up the jockey agents were. Agents are solicitors for mounts for a jockey. You gotta know breeding, be an excellent handicapper—which I was. It looked like dream street. The end of the rainbow! (St. Pat is standing now, hollering, rummaging through his pockets for a cigarette. I offer him a pipe—no good. The stub of my cigar—no good.) I'm alright! I'm alright! Let's go. I gotta sell some more damn tickets!

"Where was I? The end of the rainbow! But little did I know, little did I know (lots of drama in his wonderful Irish storytelling voice, lots of facial expression) that the jockey agents were mostly broke! But anyway, I moved out of the barn and into a hotel. And I met a jockey, Eric Guerin, who went on to win every major stake in the country. And I was with him for 14, 15 years. Hialeah, New York, the Jersey circut . . .

"Goddamn it! Doesn't anyone have a cigarette? It's alright.

"I learned about the fast life—booze, broads, the good times. A beautiful woman in every city. Nice ladies. Mucho women. But they weren't promiscuous women. I made them that way!

"At one point my jockey couldn't make the weight anymore. And I felt I never really wanted another jockey because we were such good friends. So I went to Palm Beach, Florida on a vacation and I met a guy, Joe O'Hara, who said he needed a bartender. I lied and told him I could do it. He put me into the service area that night. And all of a sudden here come 10 professional cocktail waitresses, and they all started ordering drinks I never knew *existed*. I said, PLEASE, GET ME OUT OF HERE!

"O'Hara asked me if I could make a Scotch and water. Hell, that's what *I* drink! Anyway, he told me he would teach me how to tend bar, but I could not participate in tips, or salary, till I learned how. After 10 days, he came in one night all dressed up with his wife. It was a Saturday night. And he said, "You're on your own!"

"I was in my 30's then. I had black beautiful hair and white teeth. The women would just roll all over me. I love all women, and no particular woman will ever catch my eye. Marriage, no. Still . . . I love kids. I would have loved to have some kids.

As for the Florida/Door County connection. Just how did that take place?

"John D. MacArthur," says Pat. "Jesus, don't you have *one* cigarette? Anyway, he came into O'Hara's. What a guy. A multi-millionaire. He once refused to see Howard Hughes. He loved people who drank. I could tell you a million stories about him. He came into O'Hara's and I was on one of my *super* highs. He *told* me I was going to work for him as head bartender at the Colonades Beach Hotel on Singer Island, a mile north of Palm Beach on the ocean. *Those* were my happy years—11 years. The end of the rainbow! Whatever I wanted. He was good to me.

"He gave me a derby hat for a tip cup and made sure all his millionaire friends took care of me. And *he* even tipped me a few times. At 5 o'clock every day, the piano player *had* to play "September Song" for him.

"It was about the time the French Canadians started coming to Florida for vacations, and John MacArthur was one of the leaders in promoting this. He insisted that all the pretty women land at Palm Springs and stay at the beautiful Colonades Hotel. The phone would be ringing off the hook for these gals. And, yeah, I was a pimp! One year I introduced 89 couples who later married. God knows how many friendships.

"At 9:30 every night, MacArthur's calico cat—who was addicted to booze—would come for a shot of anisette. And if the cat didn't get it, somebody on the staff would be fired! Of course I kept the cat happy!

"Pet ducks walked through any part of the hotel at anytime. He loved animals. One day the calico cat disappeared and he hired *three* private detectives to find it!

"Mrs. MacArthur, a low-key person, a lovely lady, would usually pass by the door at 1:30 in the morning, and I'd always try to be there to say hello. She was special to me. Not a drinker like the old man. He drank a fifth of Grand Dad every day. And he *insisted* that I join him. And I became addicted to at *least* a fifth of J. & B. Scotch a day.

"Some of the famous customers I served there . . . Bishop Sheen, a CC Manhattan with a water back. Jack Kennedy. I trembled when he came in. Dewar's White Label Scotch on the rocks. Always some joke. The latest joke. Jackie Gleason and his beautiful wife would sit at the bar and make my day by ordering champagne, $75 a bottle. I was very low key with him because I was always nervous when he came in. And he always shook my hand when he left—with a crisp C-note for the Saint!

"The name! The name! Saint Patrick. How I got my name. There was a theft at the hotel of towels and sheets—I mean, more than usual. And Mr. MacArthur hired some detectives and a lie detector expert to case the hotel. One day he came up to me and said: 'Patrick, you really are a saint.' I was clean. The detectives had watched me, cleared me. Little did he know I have a 6th sense about strange people watching me!"

And *then* you came to Door County, I suggest.

"Wait! Wait! The girl jockey. I gotta tell you about the girl jockey! I took a year off to handle a ————— fat —————. I could a been a millionaire! If only she would have watched her weight! She was rejected by everyone but the owner of Tropical Park Race Track at Coral Gables, Saul Siberman. Her name was Barbara Jo Rubin. The owner retained me to get her started. All the jockeys were unhappy with her. The *first* woman to step into their territory. After working with her in the morning, I knew she had the talent to compete with the boys in the afternoon. After many setbacks she won the first pari-mutuel race by a female anywhere! At Charlestown Race Track in West Virginia. The 7th race. The horse was Cohesion. Paid $3.80. I don't bet on favorites. That's for suckers. The telephone started ringing the next day. She had every newspaper in the United States. Deals to appear at car washes, TV shows, the Kraft Music Hall, all the talk shows. I *demanded* exuberant fees for her engagements. And of course she would rather be riding horses every day.

"Now hear this: Aqueduct Race Track. A trainer who apparently wanted to cash a big bet on this filly called me and asked me if she would like to ride at Aqueduct. Aqueduct! The 'big apple' brother! Hey, is this it? It was a weekday and the average crowd on those days was 28,000. Well, 50,000 people jammed that track to watch her ride. The name of the horse was Bravy Galaxy. The horse romped by 11 lengths. He paid $28. St. Pat was smiling from ear to ear and buying drinks for all his friends. $100 bills were in the minority. I had $2,000 riding on her that day. Back to the hotel, and *on the town!*

"Her picture was everywhere, every newscast, international coverage. Advertising companies calling up for commercials. Newspaper and magazine articles. The Ed Sullivan Show. I was going mad! And all I saw: This is *finally* the end of the rainbow.

"I had simply forgotten a thing called weight. The poor girl could no longer make the weight. From 111 she blew up to 130 pounds. I called the suicide prevention bureau, and they put me on hold! That's how bad my luck was going. I went on an *enormous* drunk in Atlantic City and somehow ended up in a hotel in Ft. Lauderdale with an 80 year old woman dressed in black at my side. I asked her, 'Did anything happen?' And she said, 'Are you kidding?' I looked around the room for money . . . how silly could I have been? I went back to old man MacArthur with my hat in my hand. I put in another five years with him.

"You build all this, and it shatters. Jesus Christ, is this happening to me? Me! It's like the end of your life . . . the lousy————[girl jockey].

"So I was back at the Colonades, and one time this couple comes in and tells me about their beautiful resort in Door County, Wisconsin. Phil and Curly Gordon, I snickered to myself and said, 'Wisconsin? Door County, Wisconsin?' After the Gordons left, a real elderly bartender, Eddie O'Brien, told me that Door County was *exactly* like Ireland. The next year, 1971, I arrived. By bus, of course, I don't have my own car. I keep my life savings in my pocket.

"I said to myself: 'This is it, brother. The end of the rainbow for me.' And I've been happy, happy, happy ever since.

"One of my favorite first persons I met here—Eddie Scheider. Fast Eddie, I call him. And Lou Braun, who worked the Baileys Harbor Yacht Club. I used to go to these guys to unwind. Many a laugh.

"Phil Gordon to me was a genius. At first I didn't realize why he had separated the bar from the dining room, but *everything* he did was right. He even had the windows of the Top Deck set a certain way so we can catch a double sunset. Genius! The man was a genius!

"One night he came into the Top Deck, I poured him his usual Scotch on the rocks, and he said: "You better have one yourself. He probably knew I already had 20. The people from Milwaukee always bought the bartender a drink. They didn't tip—but they bought you a drink. Sure! Always. It's an inside joke among the bartenders. We call them the F.B.I. agents because all they ever leave are fingerprints. And you *must* drink it right there. You can't tell them you'll have it later. They *insist* you have it in front of them. You see what Milwaukee's done to me? I love 'em.

"Many, many a night Phil Gordon and I sat alone in the Deck and drank till 7 in the morning. We discusses the world at large. He liked all the philosophers, and I liked Tolstoy—because he made love to every woman in sight! I loved Phil, Curly, the whole family.

"Where's a cigarette, a cigarette?" He's pacing the beach now, a determined man. "A butt, a butt. Isn't there one stinking butt on this beach? See how clean this goddam county is! Can't even find a cigarette butt here!

"My kind of bar is a one-man operation. It's hard to work with other bartenders. I take charge of the room. I can see any argument starting in any part of the room. I eject them. No crabby people. Strictly happy people. I try to generate love in the room.

"The Top Deck is a finger-touch control bar. Phil created it. The view is the most spectacular view in Door County. But the magic about the bar is the customers. Not just the hotel people, but the people in the county. And Chicago's Northside. My *favorites*. Because they're outgoing, likeable people, and it's easy to make them laugh. If crabby people come in, it's a personal challenge to me to make them laugh and enjoy themselves—because they'll come back and tell their friends!

"If they're all having fun and they don't get argumentative, fine. If not, then they have to deal with the Saint who will chop them up with words and bring tears to their eyes. I tell the drunk to go home to his wife and family. I'm responsible for him on the highway. When I say 86th Street, that's the end for the evening. Every bartender knows that.

"My famous customers at Gordon's: Jane Byrne, number one. She was in this year. I love her because she's a gutsy little Irishman who stood up to the political machine and showed them all how the city of Chicago should be run. She walked right into the Top Deck, and I did not recognize her at first—an especially busy night. When her party left for dinner, she came up to me and said: 'You Irish bullshitter. Don't you recognize me? I want to thank you for all the nice things you've said about me.' The next 15 drinks were mixed wrong. I broke 8 glasses and forgot to pick up a friend at the airport.

"She came back after dinner to the anchor out front—a favorite meeting place for lovers—and waved me out. I had a warm and interesting 11-minute conversation with her. I walked back into the bar and told Andy and Lou Foster that my life was complete. The end of the rainbow! I fell in love with her. Besides, if she ever becomes mayor of Chicago again, I want to drive her limousine. Or be her personal bartender!

"Frank Sinatra. Yes! No B.S. Jack Daniel's on the rocks. Sally Struthers . . . Hell, I can't remember them all."

When the doors to Gordon Lodge and the Top Deck swing shut in mid-October, St. Pat is on the move once more. Time to pack the suitcase again. Time to board the bus. Take the act back on the road.

"Then it's *my* vacation time," he smiles. "After the season at Gordon's and before coming back up here from Florida, I always hit Chicago. With my savings from both resorts in my pocket, I become a bartender's delight. I check in at the Continental Hotel off Michigan Ave. All the staff, the help there know me. Gratuities flow like buttermilk. I can get any girl I want in Chicago by saying three magic words: Here's a hundred. I high roll it!

"After about 7 days—the semi-annual collect call goes out to the good father for the *non-transferable* bus ticket to either Florida or Door County."

The "good father"? "The Rev. H.J. Fagan, pastor of the Immaculate Conception Catholic Church in Madison, Ohio. My brother. I call him Harry. He's a top fundraiser like myself. Once in a while he tries to hit me up for something. And he talks almost as fast as I do."

What's St. Patrick like, let loose in Chicago? His eyes light up again. "My first stop on the Chicago hit parade: Pat Harah's, a little dinky bar off Rush. Seven in the morning. All the night bartenders, young guys, are coming in, telling their stories. And me and the old bartender there, we just wink at each other because we've heard these stories a million times. Then I hop over to Butch McGuire's, my favorite saloon, to be with the young and up-and-coming politicians, to listen to their banter about the city of Chicago. In the afternoon I stroll through Saks Fifth Avenue, looking for a nice eligible lady to take to dinner the following night. Before you know it, it's time to walk up to the Pump Room and be sure to get there in time for the 4 o'clock cocktail hour. I'm trolling for broads now, and I'm hoping I might find a promiscuous lady so I can save that $100! I might go off to the Cafe Bohemia then. A lot of places. Usually about 7 I hop a cab back to the hotel and step into my one and only barrister-type, pinstripe suit, then check the desk only to discover that none of the ladies I have bought *numerous* cocktails for have called! On to the Cape Cod Room where a 100 people are waiting for dinner—and the *maitre de* spots me and says, 'Right this way, Sir.' And brings me to a 4-top table that would knock your eyes out. Of course, there was $20 in my hand when I approched him. Lobster! What the hell else is there to eat? And an *enormous* tip for all the service staff.

"Of course by now I've handed out at least 150 brochures to Gordon Lodge. You will never know, that no matter where I am for the winter, that not a moment goes by in any day that Door County doesn't enter it. I've *found* my paradise, brother. This is my home now. The end of the rainbow. It's a mile and a quarter to heaven. It might be heaven! I tell people who come here, 'You think you came here by choice? You were destined to come here by the Power above!' "

We're heading back to town now. Lunch at Al's. A pack of cigarettes for St. Pat. ("Camels! The humper. Five packs a day!") He must open the Top Deck in a couple of hours, but from now until then he's pushing tickets for the Roast. As for the origin of the Bartenders' Roast:

"Digger and I were having a drink one night at the Baileys Harbor Yacht Club. And there were two gift shop people there who hated each other. Digger and I decided we would buy each of them a drink, but have the bartender tell them that each guy bought it for the other one. That's how it started.

"The first Roast was for the former owner of the Baileys Harbor Yacht Club, Joe Smolenski. Let me tell you, those were *tough* tickets to sell! This is the seventh roast though there hasn't been seven. We've skipped a few. Last year it was Wink [Larson]. Let me tell you. He's got enemies too! Great guy. And last year the benefit was to Help Move St. Rosalia's Up the Hill. It's up there, ain't it? Stick with the bartenders. They're the lifeline of the community. Every bit of news that passes through a community first goes through a bartender. Someday this roast will make $50,000 for some charity. I hope it's St. Patrick!

"But this will be the biggest Roast ever. Al Johnson—my kind of guy. I was dumb till I seen him work. I've copied him. He is *the* top restauranteur. That's why I respect him—because I only like winners. His people all love him. Love him, are you kidding? How's this when I help to introduce him: Al Johnson's driving up to Door County, and this beautiful hitchhiker stops him. 'Say,' she says, 'Do you go all the way?' And Al drove her to Washington Island."

Time for an early afternoon cocktail. And there's smiling St. Pat behind the large window of the Top Deck, swinging two bottles of booze, always luring the customers in.

"Ah, the Fourth Estate," he says, with "your" drink (once he learns it) already

64

poured. "People come to bars not to drink," he tells you. "They come to meet and have good conversations. Talking to each other beats 90% of the entertainers. 99% of the people in Door County conduct themselves like gentlemen and ladies at the bar. Brandy Old Fashioned Sweet, the number one drink. More brandy is comsumed in the state of Wisconsin than anywhere else in the world.

"I will not mention my favorite drinkers, but Saturday night at 10 when the regulars appear, that'll be a VO and water here, a VO and water here," and St. Pat goes on matching the drink with the empty place at the bar till he's damn near filled the place with his friends. "A bartender must be discreet. His vows are stronger than the priest, stronger than the seal of the confessional. Yes. I consider myself like a priest. I deal with more people than they do. And one-to-one!

"A lady comes into the bar one afternoon and tells me she doesn't think she can go on. She lost her gusband six months ago. I told her to go out to the end of the dock and touch the last bench. She would meet someone real soon. That afternoon she met a salesman! She came back a couple of days later and told me she was getting married. I can't tell you how *many* matches I've made!

"Touch the last bench . . . they all do it here. It's a ritual. St. Pat's version of the Blarney Stone. Good luck, good fortune. *Anything* can happen.

"A bartender must be a good listener," he continues. "He must be able to listen to five different conversations at one time and blend them all into one so that you have 10 happy people at the same time. Never discuss religion or politics. Memory! You must remember their drinks. And sometimes you must remember to forget who they are drinking with! And for my beautiful, beautiful ladies, I give them titles: Countess, Princess, Queen. Because I really believe that's what they are."

The banter, the blarney, the bull—the magic of St. Patrick. It's irresistible. As addictive as alcohol. A double-whammy: St. Pat and a drink of your choice. He's working some out-of-town customers at the bar now, charming them all. One guy, who finds St. Pat's hyper-delivery too incredible for words, finally asks: "How long can you keep this up? How long do you work?" "All afternoon, all night," St. Pat answers. "Six days a week." The guy shakes his head in wonder, and keeps drinking.

It's the Irish in him, I suggest.

"Just like my mother," counters St. Pat. "She was a fast talker. A politico. Banging doors. Dragging me along with her. Talk to the people. It's our heritage. You're brought up to be proud of being an Irishman. I've worn green all my life. Of course the Irish build castles in the air. They're all daydreamers. It's a magical feeling. The outgoing personality . . . sometimes overpowering to some people. I can't explain it. A lot of dopers ask me what I take. I tell them I'm on a natural high. And I love it, this way. I'm like this from the moment I wake up. I'm down very rarely. Only for 30 seconds. Then I lift my bootstraps right away, and I'm off to the races! It's another hill to climb—make that a mountain."

Russ Stemper comes in. "The world's oldest piano player," announces St. Pat. "A Notre Dame graduate. I love this guy. My favorite piano player—next to Barbara LeBreck. Who I really love too. And Lou Foster—the one man band! Frank's [Sinatra] looking at a song of Russ' right now. Right? [Russ waves him away.] I'm gonna call the guy tomorrow. Frank records that, and it's the end of the rainbow, buddy. Who are the greatest tippers in the world?" he asks Stemper.

"The Northside of Chicago," Stemper replies.

"Just listen to this man! Didn't I tell you?"

And what's the biggest tip St. has ever received?

"$300 one night here in the Deck. They guy smiled and said he finally met a bartender who could high roll it. His tab came to about $600. He gave me a thousand—keep the change. How about you, Russ? What was your biggest tip?"

"A hundred bucks."

"And who gave it to you?" asks St. Pat.

Russ points his finger at Pat. "And the next day he was at my door to borrow a hundred," says Russ. "I kept it for three or four days."

"One night I asked Lou Braun for $20 at his bar," says St. Pat. "I already paid the tab, I told him. This is your tip. The biggest tipper in Door County! You're looking at him. That's why I love the wealthy—they taught me how to tip!"

In and out the door many times, St. Pat reflects: "I've been fired from Gordon Lodge 36 times—and rehired the next morning." And if by chance some day he awakes to find the door to the Top Deck closed to him for good? "I'll come back and be a doorman at Al's. Just to open those doors for the people, I'll pay *him* a $100 a week! Or I'll shine shoes. I've got a lot of pride, but I'd do anything to be here. I'm going to live to be 93 just like my fast-talking Irish mother. The man upstairs told me. So get used to me."

Though there was some speculation that St. Pat might be a goner for good after last year's season, he is on the mend. Amen. Off the hootch, since last year's celebrated Door County Bar Hopping Trolley Ride (organized by who else but the Saint himself . . . purely for the benefit of good spirits).

"I tell you, if I drank one, I had 50 J.B.'s and water. I fell asleep on the steps at Leroy Logerquist. They thought I was dead. *I* thought I was dead! I don't want to talk about health!

"The saddest time of the year coming up for me. The end of the season. The last two nights here. I miss the customers. Even the ones I don't like! People drift in and out, 'So long, St. Pat. See you next year.' Next year! I mean, who *knows*? Who *knows!*"

One version of the end, according to St. Patrick: "We will all be greeted by a *green* police unit, for Sheriff Baldy will have St. Peter's job. And for those who behaved— a clear path on clouds 42 and 57. I prefer 57.

"I will definitely be buried in Door County, and I hope the good people here will hold an Irish Wake Roast for me—with me in attendance, of course—and provide a shaded lot in a Catholic cemetery.

"And on my tombstone have it writ: He Carried His Life Savings In His Front Pocket To The End."

A Death in the Village
(A Mourner's Tale)

Though the county seems large, made up of many villages, separated by farms, fields, woods, hills, bodies of water, the death of any one person is news to us all and affects us with varying degrees of remorse.

News of a death travels over the air waves of the local radio station and appears in the obituary section of the local paper. We consult both these sources, however, as after-the-fact. They furnish us with the age, the names of the immediate family, minor achievements within the community, and the details of the wake, church service, and burial.

The initial impact of Who Died, or Did You Hear About . . . ? is as immediate as a phone call, minutes after the death, or the first person you meet in the village at the post office, the store, the coffeeshop.

The first reaction is, understandably, surprise and feigned shock, but very little feeling, depending, of course, upon how well we knew the deceased. It's the "news" of the death that is news, that is preeminent. And we, who think we heard it first, seem content and fulfilled as mere messengers of death. It is a role, and a necessary one, that we all play on various occasions.

It gives us an air of importance at a time, in a moment, perhaps, when there is very little going on in our own lives, in our own village.

It conceivably blunts our own fears of death. We love wakes and funerals because they confirm our own existence. *That* is not me.

And it gives us something, within a village of little news but ourselves, to talk about.

Talking about the death, in fact, occupies much of what passes for sorrow in the village life, amongst those who knew the deceased personally, or only knew about him. This can last for days, and extend into weeks or months beyond the burial, depending upon how dramatic the departure. Accidents, murders, suicides, haunt our memories most perniciously and satisfy a human need to lay blame or find cause. Years later we may resurrect these events in the aura of history, legend. Murders and suicides become our literature.

Upon the notice of anyone's death there is the usual acknowledgment of a debilitating disease (It was cancer. She has a bad heart), when disease or old age (He died peacefully in his sleep) is the only final judgment to be made. And following that (depending again upon one's personal relationship to the departed) the common condolences which might serve as the epitaph for almost anyone: He was a good man; she was a hard worker; he did much for the village; she will certainly be missed. And then the memories (if we hold them), the good memories, the pleasant anecdotes, even the humorous incidents regarding a certain fire in the dead man's soul that will not be extinguished for as long as we remember to honor it.

We wake the person then. There is a gathering of family, friends, and acquaintances at the local funeral parlor. There is a certain awkwardness, almost an embarrassment in being present. (Who else is here? Am I dressed properly? What do I say? How long must I stay?).

Local farmers with hands tan to the wrist, face and neck rubbed clean and red. Clumsy in shiny old black shoes with broken laces. Buttoned-at-the-neck sport shirts with ties the color of rusty emery cloth. Hair, ragged-edged, rimmed from the pressure of a work-a-day cap. Occasional grey, tobacco-stained beards.

Women with grey, black, or flowery back-of-the-closet dresses, altered the last minute for the occasion. Their wrists strung with black leather pocket books.

All of us seated or standing, releasing our voices in whispers.

Gathering, still gathering. Not unlike a church social one is expected to attend, and attends because one is expected to. So few of us are here at the wake this evening because we want to be here. We are nervous, fidgety, unable to keep our minds on things, and look anxiously around for a neighbor to talk to. Anyone to take our minds away from ourselves, from the necessity of being here and acting in some way sorrowful, grievous, sincere.

We are all bad actors before the casket. We call up prayer in earnest. We frame our sympathies without thought or soulful meaning. We do not know what we should feel. But there is a pretense of sadness to our faces while we circumspectly check our watches, hopeful that within the hour we will sit comfortably within our own homes again, watching television, recounting something overheard at the wake.

This is not to denigrate the emptiness, the tears, the unexplainable sorrow experienced amongst family and close friends. There is that too, audible, visible. Someone, someone else loved, is indeed gone. Human loss is insufferable. Final.

But most of us (all of us at one time or another) are merely paying our respects. Uncertain if we really belong here since, after all, we hardly knew the man. Or we knew him but never knew him. Or we knew a member of the family.

Still, we wish to be seen. Want it known and recorded that we were in attendance.

And then we gather at the white church the next day to lend dignity to the loss of human life, to raise our voices in prayer and song, to give God his due. To ask forgiveness for the departed, peace for the loved ones, and understanding for us all.

We are still looking across the aisles, up and down the pews, for familiar faces. We grieve for the family in black, heads bowed, a muffled sob. We visualize the departed resting in the closed casket, the candles flickering. We have congregated around a human body—the movement, the sound, the texture, the vision, the light gone out. We weigh the balance between a living body and a corpse.

We gather, on our knees, primitive tribesmen in our store-bought clothes, beseeching ancient, mystical connections to spirits eternal. For we do not believe we die. For nothing. And live to suffer.

The sonorous tones of the Ministers of God eulogizing the deceased are a comfort to the man in the pulpit before the eyes of the Almighty with whom he does commerce. We listen. Eulogies warm the hearts of the living, not the dead.

We bask in sacred sounds, our eyes raised to the roseate window shining above the altar. We drift through fields of glowing glass—red, yellow, green, blue, purple, gold, white—till our eyes are pools of color. We are away for a while, brought back to the service, the brass handles of the coffin, by a child's cry.

We tell ourselves all kinds of tales with happy endings before Death's door. And the various ministers of various gods have their variations on a familiar theme. But the ending, matter-of-fact, rises beyond the language of the campfire, deeper than the drawings on cavewalls, inhabiting the holy space of something no longer there.

We gather, finally, at the burial ground. The small graveyard of stone crosses behind the white church on the hill. The cemetery down the road under the stand of birch and pine.

We walk in a light drizzle of an overcast day shadowed by crows. We walk on freshly fallen snow. In either case, in all seasons, the weather is black and white and grey inside ourselves.

We trudge up the hill, all of the villagers, one at a time, in pairs, in small clusters. The tolling of the bell is superficial, overly dramatic, and proper—keeping us in step. What we need and expect. For the men whose lot it is to direct the final act of funerals (Ministers of God included) are mindful of the rituals common to the grieving human heart.

Approaching the gathering of mourners who have stopped in their tracks, we read the names around us carved in stone. We observe that the earth has been opened, and that the gravediggers (ubiquitous—farmers, tradesmen, villagers amongst us in our daily lives) lurk somewhere in the distance behind trees. Their torn jackets and muddy overalls, hands resting on the smooth wooden handles of gleaming spades, their work only half done.

We gather only briefly for the last words. Men holding their hats. Women clutching the arms of those nearest. Let us pray. We rub tears into our handkerchiefs, strew flower petals over the casket, grasp the hands of the immediate family. White handkerchiefs flit like cabbage butterflies. The grey gloves of the pallbearers rest on the casket like the ashes of so many hands.

The mourners disperse. The rain has let up. The sun has broken through the clouds. Snowflakes fall one at a time, resting on the sleeves and collars of our dark coats. There is a lightness to our steps. A quickness. The satisfaction of a duty performed (I was there), and a feeling that a return to routine will absolve the emptiness. Though one does not feel the way one always feels, yet. *Something* different remains. And will not go away.

The mourners disperse. Some go home. Some return to their work. Some gather once more in the church basement or the home of the deceased, with family and friends and sip coffee and eat homemade baked goods donated by the ladies of the church, the thoughtful friend or two who, because of bad legs or a bad heart, could not attend the services and so stayed behind to bake, to prepare a table for the mourners' return.

The voices are less constrained. A smile or two sometimes gives way to laughter, though always mindful of the occasion. We do not talk about death or the departed. We return to the ordinary burden of explaining our own lives through weather, crops, business, gardening, children, plans, and what we know or have heard about some of us not present.

We are beginning to forget.

With the news of a death in the village there are those among us who are not in attendance, who mourn silently within ourselves. Who either cannot make the services or decide not to. We feel we did not know the person well enough. We feel we might be falsely or aptly accused of busybodiness. There is something else we must do, somewhere else we must be. We may send a card of sympathy instead, or intend to and forget. Though we do not forget.

The easy death—old age, bad health—pass soon enough. A general expression of sympathy. That presence of a life (well known, hardly known), a face, a gesture, a story we file, and possibly forget, in our personal history of the townspeople. Rest in peace.

But the victims of accidents, of rare, village-life crimes, of self-inflicted wounds . . . these, strangers or friends, stay with us most fitfully day and night. Haunt us into sleep.

The men who go out in fishing tugs and do not return.

Children, right before us, taken away by an undertow.

Men disappearing through ice.

Road kills: drunken drivers hitting deer, hitting trees, killing others . . . asleep at the wheel.

Crimes of passion.

The unloved taking his or her life . . . for love.

We gawk in amazement at the empty chair. The room in the house, unlit. The car crushed beyond recognition. The stain on the road. The beam in the barn where the rope still hangs. The infinite capacity of water to reflect everything but remorse.

We pass the house of the bereaved, the soul of the departed, driving alone down dark, winding country roads at night. Our eyes twitching. Our breath, short. Passing the light of the kitchen window, we leave our drifting bodies to join whoever in the family sits inside. We *cannot* know what he feels. But the emptiness of unlit windows returns us to our selves, fearful on a county trunk marked Z, lit now by the gold eyes of cats stalking the grassy ditches.

This is senseless. We mourn in secret a life we did not know. And even our deathwatch, after death, is suspicious. What is it we seek?

The mind wavers. We've lost it temporarily. We are dead to ourselves. Then return with a stab of pain to the skull, above the eyes. And we look for home. Uncover our beds. And make a pact with prayer for a sleep of no dreams.

But we open the grave again, from the dark bottom of our bedroom where we lie, where we tempt somnia looking up, where we imagine what we see inside.

Are the limbs attached? How much water can a body hold? Where do the eyes look? Does the ring still remain on her finger? How long, really, before a body becomes dust?

Invitations to nightmares.

The village is the same. The mourners, family, and friends, have returned to themselves, but do not forget. Once a year the news of the death, the date of departure, is recorded in the local newspaper under classified ads. In Memoriam:

More and more each day I miss her,
Friends may think the wound has healed.
But little they know the sorrow,
That lies within my heart concealed.

In loving memory of Clara who passed away October 3, 1956

While the silent mourner, who can never quite bring himself to honor a death in the village amongst family and friends, rises before dawn a day or two after the burial, puts on his ordinary gray clothes, and proceeds with caution through the early morning haze, down a ragged route of backroads—curves, deer crossings, deadends—seeking the graveyard, the mound of fresh earth and wilting floral wreaths, the site of the final rite he could not attend. Death has a hold of him and will have its way.

He loses and finds and loses himself trudging up the hill through ground fog momentarily separating him from his own legs. His presence alone seems almost assured, there being no news of any other deaths today.

The gravestones are alive in dull and shiny light. He is aware of their forms but does not read the names. What he seeks is easiest to find, the unmarked grave. The earth overturned where nothing yet grows.

He stands at the foot of the grave, not unlike the village fool. Not even a hat to hold. Nor a prayer on his lips, or a flower to leave. No reason for being there. He has forgotten his own name. His whole body seems out of proportion, deranged.

He attempts to resurrect the face beneath, the time of life, the cause of death, and nothing comes but tears. Bending down, he finds the whitest pebble on the mound and washes it in the wetness of his fingers till it glistens.

He circles the grave, his foot slipping and sinking into the fresh earth.

I loved you, he says, kneeling, covering his mark.

Back home, he sets the white pebble on a small mound of other stones gathering dust on the windowsill in his rooms.

Crow Lady
Maggie Perry

She was Margaret Lives at birth. She was Peggy Lives in Wauwatosa, Wisconsin, and Milwaukee, where she grew up. She became Peggy Perry in marriage, in Milwaukee, in Mequon, in Jacksonport. In a subsequent state of separation she began searching and has retrieved that part of herself, her spirit, which is now Maggie. Crow Lady is yet another name for her.

The transformations are endless when one heeds the need for change.

She likes the water. Sometimes you will find her there, gull feathers, wet sand, smooth pebbles, walking the early hours along Lake Michigan's shore. She likes the fields, and sometimes disappears there. She's a city woman, a country woman. She's been a back-to-the-land housewife living on a small farm in Jacksonport, a counselor and teacher for women's support groups in Sturgeon Bay, and a poet living alone in a granary. She's a child of the 60's in some ways, and in other ways she remains a woman with social commitments.

"My dad worked for the electric company as a lineman, then as a foreman. He was a union man, always very involved in strikes. He did some neat stuff that way, always politically conscious. My mother was . . . she pretty much took care of the whole family—three brothers, one sister. Five kids. She was just the typical stereotype 1950's mother. She was and she wasn't. She just tried to fit in that. She was actually a tough lady. If I learned anything, it was from her—how to be tough, how to be strong.

"He, with his drinking, taught me too in a strange way. He was real violent, but there was a sensitivity to him. In his union work, he *felt* for those people. So she just took care of my dad. He was really a heavy drinker. And she took that responsiblility of taking care of him and the five kids.

"She was a writer. She always kept a journal. She's still doing that. I don't remember her ever reading a lot. She never showed me what she wrote. She'd bring out books like Edgar Guest. She went to college for a while. She'd talk about Shakespeare. I think she talked a lot about writing, about authors, rather than showing me. She saw names or photos in the paper and she'd say things like 'That's Robert Frost.' And when you're 8 years old, you remember that.

"My father was like that with painting. He'd mention names like Gauguin, Van Gogh . . . then I'd go to school and mention those names and they'd say 'What the hell are you talking about?'

"She also studied opera. She sang, she danced. She used to always say her voice teacher said she had a voice like Lily Ponds, and I didn't know who the hell Lily Ponds was! We always had a piano in the house, and we'd sing. She's thinking of selling the piano now . . . 'I'm going to sell that damn thing and get some money!'"

There is much laughter to Maggie, whether imitating what her mother said, or finding endless humor in her own condition: "Always the kid," she laughs, reflecting on her own behavior in a situation. There is sadness, too, at times often evident by quietude or revery.

"My family, I think, was wonderful at that point in my life—high school. And even before that. I always remember their leaving a lot of decisions to me. And they put a lot of faith in me. Like going to a free school. How many parents would let their kids go to a free school, an experimental high school that was started and pretty much run by the students who went there?

"I learned how to make decisions. I learned how to be disciplined. That's where I really began to write. I had the time to do it. I'd spend 6 hours a day writing. And I learned, learned how to sit at a desk and write when I was 16 years old.

"I learned from a lot of different people. We had a lot of sensitivity training, gestalt . . . I got to know different people in the community. We had a staff of six who did primarily guidance work. They'd help us design a program. But they didn't teach so much. We had a file of people who would volunteer from the community at large to come and teach.

"I went three years to that. I got a diploma. But the place wasn't accredited, so officially, I'm a dropout. I learned a lot about responsibility going there. If I don't make an effort to change, to move, no one else is going to do it for me."

The spirit of a writer seeks nourishment where it can, especially in those early stages of childhood. The writer is mostly unaware of the shaping process. Maggie recalls a moment in childhood:

"I remember reading this story I wrote in grammar school, 6th grade, and everyone loved it. And people responded to it, just loved it! My reaction was immense pleasure—I'm good for something!"

Around the age of 13 she went to a six-week summer program for teenagers, Adventures in Creativity, at Cranbrook Academy in Michigan. "That really changed my life. I studied drama and writing. I went two summers and I had some really good encouragement. Between that summer and the next, an incredible change happened. I didn't even want to go to high school after having been exposed to Cranbrook the first time. And that's when I got involved with the free school (Milwaukee Independent School). I worked a deal with my parents. I tried regular high school for one semester and then went to the free school."

One of the poems that came out of that was a long, rambling poem called "The Third Street Gang," a portion of which reads like this:

> Please
> deliver the flowers
> with love
> the love
> i still have the note . . .

> in a cold empty house
> at 7 in the morning
> we were born again
> blowing candles
> holding holding onto each other
> to things near us
> to trees to house to chairs
> and letting go
> blowing
> falling off the edges

reservoir st.
is grey and dying
it is ghetto
through broken beer bottles
and black pimps
we came with our candles and flowers
and
we were ripped off ripped in and ripped out
: lesson one:
'not everyone loves ya, kid!'

She also worked with Milwaukee poet, Jim Sorcic, around that time. "I started writing a lot better stuff. I got something published then. My work completely changed. Something had a big influence on my writing. Mainly it was exposure to other writers—which is all I needed. Just open the door, and I'll walk right in."

The presence of parents persists in a writer's psyche from early on. And one way or another it must be acknowledged, reconciled.

"I think my parents were pretty excited about the free school, pretty proud of me. We'd hold meetings at the house sometimes from our school. They trusted me. The thing that was neat about them is that I started trusting them."

In 1970, still in her very early days of writing poetry, she wrote a poem called "Picture: My Father & My Mother":

he always turns away, he always does that,
laughs and turns away
like she was making a joke or something
ha ha

their love is
such a falling down thing
falling down and getting up and falling down again
a pile of limping dogs
falling down getting up falling down getting up
on and on and on
laughing

"All that time, too, there was conflict. I'd pick a fight with my mother . . . all that stuff you work out in your teenage period. But it always seemed because of the trouble with my father, there was that need to work together. There'd be the fights between her and him in the middle of the night. That was horrible. I think I'm basically really suspicious and untrusting. I'm real careful. All this because of seeing my parents in their relationship and how it developed. The way they hurt themselves and still do. For so long I just hated my father. I'm starting to love him now, and that's kind of nice. I think my involvement with the whole women's movement came out of that. Because when I was young, my dad was always the bad guy, and I was sticking with my mother. And then there was my sister, and we were like a team. It seemed like there was always my mother, my sister, and me. I remember feeling very protective of my mother. And I think I got to feel a strong sense of that 'sisterhood' or whatever, and I've always been a lot closer to women than to men."

Social consciousness, which may sound passe in a society reverting to selfish conservancies and moral majorities, remains part of this poet's concern, her daily living, and reflects, perhaps, on her parents, her past, and her coming aware in the 60's.

"In Milwaukee I worked as the youngest draft counselor, 16, during the Viet Nam war. I was really against the war and trying to find a way to work at it rather than going to all those goddam marches and getting beat-up."

And in the way of many of the young people of the 60's, the 70's. . .when the war, the society, nothing seemed to make much sense, a search for inner peace became necessary in Maggie's life.

"The last year in high school I had been meditating regularly, and I knew I wanted to go to India. I got involved in the Divine Light Mission, and there I met Whitey [her future husband]. This was about 1972. The Divine Light Mission was something to hang onto—instant enlightenment! If you will just follow the guru, you will find the answer. I was just tired of that shit from home, and here were all these happy people. So, I 'bought it'. I did learn to meditate. I also learned about gurus—there is no such thing.

"I think I'll go back to meditation some day. Go back to India. There was a deeper reason I was first attracted to it. I went to India for about 6 weeks. The biggest impression I had was realizing how people could live on so little and survive. Coming from Wauwatosa, I never saw anything like it. We don't know what poor is. And some of them are actually happy! It was the whole thing about the material world and it being mostly an illusion.

"In a lot of ways, I was really ready for that whole experience. I want to go back now that I'm a little older. There is a lot to learn from people living like that.

"Marriage? It wasn't my idea!" she laughs. In 1972, though, having returned from India, she looked at in this way in her writing:

> married?
> i find myself clambering over the words and gestures that make
> a word of this sort even acceptable to the human ear.
> me, 19 years of life that never expected children never expected
> husband never expected to let a silver band to wind itself
> around her mind or finger.
> a strong 19 years of life
> a happy 19 years of life
> that puzzles over such a queer sounding word that every woman
> on the face of this earth worries and breaks out about until she is
> securely certain of its meaning and its safety.
> i have not seen it in the words of any others either.
> and this 19 years when they are 50 years will not be bound by
> silver rings or silver words, this 19 years will travel as
> freely or as captively as always.
> no, I will not be married. for all the silver bands there
> are to weight a woman down, i will not be weighted down.
> i was married to one of infinity several months ago, the only
> marriage i will ever admit to, and one that wears no rings or words.
> so married?

i don't care. do what you want to do with these 19 years, there is
something very happy much farther beyond this 19 year, there
is something very happy much farther beyond this 19 years,
beyond all this.

"I think it was just really special to have someone who cared about me, and I just didn't want to lose that. Want to be alone. A part of that was I never dated. I was never part of that whole scene. It all seemed just so silly to me. The worst thing in the world was to grow old alone and not loved. And I would starve to death without approval. And so, I did it. I really latched on to something permanent. And I really got into it. I was really a good wife. Worked a part-time job, made fantastic meals, gave parties . . . moved to the country, first to Mequon, then to Door. And then it all started falling apart.

"I started moving out of the marriage about two years ago—my whole process of building a little support system of my own. I relied on my husband for everything, and you can't rely on one person that much. It's ridiculous. I remember saying: I can't live here anymore. I want a place of my own for the winter. And that winter, in Fish Creek, I began living alone.

"I learned I like it, but also that it's hard. I find it really hard to live alone. In some ways it's everything I want, but I really miss that closeness of another person who lives with you, knows you. Loneliness, I guess, is what it is. You had it! That's the hard part to answer. Why don't I live with him? He's a nice guy, a wonderful person! He really is. But goddam, it's not even a matter of happiness. I mean. . .I'm lonely when I'm with him! That's incredible! And that's me! It's not something he's done to me. I do feel whole when I'm alone. And the writing thing . . . that was all so fucking hard. I tell you, I sure respect people who stay together over the years. And stay friends. That takes two really compassionate people to do that. To stay married and be friends."

Not a great deal of writing came out of those early years of marriage. The writer, the poet in Maggie, as in many women, was stilled in respect to making a marriage, perhaps beginning a family.

"When I first got into the whole spiritual thing, I sort of had this whole thing in my head that I'm going to give this writing thing up. If I can't write about the guru . . . that it's all such material world bullshit anyway.

"I was starting to have some success at it before then, and I think I shied away from it. There was a commitment to it. And this was the easy way out. I was starting to get deeper in myself, so I stopped writing for a long time. Five years at least. And I just started writing again when we moved up here [Jacksonport, 1977]. I think it was the first winter I wrote this . . . actually, a Door County poem, one of the first:

it is so quiet
so grey
so november
wisconsin november
cold wet air
weeks of it
here in my house in the country
i light a fire for warmth
i read magazines for companionship
i listen to the endless buzz
of half alive flies

left-overs from the first frost
so it is grey and quiet and empty
me and this november world
we wait anxiously to be filled
with the frothy swirls of snow
to be made a color once again

"There were little bits and pieces of writing. Then I took one of the NWTI courses from Hal [Grutzmacher]. He gave me so much encouragement. But I had started again, before that. I had already made the step."

Married and living in Jacksonport, Maggie found herself involved with organic gardening, the whole 'back-to-the-land' movement of the 70's, which captured the spirit of many of the younger people living in Door County.

"One idea in coming up here was to become more self-sufficient. I think it was primarily Whitey's motivation. He was always very attracted to that kind of vision. It was more or less my willing to go along with it. And that was the thing then. Everyone was doing it. But I remember being very worried about leaving the city, all the excitement. And what the hell would I do here? There were distractions in the city, and it was pretty much our being alone together. But I'm glad we move here. I certainly wouldn't move back to the city unless for financial reasons. I'm centered more in the country. This is much more conducive to the discipline of writing than the city. I just don't have the distractions here. They're hard to find.

"I think the 'back-to-the-land' thing was really a romantic vision of pioneer women. It definitely wasn't based in reality. It wasn't 'living the good life'—Helen and Scott Nearing. We were just going to go there and do it. We were getting away from the stress of the city. But we ended up working at more jobs and different jobs. We ended up having less time to do the things that we wanted to do than in the city. And we never did it. . .not entirely.

"I remember Liz Schmit saying about your whole life being self-sufficiency! It was fine learning I could live like this—without toilet, without running water, without heat. We had a big garden. We grew over half our food because we were vegetarians. But you don't get a whole lot of art done. Maybe once in a dark winter night you pick up some embroidery. You just don't have the time to put into your relationships with people. There is no time for anything else. The only time there is, is to survive. Plus you've got to work a side job too because there's never enough anyway.

"Whitey's still doing it, but he's tired. He's burned out. I miss my fantasies about it. But when I think back of the realities of it, there's not much I miss. Like a big snowstorm when you're huddled in your house . . . and the snow's coming in under the door because it wasn't fixed. A lot of struggle, a lot of doing things I didn't want to spend time on. But then . . . I figured this is what I'm supposed to do . . . the Pioneer Woman!

"I miss the garden a lot. I feel a real desire . . . there's something about gardening, working with the soil. It feels right, real whole to be in touch with it. That's the trip there—growing food. It puts one in touch with reality too—all the little battles going on between the bugs and the vegetables. I'm really drawn to going back to that someday. To just get rid of the 'stuff' and live very simple and just work. Have a stove, have some wood. Very small. A few books I need. Even just one room with an outhouse."

Her life and poetry begin moving closer in the latter years in Jacksonport. When the poems come, they are single poems of isolation, nature of emptiness:

Spirits

you would be four years old today.
you and i and whitey would walk
through the cold morning
of the first fall frost.
we would touch the garden
plants and shiver,
our feet wet.
this house wouldn't seem so empty,
sharing the wood heat
i could tell you stories
of the snow.
this is not how it is, i know.
this is a fantasy,
a dream.
stars and darkness in my mind.
a child never touched or seen.
being who took up residence
in my warm womb for only
a short time,
then decided rather abruptly
life wasn't worth the work
of being born.
there are better
places to be, i suppose.
i thought about you, the loss,
as four frosts' worth of memories
stir around inside me.
lame butterflies,
survivors of the cold.

And poems of woman-ness:

i admire women who move easily
through the grey steady world of tall men.
share swaying dancing close
i've never known.

this is a new land to me,
a new language and customs.
i've grown old in a house
of women.
how does a woman hold a man?
different from a child or a loaf
of warm bread? how does a woman
learn to move easily among men?

Gradually moving away from her marriage, then, the poet finds herself back among the work force. Identifying, readily, easily, with the women's movement in her own, immediate, Door County terrain. . .and working with them.

"My position with the Women's Employment Project [Sturgeon Bay] initially started out as an instructor. I actually started doing volunteer work there, and they then hired me on a part-time basis. I went through one of those courses as a participant and then began helping out in the teaching. I also worked at the Project as a para-professional counselor about 6 or 8 months.

"The Project is to assist low income women to become employed and self-supporting. We teach basic skills: interviewing, resume writing, assertiveness, communication, for women who have never been exposed to this. Some of them don't even know how to read or write very well, let alone handle an interview. So basically, just helping them get their feet in the door so they have a chance.

"There are also well educated women who have just lost confidence in themselves. A divorce can put a woman through a lot of changes that she's not chosen, and this can make her very insecure for awhile.

"What the women all have in common is lack of self-confidence. Just a sense of self. A sense of who I am. They're primarily low income. They have to be to qualify for the program. A lot don't have any money and are just getting by. Some are divorced or widowed or unwed mothers.

Crow Night   N. Blei

"When we start talking to women about going to work, we start shaking things up in the home. Sometimes it upsets the husband who doesn't want his wife to work.

"There are politics involved mainly in regard to funding. The federal government has to fund it. The local government wouldn't."

Her social commitment in this area of women's employment, her concern once again for the human condition, seems a natural outgrowth for a union man's daughter, for a child who experienced personal problems in her own family, for a young girl who supported anti-war causes, for a wife/woman/poet now separating herself from marriage, on her own again.

"I did it [the Women's Employment Project] personally for me. I learned a lot. And I like helping people. I learn so much from this just about myself, about working with other people. It sounds like a circle. It's just, in these classes, the kinds of feelings that happen between people. We talk a lot about things we don't talk about out there. There's a trust and a feeling that I'm hungry for. They're learning how to live, and how to survive. Sure, I can learn this from waitressing, but people aren't focused on self-awareness in jobs like that. Whereas in the Project, that's the focus of the whole class. And I'm reminded of that, and that's what special for me.

"On the other hand, it's also a burnout. It's also being open to a lot of reality. You see other women in these incredible situations. One woman, how she lived off 50¢ for three weeks! Maybe I've seen two or three women who were abusing AFDC (Aid to Families with Dependent Children), but there are hundreds and hundreds out there who really need it. So many of them with kids . . . they're up against so much! It's not a self-pity thing. They've got a lot of fight. The thing about the course is that it gives women back some strength—dealing with all the irate employers who don't want to hire women. And the whole employment scene up here is pretty bad for anybody.

"I do identify with these women a lot in my situation, especially right now, going through this separation. Just that general feeling of being alone and taking care of oneself. And women, a great deal of the women I know are just so dependent upon men, and it's not anything men did. It's just the way we were brought up, to be so dependent upon them. I guess that's the thing that binds a lot of us together. And learning how to live alone. It seems men can do that so easily . . . to handle that whole ocean out there. But women are always looking for their white knights. Some guy to rush in and save you.

"It's kind of neat to learn how to live alone. To learn how to reach out to other people besides just one person. 'Hey, I can reach out to someone else too, if I need to know how to change a fuse!'"

The poetry, too, changed, began to show a greater sense of self. She reached back into the past for a significant poem in her development, a poem reflecting a father and daughter relationship.

"I wrote this poem about my father and that was a very important change. Till then it seemed I was always writing outside myself, and then I wrote this poem about him right after he had gone through the first withdrawal that I was involved with. That was a real change for me. I was drawing from personal things in my own life. I was drawing from me, rather than 'the sun shining on the lake' sort of thing. I began writing now from my own experiences. People I knew.

His Daughter

My father was a strong man
with gnarled legs, large tree trunks.

81

Massive bent nose under
A combination van Gogh and Hemingway.
He climbed utility poles
for the power company.
Late at night,
when the lightning, the rain, and the thunder
scared us children under the sheets,
he would go
climb dead creosote trees.
Repair fallen, sparkling, electrical lines.
In the morning,
we would look up from breakfast
to see him come home
weary, smelling of beer and sweat.
My two-fisted father . . .

now, at sixty-five,
lies in a county hospital bed,
incoherent.
Screaming, yelling, crying
broken old man, drooling.
Grey hair, grey complexion,
empty grey eyes.
"It's the Librium," my mother whispers.
There are moments,
moments when he holds his head
in his hands
and weeps with realization.
My father

and i
i am here
far away,
as always. You see,
i have a hard time
relating
to those "two-fisted" types.
I have a hard time untangling the words,
the meanings, the feelings.
i hated him, once. i hated
his power as he stood,
a huge resonant voice
at the top of the tall staircase,
shouting his way into my small
world.
i have tried to deny
the blood, the genes
that flow in my body.
20 years later, i still
try.

i watch him
spouting obscene fantasies
from his hospital bed.
The mess, the coping, all
the irony of being grown old.
i still find room to love him,
my father. There is relief
in that thought. A silent,
shifting, movement.

You see, i've been taught
to listen, to understand . . .
all the workshops, the seminars,
the people. But, i never asked
him about his life. i never
told him that i cared.
i never asked him if
he was lonely. i never asked
him why he chased us all away,
and then cried.
Maybe, i will try to talk with him
like i would have tried to talk with
anyone else. Maybe,
give him the chances
i would have given anyone else but
my father.

"Before that poem I was doing a lot of stuff that was outside my self like 'the pretty cactus blooming.' I was still being cautious about putting myself in poetry. Writing stuff I knew my mother would like. If I talk about pretty flowers and blue skies they won't see that underneath is that . . . crow lady . . . this other side of me. That was really my Door County days . . . fitting in the neighborhood.

"But in writing about my dad in a personal way, there were a lot of things I had not admitted to myself. I wanted to share that part of my life with people. It was really a hard poem to write. And I wrote it for him too, because at the time I didn't know if he would come out of the DT's and I wanted him, if he came out of it, to be able to read it. I told him I loved him in that poem. Up until that poem I always thought I hated him. That poem changed our whole relationship.

"I started getting more in touch and more in tune, which also resulted in a lot of self-exploration that whole year. I went in therapy, I got in women's groups, I was in Al-Anon. I wasn't spending a lot of time outside myself and the place I lived in, although I did write some nature poems, although they were poems of me staring outside myself, looking at nature, not becoming a part of it. The cool observer. Bly [the poet, Robert Bly at a workshop in Rhinelander, Wis.] came along and Jesus, if that didn't change things.

"One of the important things that stuck with me . . . he talked a lot about women writers like Anne Sexton. He had this belief that you can look inside yourself too much . . . and eventually you'll kill yourself, looking too much inside. But to become part of that object . . . to become connected . . . that I am connected to all these things around me! And I can see that with women's writing, so focused on all the inner pain. No joyousness. The Sylvia Plath stuff—and she killed herself.

"There was still a lot of inner struggle about the writer who was inside of me— Maggie—and the person, Peggy, who had been the nice woman, the mother, the fixer, the wife. There was still a real struggle: the side that was honest and the side that was dishonest. I was going to have to make changes in my life, changes that were going to affect people in my life. I just felt like such a dull person."

She left her husband and home in Jacksonport for a winter of going it alone in Fish Creek. "Living alone that first winter I got a lot of work done on my writing. In the house it was just physically impossible to be alone. There were literally no walls, no doors in the house, and for me it was impossible to write. Too many distractions."

And soon after, returning to Jacksonport, giving it another try, she rented a small office in Sturgeon Bay where she could pursue her writing. "When I had the office, which I rented almost right after moving back in, there was no distraction. I shut myself in, and I had to write. That was all there was to do there. And that was the real turning point. It was also the monetary thing, because it cost me to keep that place. For me it was really a commitment to say: This is important enough that I want to take something from the farm, the house, and put it into my writing, my work, even though I wasn't making any money from it."

From there it was a living and working place of her own, the granary: "It was so wonderful to have some space to work again, to get disciplined again. How great it is to be able to go in a room and close a door. That I can work in a place and shut a door! Though, I like open doors too. And I'm confronted with the same problems as before I got married. Now I'm confronted again with the aloneness of the writing and the commitment to it as when I was 17 or 19 years old. But boy, I sure feel a hell of a lot different. I'm living the way I want to live now."

She claims she is still far too young to have reached any great conclusions about herself, her life in general. She might tell you in letters:

> I realize I just don't talk well . . . I've always been too young to talk . . . people shouldn't talk till they're in their forties . . . then they begin to say something that matters. But . . . that's different, a different thing altogether. Writing is where I speak. Writing is me. I'm nothing else. I never will be anything else. I'll die in the pollen of my words, dust, wings, and dandelions . . .

Or she might tell you to your face: "I don't have the maturity yet. Oh, I do to some degree, but I haven't gotten much living done in me yet to express what I want to say. I can sense things, and I can know them and feel them, but others are much more able to capture these things eloquently. I'm so fucking paranoid all the time, reaching into things. I think when I get a little older I'll be able to mellow out . . . clearer insights . . . more profound."

Yet she can tell you what she sees in marriage: "The contradiction in it. Trying to form a perfect relationship with some permanence—which is a contradiction in itself. I still have a part of me that still wants that permanence of a private relationship, even though I feel real spent from the one I've been involved in. It's like the neatest thing in relationships with other people—yet it's the most frustrating. That's the thing I seem most drawn to—involvement with other people. And marriage is that—deep involvement. Right now I don't see myself ever getting married again.

"The thing I want is just recognition of the different parts of myself—sometimes I am a bitch, sometimes a virgin, sometimes I'm a working woman, sometimes a city woman, sometimes a country woman. Sometimes I want to be strong. I want to be weak sometimes too. The acceptance of that . . . the contradiction . . . that will give me room, that will give me space. Yeah, that would be nice. Just like Whitey . . . he wanted me to be a certain way, and suddenly, I wasn't that woman anymore. That's pretty much what men want too . . . some men.

"Men, well . . . I've had a hard time with men. I really identified a lot with my mother when I grew up because dad was a frightening man. I never would sit on his lap. I never wanted to be close to him. So I got this feeling that all men were creeps. Don't trust them. I really learned that at home. It's just been the last couple of years that I've felt more integrated with men . . . trusting them, forming some good friendships. And seeing that in myself . . . the parts that are more masculine. Because they are there—the man and woman parts. And it's kind of neat to see that."

And she can reveal, too, as she does in some of her recent poems, just how she continues to come to terms with some of this:

Companions

"madness has its place too, you know."

i tried to explain,
but he just kept fingering the telephone
black cord
and talking about hospitals

so i hear voices!
voices are good . . .
what if i heard
car accidents or snakes singing
or tomatoes tapdancing in the icebox?

last night she told me to dance
naked under the moon and
i did. the frost hung jewels
kissing my silly, bare feet.

i laughed and sang until
he turned on the porch light
and called me in . . .

"what if the neighbors saw!"

(what would they see?)
a winged woman with stars
on her breasts. they wouldn't
believe their eyes, the same
way they don't believe their

85

dreams.
but i came in
like a dog with a dead rabbit.
i dressed in my flannel nightie
with red roses and he said,

"tomorrow i'm calling the doctor."

i fell asleep
naked under my clothes.

"That was a real fantasy thing. Sometimes I write stuff I don't know where it comes from. It's just a story and sort of a feeling I was having about my relationship. The whole idea the woman is being something different from the woman he was married to . . . 'Well, she's crazy, this woman!' But madness is another escape . . . a lot of women use it . . . it's a way for women to remain dependent."

"Then we were doing that thing about dreams at the clearing. And this poem came out of that:

Now That She's Got Your Approval

disfigured face,
she hangs from a meat hook.
red sweat shine,
soot city yellow stairwell
tomb.

the cuts aren't clean.
nothing's clean.
two men with cameras,
glass eyes,
canes.

"she got what she wanted"

she IS the image
of success.
the best.
the finest.
jesus does she GLOW
she's everybody's favorite.
look at her smile.
can that babe smile.
everybody loves her,
wants to eat her up
alive.

but all the photos
are black and white.
there isn't any color

till the dead crow night
opens the wet alley brick
with one eye
and i bleed into cement.

"It's a deeply personal poem. It's like working on something a long time and finally it's out there in the open and I'm finished with it, and I want to share it."

And through all this living and writing, a slow but steady growing, searching, for self, for words, for forms, meanings . . . even myths.

"So many things came at once; it's hard to separate them. Now with the summer, this fall, everything started coming together with my writing, my career, my homelife. All this began to merge. I'm starting to feel . . . it's the whole 'Maggie' thing. That was the turning point. That's me now . . . that's all of me, the writer. The merge. I still separate it at times. I can always tell—when I start watching my cursing. Or getting involved in stories that are not ladylike. Trying to accomodate other people. Being who I think they'd like to see—not Maggie.

"So my writing is more honest now . . . that part of me that is dreamy, crazy. The sexy side of me. Women . . . we can write sensually, not sexually. It's been just very recent that women can write sexually. Women writers like Erica Jong and Elizabeth Sargent . . . they have the courage to write that way. To be able to write about my erotic side, that's important to me. More love, erotic poetry.

"Crow Lady . . . Oh, God, Crow Lady. What's a Crow Lady? She fits in. She's tough. Where did she come from? She flew in one day . . . all of a sudden crows were showing up in my poetry. And I was sitting there at the typewriter one day and all of a sudden, there she was . . .

Hungry Crow Lady

she leaves
bits of flesh
hanging on nameless trees
for the autumn crow man

in strange blue caves
she flies the edge of dream

she gives herself away
as satin leaves
watching the moon
open white swallow
the sky the world the whole
field of her
in one
wide
gulp.

"That was Crow Lady speaking. She's my fantasy, you know. She's my myth . . .

Crow Lady Walking

black crow man
sitting up there
moaning wounded cat
the gang flies
black clouds over morning corn
sun comes up
red/orange lobster eye
boiling
in the purple water sky
i stand waiting
all you are is shadow
memory of past
everything is fiction
except my feet
on this gravel road.

"Something about crows . . . I used to hate crows. Crows were birds that ate corn out of my garden . . . they ate carrion . . . And now, now I like crows. There are summer crows, and they're here in the winter. They do what they have to do to stay alive. They're not evil birds. They're just survivors, they really are. They're watching all the time. They're always out in the trees talking to each other. They're always watching people. But I like that. They appeal to me. And they're really very vulnerable too . . .

Crow Lady Takes A Lover

lost
in the pattern
of unending days
floating one grey
egg yolk
after
another
marking my place
with a thin
black
pencil
i traced a line
on your tired
face
in your eyes
twisted dreams of butterflies
orange/black
and beating

"Of course, I've never seen a dead crow . . . but when they fly against the sky, they have such *presence.* Like hawks they have that same presence. I want to read more about them in Indian myths. I feel always like I'd just like to fly with them. I love lying in the corn in early fall, listening to the sound of dry corn stalks in the wind . . . it's a crow sound . . .

Crow Lady's Visitor

we talk safe today
facts stories
great bowls of fruit
untouched in the sun

inbetween sift dry leaves
falling heavy with frost
crickets at dawn
drops of rain on a stone

all these things
run through
your fingers

i look for stains on the rug
wash my empty cup
close the door
to soft wings and wind

"Does a woman need a myth? This woman does . . . I don't know about other women. For me it really creates a connection. Now I've connected with crows. I can make that leap now between the very physical side of me grounded on earth inside this body, Maggie Perry, and expanding out into the trees and birds and water. I become that Crow Lady, and I'm not bound by this body, this person, and I can be anything. That's why fairy tales are so great. Kids are really in touch with that.

"I'd like to succeed as a writer, but I'm not really planning on it. I'm not as interested in success in the sense of publishing as I used to be. I'm trying to write for myself now. Like Georgia O'Keefe . . . there was that time when she stopped listening to what other people had to say. She used only black for awhile. 'I stopped using all other color,' she said, ' . . . and then I used blue.' She couldn't show her work to anyone.

"I'm trying to keep things very simple. I don't have to force myself into anything. Not writing for me, but in me. I pretty much see this writer as wanting alone and using the time I have to become more productive and more disciplined.

"I want to stay in a rural setting. And that's a real change, since I was very hesitant at first about moving up here. It's the whole lake thing. I grew up on the lake in Milwaukee, so I don't like the idea of ever being very far from it. I really like the idea of Door County being surrounded by water. The unpredictability of the weather here. You can't count on this peninsula for *anything*—even food, because there are so many fucking rocks in the soil!

"As for writing, I've never written the way I have since I moved here. Part of it has to do with just roaming around. I like the fields and beaches and woods. I like to wander around like some kind of animal. You can't do that in the city. You'll get attacked! The realness of it. There is a respect for the recluse here, which I kind of like. I feel drawn to that. Having 'alone' time. Distance. Days of alone time. Physically alone. I really appreciate the vastness of winter. You can get lost in the county sometimes in winter. I don't much get into the people of the county. I guess that sort of something I missed out on. I don't know a whole lot of people in Door except through my work. I kind of like being unknown for while. At least pretending I'm not known.

"Now is the prime time when I could move back to the city, but there are still too many distractions there, and I write here in the country. I feel more centered here. But I don't know if it will always be Door County. I love the lake. But sometimes I feel really starved for my kind of people . . . people who will accept Maggie . . . who will accept Crow Lady.

"I really believe in karma. It's just true for me . . . living out life after life for some purpose. I'm more attracted to the Eastern beliefs that we go through many lives before we reach enlightenment. I think I've had a lot of karmic experiences . . . places I've been . . . meeting people . . . an immediate recognition. No logical reason. But people I've worked through some very important lessons in my life. Like my marriage. My whole marriage to Whitey was working through something that perhaps we worked through in another life and it's still unfinished and we're working it out now. I really, strongly believe in karma . . .

Crow Lady Karma

if i follow down
your sad brown eyes
will i find a field of wild horses
or moon spirits flying wings in the wind?

all the ghosts
of your lovers
run fingers through my hair
tell me to forget
the scent of you
burning grey cloud man

losing myself
in the low flight of crows
green eyed bandits give birth

what about the lives of other birds?
how do they eat? sleep? love?
i
circle black
against yellow sky

you beggars of light
laughing fools
hang your silk legs out to dry
tonite snow! nothing moves
in her secret
ice
lace dreams

spin fine webs
of old crow man hair
and hang red flowers
from dying apple trees

i will find you

The Clown
Ken Zilisch

I myself laugh at everything, for fear of having to weep.

—Pierre-Augustin

I feared the dark from early on, and as a child, certainly feared clowns. There was once a Chicago clown called Coco, I believe, who appeared at the annual Christmas party given by my father's employer. As much as there was joy in that season, at that festivity, there was also fear . . . fear of the clown's return.

Though I remember some of the clown's costume—large, saucer-like cap, wide pants, sharply creased like half-moons, big shoes—what I recall most vividly, was that he was all white. A white that glowed, that burned, that haunted me for nights like a vision. Spirit, angel, ghost . . . it addressed something surreal, primal in the psyche, something that I had no words for yet and perhaps never would, surrendering to it that space, that life, where imagination dwells. Allowing it, as I grew older, whatever metamorhosis it demanded—angel, devil, spirit, woman, death. Anger? Joy? Always the unreal. Fear. Mystery. Maybe even love—for the darker side within.

If there was laughter—it came later. Then the clown was "understood." Then he was "real." And then, in many ways, he ceased to be a mystery—the nothingness, perhaps even the fear I found necessary never to be understood.

As a grown man, I was aware of the clown's return to my periphery. Once, late at night, I was driving home alone through a rather deserted Chicago neighborhood, quite lost, a bit too much to drink, uncertain of the empty streets that might lead me back to where I came from.

I recall stopping for a redlight, waiting an inordinately long time for the light to change, and out of the corner of my eye . . . aware of another car creeping alongside of me. Turning my head, I faced a white clown watching me. Fear, reaching back to childhood and beyond, ignited me.

Some years later, when I first began to write, I picked up an unknown little magazine of some literary quality to read an unknown story by an unknown writer. The story so filled me with despair that it has affected my writing life ever since.

Simply, as I recall, it was a story of a man who had failed in life so many times (and any writer, especially a young one, can readily identify with that) that in the end, awakening from a drunken stupor, he finds himself alone on a train. Strangers begin to appear . . . carnival people. Catching his own reflection in the nighttime window of his own compartment, he discovers a clown's face . . .

Colorfully striped pants and coat-of-tails, top hat, white gloves, tiny umbrella, big red nose, white face and painted smile . . . he's the beginning, the middle, and the end of most Door County parades. "I'm the kind of clown that starts a parade, works his way back, then finishes the parade. That's my trademark." A gentle clown. A silent clown of unspeakable acts. He will tell you nothing in disguise. His name is Zero. And his name is Kenneth E. Zilisch, of KD ad-ventures, artist, clown, born in Beaver Dam, Wisconsin, in 1942, living in Sturgeon Bay since 1970 with his wife, Diane, and daughter, Cara Jo.

"Clowning allows me to get attention," he will tell you. "It is an outlet. You can do crazy things. You can hug people, and it's all right because people are only hugging a clown. And, after all, a clown isn't *real!*"

Which is part of the attraction. The mask we all tend to wear upon occasions. Our dual natures. To be, if only for awhile, that part of our spirit which we keep hidden inside. (The clown of the American Indian, called the Koshares—the sacred funmakers.) The costume party. Halloween. Mardi Gras. A very primitive instinct. The carnival, the circus, the fair, the fiesta, the parade, the whatever-the-occasion to get out of myself and be 'the other'. Often joyous. Sometimes sad.

Some, indeed, say the fool is sacred. Cervantes claimed, "The most difficult character in comedy is the fool, and he who plays the part must be no simpleton."

Ken says of his childhood, "We were a very low income family. We always worked before we played. All my aunts and uncles were farmers. My dad worked for the Kraft Food Co. for almost 30 years. I'd say, all in all, Mom and Dad did a terrific job with what we had. We didn't know what we were missing because we didn't have it."

Enlisting in the Air Force in 1962, he remained for four years, learning the culture of the Far East, intensifying his own interest in art, and finally discovering the clown within himself.

"It was in Okinawa where I started Zero. I spent a total of three years in the Far East which was absolutely fantastic. It gave me the greatest education I've ever had. I found out people don't have to be white to have feelings. That no matter where you go, all the people believe in a Supreme Being, and that Supreme Being has many names. And if you treat people the way you want to be treated, you get along real fine. I even had people save my life—people that were from another country.

"Being brought up Lutheran, it brothered me when I got back from there. I was sitting in church once, and this tall, dark minister was putting down the Oriental people. I wanted to scream out, 'You're full of shit! You're telling these people a pack of lies. We got more letters and more support from people from my church when I was in the military, than these so-called Christians here. Don't give me any shit about who is a Christian and who is not because they don't go to church.' I got so angry I never went back to church. I would get up and leave every time he got into the pulpit. He is no longer at that church.

"It took me years to try to be assimilated back into the white culture. The people over there affected . . . the arts . . . the food. It left a definite impression on my life. It proved to me that if I'm going to get any place in life, the main person I'm going to have to rely on is me. They *allowed* you to be human. They *allowed* you to really feel.

"It was important to be able to listen to the bells. You go to Thailand and you listen to these things all over. You become *aware* of the movement of the wind.

"Fragrance. The lovely fragrance of flowers. The aroma of food. The touch of a child.

"I guess I was not the typical G.I. who would spend all his money in bars. I took my camera, my sketch book, and learned enough of the language so I could understand what was going on.

"Zero happened in Okinawa. It was the time of Obon—harvest time in Okinawa. Big parade. Big festival. I watched it. There were a bunch of clowns who looked like they were having a good time. One of them was named Tillie. He was having a great time. He was tall—about 6'—had enormous shoes, red hair, red nose, red suspenders, and red baggy pants. Funniest thing you ever wanted to see. I was in stitches.

"A couple of weeks later I saw this nametag in my barracks: 'Tillie.' I asked him if he was the same Tillie. He was. And I came to find out he was part of a group known as the Island Jesters. He invited me to their next meeting.

"I designed a costume. I bought my materials—buttons, thread, everything I needed. It took me a full day to find a tailor on Okinawa who would do it. And within a week I had a costume, and it was neat. Same design as I have now. Wide lapels, cut at the waist, tails, and, of course, my stripes. He made me one in blues, and the other in reds, yellows, oranges.

"The name came from my last name, Zilisch. In the military they would sometimes mispronounce it, and it would come out 'Zilch.' And sometimes they would just yell out, 'Hey, Nothing!' And, of course, from 'nothing' came Zero!

"I covered my head white. I had a white face. I also wore a little bitty bowler then. And that's how I would clown around. You had to be careful the way you designed a face in the Orient, so you didn't look like a demon.

"The Island Jesters taught me how to mime, clown etiquette, juggling, and they tried to teach me sleight-of-hand. Two of the clowns used to be with Ringling Brothers, Barnum and Bailey before the Korean War, I believe. They were our instructors. And we were a co-ed group. We had military personnel and dependents. There were about 30 of us in total.

"I didn't want to be an Emmet Kelly. I wanted to be a happy face, and I didn't want to look like anybody else. There is no way I would want to be a sad clown. We have so much depression, so many down things in our life. We don't need it in a clown too. In Emmet Kelly's time he fulfilled a role as a sad clown. He was able to show humor in his sadness. He had people laughing with him instead of at him. And that was important. He was a clown of his time as I am a clown of my time. Each one serves to fulfill a need.

"It was a lot of satisfaction, my first days of clowning. You made someone smile doing pratfalls, tumbling, tricks, begging for food. The only difference now . . . I now wear the military brogan (Air Force drill team boots), a black top hat, and a big red nose. I performed whenever there was a call for a clown . . . any kind of a parade, also hospitals and orphanages. The greatest thing the Island Jesters taught me was how to mime. Because then you could talk in any language.

"I chose to be silent. It's very satisfying. Sometimes it's very difficult—two to three hours without saying a word. But I can do it. People, when you do not talk, make a definite effort to listen. They're more attentive."

Returning to Beaver Dam after his time in the Air Force, Ken first went to work as a painter. "Painting houses and barns—all of that." He recalls going to an art show at Wayland Academy in Beaver Dam and saying, "I can do better than this stuff."

In Okinawa he had done photography, sculpture, sumi, calligraphy, and oil painting. Through the encouragement of a friend, Bev Dohmann, he enrolled in the Layton School of Art in Milwaukee, where he graduated with honors in graphic design in 1970. "It gave me great pleasure to send our announcements to people who never thought I would amount to anything."

He married Diane, also a student at Layton, in 1967, between his freshman and sophomore year. "Diane was born and raised in Sturgeon Bay, the daughter of Floyd and Florence Dickinson. We'd just come up here from Milwaukee every now and then. Between my junior and senior year at Layton, I worked at the *Advocate*— graphic design and layout."

Zero emerged for the first time in this country: "At Horicon Marsh Days, a few months after I returned. I didn't get paid either. He was fantastic! I had a nose then, a little rubber ball. The way that I was received from the people was very encouraging. And I got my picture in the Horicon paper for the first time! I remember asking my mother, 'Do they have any clown there?' And she said she didn't think so. 'Well, I'll put on my stuff and do it.' She was surprised too. It was the first time she saw me perform.

"The Egg Harbor 4th of July parade, 1968, was the first year I clowned here in Door county. Bob Sawyer hired me. I have been at the Egg Harbor 4th of July parade ever since.

"We chose to come to Door County in 1970, to move up fulltime, because we felt the county needed our services—graphic design. People could have quality work for a reasonable rate. And we're still doing that."

94

Listening to Ken Zilisch in his studio, observing his gestures, his facial expressions, I find myself continually in search of Zero, the clown inside. Just how a man harbors "the other" one. Occasionally glimpses of Zero are revealed . . . mostly in the face, sometimes in the way he carries himself. What they both share, however, is a concern for human beings.

Ken speaks of clown etiquette: "You don't harass people. You don't sexually assault a person either, in gesture or by contact. I try to make people happy. Try to get them to smile, to forget troubles, worries of the day. To relax and to be.

"I'm billed sometimes as a clown for kids, but I'm not. We're all kids when we allow ourselves to be. But our society robs us of that. 'Act your age!' That's why I'm a clown because when I'm really my age, which is . . . pick a number. I don't have an age when I'm a clown. It's right now."

Which sounds like Zero . . . a sort of Zen clown. If Zero could talk. Silence. Nothing. Now. It all adds up . . .

"People tell me, 'Do something funny.' I look at them and smile. You don't know what you're going to do as a clown till you do it. Even hugging Baldy [the local sheriff], even though he didn't like it. But at the end of every parade there was a handshake for Baldy.

"Zero's within me—and probably with thousands of people who have seen me. Every person I have touched or has seen me, I have changed their lives in some way. I know that for a fact. They've told me so.

"Zero is a gentleman clown. That gives him lots of latitude. The tipping of the hat, kissing of hands, the bowing, you-go-first type of thing. I try very hard to be respectful of other people. How they feel, and how they feel towards me. And sometimes it doesn't work. Sometimes it's impossible to be a gentleman with some people . . . men, women, children. I got kicked in the groin once by a 13-year-old girl—on purpose. She was on a dare by friends. That's one of the times I talked. Both her and her friends know that if any one touched me again I would sue them and their parents for bodily injury, and she personally would be polishing my boots for the rest of her natural life.

"Now I'm more in tune to people around me and their movements. One of the things I'm able to do: I can actually tell what kind of a person one is from the backside of him. It's like animal instinct. You know who to trust and who not to trust. I've defused a lot of situations prior to their happening.

"I've been stepped on, pinched, grabbed at, and one fellow who shook my hand so hard . . . he was trying to show his friends how strong he was. With one slight move of my umbrella . . . he needed his hand to hold something else.

"It all goes back to 'a clown is not real. A clown does not feel. So therefore I can do anything to a clown.' But a clown does feel! I feel that I'm a pulse of the people at that particular event."

Ken Zilisch as Zero, Zero as Ken Zilisch?

"I don't really think there is any difference. Many times I'm as nutty in real life. But others do, some of them, know what this town clown is really about. Little do some of them know that this town clown also has talent. 'He's just a clown.' I laugh about that all the way home. I cry too.

"I'm touched . . . People who tell you how you've changed their life, and thank you for it. Or a note from a little child. Or an older couple who came up to see Zero and say goodbye for the last time. They were both old. The wife had had some serious surgery. The husband had suffered from a heart attack. I had danced with the woman some years earlier, and they were hoping Zero the Clown would be at Fall

Festival (Sister Bay) for one more time. There are so few people who say thank you. I wish people would say thank you while our ears can hear it rather than paying regrets."

As for the artist within the clown, within the man . . . "Zero and the artist are hand-in-glove. It's sensitivity to people. It comes out as sensitivity in my portraits, in my drawings. My works have little stories about them."

One of his paintings, based upon the serious illness of his daughter at one time, he calls "Between Life and Death." "The painting is a tribute to womanhood. Women, in the religious aspect, have sort of been the forbidden fruit. And they're not. They're beautiful, viable and important to our total being and life cycle.

"The only person that was around me to any great extent was my mother. My father worked and worked and he slept and then he worked some more. The woman was always around.

"I can relate better to women because men don't want to take the time to listen, and the woman knows how to listen. Men don't listen. Look at our government situation. The bastards don't listen!

"Zero is in tune with people's feelings. I seem to be at a particular place and at a particular time to fill a need for persons. Over the years this pattern has been brought to my attention by the people I have touched. A burst balloon, a dropped ice cream cone, a harsh reprimand that I've sort of been able to smooth over. Spats between individuals. I just happen to be there—as a woman, as a mother, as a parent is expected to be there. If you look at all the animal life forms, teaching is very essential to their well being. That's exactly what I do as Zero. As an artist. As a parent . . . ."

As a human being? (Ken/Zero nods in the affirmative).

He appears somewhat shaken at the moment, this artist, this man . . . as if the silent clown within him is hearing his own voice for the first time.

"You know, my Dad was a clown once," he confesses, his eyes beginning to tear in the old and true spirit of the clown everywhere. "And I thought he was crazy! I was ashamed of him. And now I wish Dad were alive and could see me clowning because I think he'd be proud.

"I've been clowning for 20 years now. As long as my legs will carry me, I will probably always be a clown. Something I feel needs to be done. My grandfather once told me, 'If one person doesn't make a difference'—then he reached in his humidor and handed me a cigar—'Smoke this in a crowded room'."

Henry Miller saw the clown as "a poet in action. He is the story which he enacts . . . The clown appeals to me deeply, precisely because he is separated from the world by laughter. It is a silent, what we call mirthless, laughter. The clown teaches us to laugh at ourselves. And this laughter of ours is born of tears."

"Sadness," admits Ken, "is something I suppress as a clown. But there are times when I take off the makeup that I sit and cry."

The joy, though. This relationship to 'the other,' the Zero inside. The moment one becomes the other . . . ?

"I begin thinking about Zero the night before. I put a spit shine on my boots. Makeup is put out. I press my own suit. Everything is laid out in readiness . . . hat, handkerchief, white gloves. It takes about an hour. Early to bed. And usually, say I have a 9 o'clock parade, I give myself an hour for travel, an hour for makeup. Then there is time for breakfast. That's when I really start psyching myself up—breakfast.

"Sometimes I don't want to put on the face because I know I'm going to have to take it off. And I don't want to. And that's hard. But I know people are waiting for

Zero, and I don't want to disappoint them. All my life, when I tell someone I'm going to do something, I do it, and I'm there!

"Putting on the face . . . I'm not aware of the transformation. All I know is when the boots are laced, the coat put on, the gloves, the hat put on and tapped . . . The hat is the very last thing I put on. When I tap the hat I know Zero is ready, and I'm ready to go.

"As I drive, it begins then . . . the wave of my fingers . . . the astonishment in people's eyes to see a clown driving a car. A clown isn't supposed to drive a car! A clown isn't real! It makes me smile . . . and the smile begins to grow from inside . . . ."

And Zero is born. Begun. Is alive in himself and within us once again.

"Joy is like a river," said Miller. "It flows ceaselessly. It seems to me that this message which the clown is trying to convey to us, that we should participate through ceaseless flow and movement, that we should not stop to reflect, compare, analyze, possess, but flow on and through, endlessly, like music. This is the gift of surrender, and the clown makes it symbolically. It is for us to make it real."

The Poet As Midwife
Sue Peterson

She is a woman in the middle of her life, and a poet only beginning to realize her birth.

An early entry from her dream journal/writing notebook:

> January 23, –8:00 (Sun.) 1977
>
> 'Sometimes you must be your own mother.' I wonder what that means. Another dream, 3 days ago. I woke up with that line in my head—and it seemed important. I saw a bent, scurrying (bug like) woman scampering in front of me, away from me and towards a door (Innsbruck type of place) heading for old used grotto-like door—arms and shoulders like mother's.
> Sylvia Plath writes of Mother-to-self?
> Poetry? Read that after dream/

Over a year later came these first lines of a first draft of a poem:

> *Dream Collage*
>
> Suddenly, the old midwife
> was there, scurrying down the
> cobblestone street like a
> bug, ~~heavy black body,~~ thin dark
> arms and legs ~~working~~ shawl flapping, . . .

And some days later, a second draft:

> *Crone ~~Dream~~*
>
> Suddenly, the old midwife
> was there, scurrying down
> the dark cobblestone street
> like a long-limbed bug,
> black shawl flapping.
> herb bag bouncing, she
> hurried into the ~~cave~~ back room
> through an archway of stone, time worn
> timeworn like her hands . . .

She will tell you that after two winters of writing classes at the Clearing it was not till after the winter of 1978 that she made more of a commitment to writing. "Up until that time I thoroughly enjoyed it, but I didn't even think of taking time from being housewife and mother. 1979 was the year I made more of an attempt to set aside time for writing . . . to just take it. Till then I considered myself a closet writer in that I didn't talk about it and kept it almost a secret. My family knew I was writing, but I didn't share it. Maybe it was because the very act of writing is a very internal thing, very personal, and it's very hard to share that in the beginning. It has to go internally first. I think there's a matter of guilt involved. I was a housewife, mother, and I suppose there's an amount of guilt to that.

"I think one of the first poems I wrote that I was revealing a lot of myself was in the second year of writing:

> *Valentine to Myself*

> Me,
> I am what you see . . .
>   plus what's hidden,
>   a shy lilac girl
>   waiting, geisha-like
>   behind the closed door
>   for her valentines of love.

> Me . . .
> I shop the village square
> exchanging chickens for flour,
> drawing water at the well,
> and when I meet
> someone's eyes, deeply . . .
> and understanding glows
> like sun on amber,
> I wrap this gem
> in a lacy heart
> and send it
>   to the flower girl
>   waiting behind the closed door
>   and she smiles with rapture . . .

> we hug and are warm
> all day.

"The idea of a double self. I don't know that I ever thought about that before, and yet I was writing about a double self, this inner person, in that poem. The valentine, the crone . . . the dream. I can see a relationship in the poems I'm now writing. It's all coming from the same place."

Though the role of the teacher, throughout her schooling, was minimal in affecting her interest in writing, she does regard her mother's influence as significant.

"My mother loved literature. She came from a family that loved to read. From the earliest days she always read us good literature. Good children's poetry, novels. I can remember being highly affected by her reading of Maeterlinck's *The Bluebird*, and how I would always cry at a certain part. I identified with everything that happened in that story. She always read to us till we were able to read to ourselves. And she read very well. My father did not read much.

"I think it was basically a happy childhood. I remember being fairly . . . not content, in a way some children are . . . but fairly happy. Exuberant a lot of the time. There was also, along with my childhood and many others, a lot of painful incidents—mostly to do with relationships. Some very good ones and some very bad ones.

"I think I was a people child. Even as a very young child, 3, 4, 5 years old, I remember defining life by the people around me, not by things, or houses, but by people. Even though I had a large family. I remember meeting, more than anyone else in the family, more people. I would just go out into the street and see them and disappear—which would drive my mother buggy.

"There were a lot of tensions in the family structure, especially during the Depression and then the war years. My father was under a lot of pressure at that time because of business. And I think I felt a great tension in the family because of that.

"I really don't think I have much to work out in my writing from that period of life. My earlier life kind of bores me. I can't imagine it fascinating others. I think it's a matter of when you reached your 40's, either you've worked out those early years or

blocked them. I personally feel that my relationships that I've worked through in my early family life . . . well, I don't see any negative energy there anymore. I've accepted the good and the bad of those times and gone on to other things. I just don't live there anymore as a writer. I'm talking about sibling relationships as much as parents.

"Maybe if I had started writing back in high school and college that's the thing I would have been writing—family. But I didn't. I started in my 40's, so I had a very different perspective of my life. I think what I find myself being drawn to writing now is trying to understand myself as well as others. Some poems, like "Flatbed," are simple observations of things I see and hear.

The Flatbed Man's Story

"This 1964 Rambler
sitting in the woods for years,
.with long chains I winched it in,
a grass snake drops off the hood, curls away;
winched it up the ramp
of the flatbed, the rocking
dislodged all the wildlife
at once . . . a rat jumped
to the ground and hopped away
on hind legs like a kangaroo.
Mice dropped to the flatbed,
saw the edge too high, ran crazy
in the shadow of the car
then as a group make the leap
to the weeds below.
Long-legged spiders drop,
cover the trunk, the cab;
a chipmunk leaps
to freedom.
Things settle, the Rambler seems to slump,
sad, deserted, chained.
A hollow wreck.
It was getting dark. I suddenly
get the hell out of there,
flatbed, Rambler, me covered with spiders.
That ain't no way to live."

"I write about others because people interest me; it all has to do with the human condition, and it explains me and life. Other people are me and I'm them. I'm interested in people seeing myself in them and they in me:

On An Old Man In A Nursing Home

Old men parchment-curled
in thin white sheets, notes pinned
to white hospital tops;

'take Jensen's teeth out
at night, he loses them
in the sheets.'

'Harold doesn't like water,
give him juices.'

Harold. Now fetal, a
fading, wordless midnight.

The wife is busy mornings
bent over the gnarled silence
trying to spoon malted milk
into his clenched-tight mouth.

The minister visits. He speaks loudly
into the blankness of that space,
    "Blessed are the meek; for they
    shall inherit the earth."

The wife weeps, "unclench your teeth,
you're doing this on purpose,
I know you're doing this on purpose."

At 9:00 evenings, the nurse smooths
white sheets, tucking in sides,
arranging his hands, limp as old lettuce,
across his belly . . . a willing package
tied with a bow.

Late at night the Rose Lady
           sneaks in,
throwing handfuls of prairie roses
and small bunches of lilacs
into the thickly silent rooms; up and down
the long dark corridor she goes,
petals flowing from her hands
like sunsets,
falling softly
like snow.

"In the first year or two of my writing, my viewpoint as a person, and therefore as a
writer, was as wife and mother. As somebody else's person rather than my own. I
didn't write as Susan, I wrote as mom, or as the wife of the artist [Charles Peterson]
in the community. And that's how I viewed myself. If somebody asked me for my
opinion on the simplest thing, I would not be sure of my opinion because I had
considered so many others' viewpoints for so long.

"I think one reason I began to rely on dreams so much is that it was my way of
forcing myself to write about something that was totally myself—to see my own
outline."

An early entry from her dream journal/writing notebook:

Dream: January 24, 1977

It is a thickly entangled and overgrown woods, but somewhere in the middle is a clearing. And in that clearing is an apple tree. A pileated woodpecker, with large black body and strong fast-beating wings, swiftly flies out of the woods through the clearing to the apple tree, where its talons grip the underside of a horizontal branch. The bird hangs there totally still for minutes, as if in a trance. Then slowly it opens its wings, which have changed to the shape of a butterfly's wings, and the coloring and texture are different too . . . now the black is softer, more velvety, less like stiff black feathers . . . and on the top center of each wing is a large circle of bright gold-orange. The wings slowly fold and unfold, much like butterfly wings just out of a chrysalis, drying itself for flight. The head has changed a bit too, looking now more like that of an insect. Suddenly this butterfly-bird creature lets go of the tree branch and gently glides through the clearing, the wing beat now slow and easy, the flight pattern erratic; it floats this way and that, and finally into the dark woods where it disappears altogether.

"I write about nature a lot. I don't think they're my more successful poems, and I don't know why that is. But I find I need to express a lot of what I find in nature, and that has come about mostly since I've been in Door County . . . since 1973.

Village Post Office: February

one man says
Whose dog was it, anyway?
and the postmaster says
No one knows . . . didn't belong
to a local . . .
but it was awful to watch
anyway, big as he was
he couldn't break through
the thin ice . . . kept swimming
farther and farther away
from the ice hole.
another man says
they tried poles, nets, everything
to steer him back
but nothing worked . . .
they could see him always
the ice was so clear.
and the postmaster says
Yeah, could even see his
dog tags . . . they flashed
under the ice like
shiny silver cleos . . .

"But it also existed when I was quite young and spent a lot of time outdoors. I felt then, as I do now, very much at ease around woods, fields, and water. I find nature

103

very peaceful. I can get my thoughts centered. I feel far less scattered. I spend a lot of time at the pond near my home. I think of it as an escape more than anything—the tensions and hectic life that often goes on in the house.

"I think one reason I found myself involved with poetry was because I was a woman in her 40's in Door County, and it is one of the best ways to survive, to be a creative individual. Drawing on your own resources to make life interesting. I was the wife of a college professor back in Marietta, Ohio, and if I had stayed, I would still be leading that life, still active on many committees, living the life of the college wife. It gets repetitive. There's no challenge to it. But more importantly to me— expressing who I am—I needed something much more personal. Something much more imaginative.

"I think every woman is her own person. She has her own needs, and her own satisfactions. I think some women here are very satisfied being . . . let's say, a housewife and a mother. I think some are very satisfied serving on committees, or with some employment that they have. And that's fine. But for women who feel a need to be creative, to be personally very involved in some creativity, the other life is not enough. It becomes very hollow.

"And let's face it. To some degree I have a choice that is not the choice of many women because there is no financial pressure on me to bring in a good deal of the income. I am free of that. I am very lucky. And so I choose to spend my time in a way that satisfies me most, and for me that's writing.

"I really don't spend that much time with the women here. I think the women I know here, roughly my age, that I have some kind of personal contact with are often at the same place I am, and I think it's characteristic of the age—40's and 50's—the sudden realization that you can't go on just turning the crank. There's got to be more somewhere. And most of these women have worked through their first great challenge, which is raising the children or helping a husband through business, and I think they're beginning to look for more, something more spiritual, more emotional.

"A lot of them, like me, want to make a more personal contact with themselves and the world. I think most of us satisfy the early challenges in life—to be married, to emotionally support one's husband or perhaps help in the business—and I think this is the crossroads time for them: the 40's and 50's. And some seem not to change— either they don't need to, or they don't know how to. And some of them get very depressed.

"I think some, some very lucky ones, don't need to and are prefectly happy sliding into old age without changing patterns. They have no new needs. I am thinking of some people I know who didn't change, while life changed around them, and they became very depressed. I think that is what a lot of serious depression among older women is about. Their life changed around them, and they didn't keep up with it.

"I don't blame Door County. I think this happens anywhere. We have survivors and we have depression cases. I think a lot of women were raised to occupy their time shopping, and if they haven't got that here, they go crazy. Basically, it's being self-sufficient . . .

"A woman comes out of 15, 20 years of marriage and raising children, having intensely concentrated on serving others—often in a fragmented way. I think of myself as having gotten rid of any strong edges. The act of raising children almost demands a smoothing, a flattening of self, and after raising them you realize there is very little self left, and you are very bland.

Removing The Warp

Sandpapering myself.
A fine process
of defining. Sometimes whole chunks
fall off. And sometimes
grow back lopsided, humped over . . . I curl
inward like a fist, grow a crooked mouth, a suspicious
lizard eye.
So, more sandpaper, more
fine tuning

    that seeks the honest contour
    of the uncurled woman
    whose clear eye knows the earth,
    the sky, the silent slide of time
    growing rich and pungent in her hands.

curling uncurling removing the warp
Somewhere a woman is clearing her garden
of last winter's stones.

"Writing for me is a very, very important thing to get into, to find my own characteristics again—to find my own face. I think the others wrote because they had so much to say . . . while I had to find what my creative strengths and possibilities were. I think it would be easy to become very bored in Door County. Door County has that attribute, unless one has something very personal to fall back upon, like writing.

On Reading Margaret Atwood's Poem

We start from the riverbank,
she the boatman ferrying me across
the broad surface; maneuvering
in and out of currents, indicating
the black mark of boulders,
she makes so obvious
the route that was always there.
And from my comfortable rattan seat
in the back of this boat I suspect
I could have found my way across
without the boatman.

Yet here I am again
on the starting bank, this time alone
and everything is remarkably flat
and swift; shapeless currents
give me no clue, I can't hear the language
of rocks . . .
I have no idea how to begin.
Do I start by walking into water?

"There are a lot of things about writing that intrigue me more than anything else in life. It's just a wide, exciting ocean out there. Everything from the real excitement of solving technical problems . . . well, it just keeps you alive. Keeps the blood moving. There's always a deep satisfaction, even a fright, to pull something out of yourself and go deeper and deeper . . . allowing yourself to find out more about yourself.

"Privacy . . . a room of one's own. I imagine there are creative women who maybe don't live in a family situation where privacy is very important. But I really need some space of my own, a room of my own, a hut of my own, which I now have! I need this, physically, to be able to get away, and to be able to work without interruption. I need it physically, spiritually, to be able to withdraw into myself and live there for a while . . . a kind of interior monologue with myself. I really need that, a lot of quiet, private space. I definitely need it as a writer, and as a person. I once had an astrological chart done, and the chart points to a woman who could be a hermit! And she was very right. Except that the chart also pointed out that I needed to communicate with people. Two very different needs.

"The room-of-your-own idea is also tied into honoring the writing process. This is especially true for a woman who has never had a room of her own. It's *important* to have it. I remember sitting in writing class, listening to other woman writers bitching about how we don't have a space of our own . . . one woman even told of her husband always taking her typewriter! And I've certainly been guilty of not demanding a space of my own. If a woman is going to write, she has to take it and herself seriously enough, and *take* her space, make her own room. I built my hut for that reason.

"The thing that intrigues me more about writing now is an awareness of the better you write, the more honest you are. It's honesty in writing that is maybe the real tough thing to face. It's like peeling an onion back. Each time a little more about the way you really feel about the essence of something. For me, right now, that's the most interesting thing about writing—getting rid of old perceptions, the expected way to react. And that's part of my background—acting the way I was expected to. Somebody else's expectation of me.

Small Joy

walking wet and naked
in the rain
I hear no one
      the women and children
      are all hidden away
      behind doors
my feet flip and shine like fish
my wet thighs glisten like salmon
my breasts are hills and rivulets
     the earth smells of mud, is all
     thick gray mist, water
              falling
my umbrella is a drum, a
bright orange slice, ribbed
and glowing, a wet dripping full moon
        beating
            beating

no one is alive
but me

"Any creative process touches upon something that is very important to me—
beauty. There is very real beauty in expressing oneself well on paper. And it's that
beautiful aspect in any well written piece that really thrills me, touches me. I don't
feel I've written that well, that often. Writing isn't just a way of getting rid of emotion.
It's also a way of creating something of beauty."

Much of Sue Peterson's coming to terms with her life, her writing, herself, has
involved a continued fascination with the dreaming mind. In many ways, that alone
has helped to set her free.

"Dreams and poetry . . . they're marvelously entangled. I think they come from
the same source. Some of my best poems come from dreams. I only became aware of
dreams about four or five years ago.

"I can't remember the first time I was told in class at the Clearing to start recording
dreams because they are a good source of images for a writer. I kept my writing
journal and dream journal together in the beginning, then separated them. I'm on my
ninth writing journal now, and my third dream journal. I recall how amazed and
delighted I was with the marvelous, crazy fantasies coming out of my head. I still feel
that way—even if they're bad dreams. It's the wonderful, sad, funny, beautiful
images. I still delight in them. And I like to use them in my writing.

"I think the 'Crone' is a poem that came out of this thing. The pure delight of the
crone, the image that came out of my head. But it's more than that, more than
mindless entertainment. If the dream carried enough personal energy to have
impressed me as much as the dreams that I work into poetry, it probably was a very
important dream for me, touching some deep source of self-knowledge. Because I
often write these poems that come from dreams without really understanding what
they're about personally. That is, I'm writing because the subject fascinates me, but
I often don't know where the poem is going. It's as if I follow it, rather than my
creating it. And it's often months and months before I really catch on to what it was
about.

"I think sometimes these poems are actually foreshadowing my life. These deep
dreams are actually aware of the directions I will soon be moving in. Dreams are
honest. They force you to see yourself honestly, and your real desires and
fears . . . and pains and pleasures too, I suppose. Why am I dreaming of dullness
all the time? Living a life of dullness is what I *really* fear."

Late Winter Woman

All my perfume is gone
    soft iris petals
    frozen deep
    under the dark snow

My bones quiet, curled
a night burial   sleep
    dry skin rustles
like old corn husks,   is shed

        abandoned

107

                last year's snakeskin
Nightdreams dig deep
into denying earth
this twelfth moon,
                          Moon of Stilled Hunger

    Late winter woman
    curled in moon
                  waiting my way
                  to new circle of sun

     She is a woman of clarity. Both a writer and a woman with a remarkable sense of
assimilating many diverse elements and then, almost effortlessly, rendering them
into something whole. The creative process, of course. But magical too, in a sense.
Even bordering, at times, on that ancient art of

    Alchemy

    In that heated dream
    we are melting
    together;
    soft silver curled
    and fusing at the edges
    like warm bracelets,
    the middle liquid, supple,
    shaped and reshaped to
    alchemic change, the sun
    pours down . . .

    Yet she remains at home in the natural world. Be it birds, bears, but-
terflies . . . she will have her way with them in words. Eventually, in poems.
    "Birds are symbols of something free, spiritual, lifting. They give a great feeling of
expansion to me. The hawk . . . powerful, in the American Indian sense. Also
different, arrogant of the human plight. Yet beautiful. Gulls are humorous. They also
have a sense of spirit about them. They soar. Crows are like gulls, but they are much
more human. I feel a definite connection with a crow or an owl. They are definitely
tuned in on the human wave length. It's almost as if they know they're there, we know
they're there, and all know each other. I don't think of myself as writing about birds,
yet I'm often amazed how much I use them. I refer to a wing or a beak or a flight
pattern.
    "If I had to use a bird to symbolize Door County, the obvious one would be the gull.
But I wouldn't use it because its been used so much. For me, personally, it would be
the owl or crow. I think crow for more physical reasons—farm fields. The owl for
more spiritual reasons—the hidden, deep-in-the-woods feeling. A night feeling.
Somehow an owl makes connection with one's soul.
    "Flowers. Queen Anne's Lace, since I've been here. It almost haunts. The star-like
patterns which fascinate me. I also love the wild rose . . . the surprise of them.
    "Butterflies . . . I love 'em! There's something numinous, mystical about
butterflies. It's almost like a secret between us. I especially like monarchs. I grew up

with a lot of monarchs along Lake Michigan. There's something incredible about butterflies. They are so delicate yet they survive a tremendous migration.

"Horses are symbols of strength, of energy, and yet, there's something very mysterious about them. Almost an uncanny beauty about a horse if it is just standing there in a field. Most humans dream about horses. They must be a very deep, psychological symbol of tremendous energy source.

"I don't have any real feeling about bears, except for three dreams . . .

Bear Dance/Three Dreams

(1)

I walk carefully in this dark
staying on the narrow strip of sidewalk
victorian feet pointed
properly straight, no side trips
or traps for me thank you . . .
so very gray this path   avoiding
       the orchard
this night closed up like fists
   suddenly fearful dark shapes
   animal shapes moving   in trees
   apple branches growling and snapping
plucking ripe apples, eating the richness of apples
Oh the wild fright of bears their fierce dark dance
Bears!! trees full of hungry bears
plucking ripe apples, eating the richness of apples
Oh the wild fright of bears their fierce dark dance
I hurry my cautious step   I panic PANIC
   yet I can't help looking back

to see a big thick-chested bear
drop roundly to the ground and move
with his strong grace, his rolling gait
towards me
he slows then he stands his ground
  swaying   what does he want
what does he want, watching me with his
thick body swaying as he stands
as if to the roll
     of thunderous kettle drums

in terrible fear I run away
on the narrow sidewalk running away
into the safe closed night

(2)

in the shadow of dusk
at the dark edge of dream
bears come out   carrying night

109

around their shoulders like a black fog
screams of "Bears, Bears!"   we run so hard
I drag my child with me she wants to sleep outside
"No!" I slam the cabin door shut lock all doors
bolt windows
  when
    a
    woman
      walks in the back door
magically appearing with smiles of ease
I ask "Are the bears still on the rampage?"
"Yes!" and she throws open a window with delight,
"Look, like a circus, one even stands on his head!"

(3)

A gypsy camp somewhere
with night warmly lit
at its center by fire
a bear and I dance without moving
in a darkness he brings
yet lit by fire
to a music not heard
yet the closeness
of thunder

"That's a very Jungian poem I wrote of those three dreams—a very strong image I had then, but they really don't have much meaning for me. I think the bear image was fear, and I came to a positive relationship with that fear."

She is an herb woman, too . . . owls, alchemy, magic, butterflies . . . the gathering and sorting of diverse elements. The transformation process. Dreams, nature, herbs, crones . . . midwivery . . . poetry . . .

"Herbs . . . they just came right along with that midwife dream and the crone poem. They're the female thing. Herbs seem to go along with the *curandera* . . . the woman healer . . . the midwife in any culture. And I love that image. I think it's a very gentle, very female image. The use of herbs, the smell of them . . . all very comforting. Whether it's herb bread or herb tea or just working with them in poems.

"I think the midwife . . . a little woman scurrying into almost a cave-like room . . . and I'm going to call her a midwife, not a crone now, because I knew she was going to aid in a birth . . . I think she is a concrete symbol of the need to give life. I sometimes wonder if she isn't something from almost a reincarnated past . . .

Midwife

    . . . down
the dark narrow street
like a long-limbed bug,
black shawl flapping,
herb bag bouncing;

110

hurried into the back room
through an archway of stone
as primitive, timeworn
as hands . . .

hands, long-fingered and
flowing, knowing magic knots
for cords, the signs, timing,
brewing teas, pushing, kneading,
drawing out life,
covering up death . . .
sprinkling the heavy air
with the ground roots and juniper,
with crosses,
rubbing skin with hazel water,
with birch branches, each branch
bearing seven leaves . . .

after the chants, the herbs,
the cries, the special knots,
  her woolen shawl
  her bonnet
  and, before leaving,

she suggests
a name or two
such as
Hrothgar, or
Gauwain

"I am now beginning to see that she is a part of me, maybe parts I am growing into.
My first birthing . . . giving birth to myself. 'Sometimes you must be your own
mother' really, for me, means that sometimes you have to become your own midwife,
your own mother . . . bringing into being that person you want to become
psychologically, spiritually. You have to deliver yourself."

Living Amidst the Ruins
Flora Langlois

Through the years, a man peoples a space
with images of provinces, kingdoms, mountains
bays, ships, islands, fishes, rooms, tools, stars,
horses, and people. Shortly before his death, he
discovers that the patient labyrinth of lines
traces the images of his own face.
—Jorge Luis Borges

I saw Flora Langlois' silverpoint drawings for the first time at Anne Haberland's
Edgewood Orchard Galleries in Fish Creek. I remember being in a hurry, and I
remember those drawings holding me, pulling me into them.

There were intricately drawn faces, figures of shrouded women. There was the
sea. There were trees, birds, nature as only a visionary sees . . . both defining and
releasing. There were towers. Ruins. The passage of time. Something both medieval
and mystical. A language of lines. There was a transparency about it all. There was
sadness and suffering somehow raised to the ethereal, absolving artist and observer.
There was loss and there was love in the fullest dimension, which mystics alone
realize in silences.

These were landscapes far beyond Door County, yet they came from a woman, an
artist, living here, discovering her own life.

This was the kind of art that always appealed to me. A touch of the surreal.
Shadows reminescent of the mystery Giorgio de Chirico. It was story, it was strange,
and in some ways even sacred. No, it was definitely not what has come to be known
as Door County art. Yet the artist, I was to learn through the graciousness and
concern of Anne Haberland herself, was actually living in Fish Creek.

She comes from Costa Rica, explained Anne.

Which explained some of it . . . the sea, the light, the seductiveness of color. The
totally alien terrain bordering on fantasy. I thought of all the rich literature of Latin
America I enjoyed: the poems of Pablo Neruda, the books of Borges, the fiction of
Fuentes, the stories of Gabriel Garcia Marquez.

I have to meet her, I said.

Yes, smiled Anne.

She is small, child-like, almost fragile but for the Picasso depth of her brown eyes
which take in everything. There is a sadness at times to her face, a melancholia, that
unexpectedly warms to a smile and sometimes laughter. Her speech, though
occasionally halting, is direct, honest, completely revealing. One instinctively trusts
her, accepts her, and admires her for all this.

Coming from a traditional, upper class family in Costa Rica (her mother, a significant painter in Costa Rica) Flora will tell you how much to her surprise, and after a rather strict upbringing including a convent-like school, her mother sent her off to California at the age of 17 to attend Immaculate Heart in Hollywood Hills. "A girl's finishing college," explains Flora. "It had to be nuns because I had to be chaperoned. Education in Costa Rica . . . like the Middle Ages, exactly. Brought up in a fort-like building . . . everything done with a little bell. Certain reverence to the nuns, to the Mother Superior. I thought the nuns were not human, did not have bodily functions for many years!

"The career was to get married and be the perfect wife. I was the only one who was different . . . very introverted, interested in the arts. I wanted to be the perfect wife also. I had all the trimmings—sewing, cooking, baking, ballet, piano lessons. You had to be the lady, beautiful. That was the ideal in Costa Rica.

"Actually, my art was at home. Mother was an artist. I was always drawing. There was always classical music going on. I was reading classic books . . . books that the church had banned. Dumas, Hugo . . . My mother didn't force religion down me. She read the stoics. She didn't go to church. She was a mystic. She is a mystic. My dad said church was for women. So I didn't grow up in a religion at home. Yet I was at a nun's school where they were so strict.

"Mother . . . I didn't get along with her at all when I was a little girl. My dad was the big hero. I went to soccer games with him. Went hunting with him. But I was not a tomboy."

It's the mother, though, who continues to fascinate and mystify her. Her mother's paintings, which Flora describes as "sort of surrealistic. She wanted nature to practically swallow the house. The landscapes that mother painted were always tormented landscapes. The sky had a lot of grey. All those years she never talked about her own personal feelings. But about two or three years ago she told me that her father once told her that her birthday should never be celebrated because when she was born, her mother died.

"So she was never very humorous. She took life very seriously. Not my dad. For my dad, life was to be enjoyed. But from my mother's side, it's been a very unique family, very individualistic.

"The only thing she used to say to me is: 'Someday I want you to go to the United States. And someday I want you to become a great artist.' But she never taught me a thing about art. We worked together in the same room, but she always had her own things. Never said anything to me. She supported me through school, through college.

"Now, every year, I go back to Costa Rica, I take my drawings down with me for her to see them, and she is a great admirer of my work. It's so strange. In my young years she was my enemy; in my later years she became my friend.

"She was very open now about my relationship with a man twenty years younger—Scott Chobot. She accepts it all. That's what makes it so strange. When I was young she wouldn't let me look at a guy, and now she accepts everything I do."

After three years of school in California, Flora returned to Costa Rica for two years and then came to Kenosha, Wisconsin, to visit relatives in 1952, eventually enrolling in the Layton School of Art in Milwaukee.

"It was my first experience going to school with males," she smiles, "and seeing nudes. It was very embarrassing at first. In Milwaukee I met my first husband [Leslie Langlois]. He was going to medical school at the time. We started dating. In about five months he wanted to get married. I didn't get married in the church because Leslie couldn't stand the Catholic Church. He was an agnostic. So I got married here by a judge, and I got married by proxy in Costa Rica because I still felt I would be living in sin. So that saved everybody."

Moving to Madison, Flora pursued her degree in art while her husband studied for his degree in medicine. New York was the next stop, where Leslie did his internship and Flora worked for Norcross.

"We then moved to Connecticut where Leslie was doing residency for psychiatry in a mental hospital. We lived right on the grounds. It was a depressing year, but that is where I conceived my Jeffery. I got involved teaching at the mental hospital, but I couldn't muster it. It was so depressing. I did a couple of drawings there . . . people sitting on benches with their heads down.

"A kind of strange mixture of happiness, that time . . . happiness in being pregnant and the sadness of the place. Also important . . . Leslie was not a healthy man. A brilliant man but frail of body. A great soul and a great mind.

"And because I was brought up with nuns, so mystic, the body part was not important. I knew there was something about the physical, but it was not there. I saw a lot of physical pain with him and a lot of illness in those 10 years of marriage. Consequently, the illness affected me too.

"He was a very difficult, very complex personality. But it was not really a happy union because of the difficulty, yet it was very definitely growing years for me. He opened a lot of doors. He showed me a lot of other religions, other nationalities. He loved people of all nationalities, all walks of life, while I knew only one walk of life— society, period.

"When he died, it was a great loss to me in that area of the intellect. But as a woman, I didn't think I really knew what life was all about until I met Scott.

"But I married again in 1975 [Francis Pauls] and it was a very bad step because I was thinking in terms of security, a good man. We had very little in common. I remember mother saying, 'Well, you'll learn to love him.' So I got married and it ended up being a disaster. It didn't last more than 2½ years.

"Leslie, my first husband, was very much into Freud. He felt the best thing you could have was to know yourself. He suggested I should go through analysis too, and I did. And the psychiatrist used to go to sleep on me."

Her Costa Rican and Catholic past, her mother, her two marriages, especially the one to Leslie, whose suffering she shared, the young man she was about to meet in Door County . . . all this would eventually work its way into her art.

Even as a child her artistic talents were evident, though her own mother did not directly encourage her. Flora was always the best in class . . . in California, at Layton, even in Madison. At Madison she recalls an art professor telling her, "Stick to your own ideas. Don't let anyone change you."

In Madison is where she first began to draw in silverpoint, a Renaissance art form of drawing in silver upon a casein or any white pigment background. "It has a shimmering quality of silver," she explains. "A delicate quality that pen and ink doesn't have. It's the delicacy more than anything, the way it is handled with small strokes. People want to get real close and examine it."

She has explored the possibilities of this form even further by adding a delicacy of color to her work which both harmonizes and heightens her images to almost magical, certainly mysterious, even mystical overtones. The process, painstakingly slow, often involves months to complete a single drawing.

"It accomodated me because I love to work with details—in relationships as well as drawing. I could really get in there, like a bee crawling into a flower. Silverpoint was just fascinating . . . to know that it went back to the Middle Ages. The technique . . . a prepared surface of white pigment, and on that carrier, the

particles of silver are deposited. You get a silver line which in time tarnishes. People find that's one of the attractions."

Her development as an artist during the time of her first marriage was, of course, a period of adjustment—woman, mother, artist. "There was conflict all the years I was married to Leslie because I wanted to be the perfect wife, a mother, and I wanted to be an artist. So I always did some drawing, but I never thought of not being a good wife in every respect regarding my husband, or letting my child walk in dirty diapers. So I always put myself second. But I did not resent this. I always managed to have a little corner of the house for my studio, so I had a little time for my art. Leslie himself said, 'What in the world are you doing sewing, when you have such a talent?' He wanted me to go to school, to get a degree.

"There was a lot of concern for the development of a little, independent individual . . . my son. I said to myself, I don't want Jeffery to grow up with any religion, just a good moral code. And independent. A lot of discipline, and a lot of love. And so there was never a big problem with him with drugs or anything. I'm sure he's smoked some pot. So have I. But no real problem. He is a business student at UW-Madison. He has his father's brain for mathematics—but very sensitive. 'Mom,' he said to me, 'I admire you because you have done so much in life.'

"After Leslie's death I kept working because I was teaching. I was drawing a lot of mother/son subjects because I was so involved with the responsibility of raising a

116

son by myself. Also a lot of Bible things because I was getting into mythology. There was always a touch of something different about my work. I could see how it evolved. The theme of Adam and Eve intrigued me because I didn't know what it was all about yet. From being very religious, very mystical . . . to beginning to question the church.

"I began to have these guilt trips of not going to church on Sunday—when I was married to Leslie—and not giving religion to Jeffery. I went through an awful lot of anguish because it was such a dramatic change for me. I started to exhibit in Milwaukee through the Bradley Gallery in summer, in '79. I had my first one-woman show there. But I was still primarily interested in raising Jeff and getting another degree, a Masters. Whenever I undertake something, it's with a lot of enthusiasm—skiiing, sailing, teaching—and not half-way. And that goes with relationships too. And my art.

"I was never competitive in art. I was very happy in just expressing myself at home. I didn't believe I was all that good, though other people kept pushing me. With the show here [Edgewood Orchard Galleries, "Inward Vision: Silverpoint Drawings by Flora Langlois," August 1—October 18, 1981] and Anne telling me of all the response. Well, I was sort of amazed. because I didn't realize it."

Describing the subject matter of her own work, Flora explains, "There were some autobiographical drawings that began coming out . . . there was one, a woman walking with a birdcage in her hand. In the arches of a building there was the whole figure of a man disappearing into the wall . . . In another, a beach, my dreams, like a sand castle that would disappear into water . . . A friend of mine said, 'Flora, your work scares me!' Why? 'Because it is so revealing.' Well, I don't know. It just comes naturally.

"I think there should be more autobiographical work, but there aren't enough people who are gutsy enough to do that. They would do it to psychiatrists or friends. But I'm not that kind of person. I'm quite open. To me art, the drawing, is like an escape valve. It releases a lot of feelings on the paper. It nourishes me. Consumes my attention completely. Involves me."

Her move to Door County in August of 1980 came soon after the break-up of her second, brief marriage. "When Fran moved out of the house, I was so depressed—taking pills that brought me up and down. Very bad shape. Contemplating suicide and everything. I had never taken a trip by myself in the car because I was afraid. But I got in the car with a suitcase and drove to Door County. I rented one of those tiny little cottages at the entrance to the park in Fish Creek. On the weekend I visited this friend of mine's farm . . . and met Scott. That was in 1978. We became involved. And that's when I started to come to Door County more. I began to outgrow Milwaukee. I liked the people here. I found this piece of land. I bought it and I built this house."

She speaks very openly of her relationship with Scott Chobot, a Viet Nam vet who lost both legs in the war. An intense relationship, as she describes it, that has marked her and much of her recent work with the pain of love, of loss, of the human condition in all its manifestations.

"In 1980 I took a show to Costa Rica—about 25 pieces. There were almost all silverpoint. Several involved mother. And several had to do with Scott. There was one of just feet. He was remembering what it was like to walk barefoot in grass. I remember saying in the program that it was dedicated to a Viet Nam veteran.

"Scott calls himself the Wooden Wonder. He is very proud that he can do many things despite his wooden legs. He doesn't want anyone to see him without his legs,

117

though. It was quite moving for me to see him that way, how he moves with his arms like a monkey, but it has never really bothered me that he has no legs.

"All my work, since the show in '79, was beginning to evolve. There was nothing very intimate in my relationships before the second marriage. When I met Scott all these feelings and emotions began to come out. Very intense. Very painful. Something I never experienced before. So I kind of opened myself to that kind of relationship. Sometimes I think, heaven forbid if I ever have to experience that again! Yet I'm not sorry. It would be a very bleak existence not to experience that. Scotty has showed me all the hues in the palette. All the colors: kid stuff to intense passion to incredible pain. And I think that's what brought out all this incredible work. And I think that brought out a great theme in my work. Scott is responsible for that. Up till then, I was always protecting myself.

"Last year I went to Costa Rica and I left without telling him. When I got home I did a drawing called 'My Time Has Past.' It has several sculpture figures. Some are either a woman alone, or a woman or man together . . . and through the ruins of a building . . . there is a little river, there is a woman looking at the reflection. And through the door there is a stream of light the shape of a cross . . . One time I told Scott he is like a crucified human—scars all over. What is left of his body is full of scars. There is another sculpture of a decapitated man. Then I did myself in another corner the bust of a woman, all in shadows. I had no feelings. So I put myself as a statue of stone.

"There was a drawing I did called 'The Spirits of the Past.' A woman who was very transparent. Her chest is open where the heart is, and instead of the heart there is the head of Scott, and hanging from her waist is a pair of scissors. From the ceiling, which is a sky above, is a head looking down—which is Leslie. Way in the back of the drawing is a little stair with a shadow projecting into a hallway. Scott had already entered the past, and I was trying to cut him out of my existence. And the windows show the same scene, one winter, one spring. So there was some hope.

"Another drawing is called 'Weather Vane.' On the crown of the weather vane is a tiny figure that looks like Scott, with a rooster tail . . . and across from him is a little figure of a female. They are looking at each other directly. It's because of the way he changed from one thing to another. From hot to cold. To very close, to very distant.

"We are no longer together I think, primarily, because Scott's needs and mine became different. He would like to continue exploring other relationships. He's just not ready to give to a relationship that total commitment that I desire. He needs a lot of freedom."

As for artists and periods that may have influenced her . . . "Boticelli . . . all the Madonnas and the transparencies. And the Gothic period—very austere. The Medieval absolutely fascinated me. Then Durer, for the detail, the intricacy, the symbolism. just fascinated with his skill. The control. The contemporary . . . a Mexican, Remedios Varo. There is a quality about her work that fascinates me. The bodies are very thin, very long, and you can't connect them by anatomy . . . more of a disembodiment.

"There is no mystery in the flesh to me. If you see a woman draped, she is more mysterious than naked.

"My drawings are not completely surreal. They're not that odd. Just more dream types. More an interpretation of feelings. And how would you do this if there isn't an amount of strangeness to them?

"A little bit of Andrew Wyeth's loneliness I like.

118

"Even though I derive my ideas from nature and reality, they are really my own concoction."

Though religion as such has little meaning in her life, her paintings are imbued with a sense of the religious, the holy, the mystery of existence. "I have shaken that part that has to do with the church. I don't feel guilty. I think deep inside I'm a mystic. What really affects me is the quietness. The tower in many of my drawings is like a tabernacle. It goes back to my Catholic church. The idea that I might be possibly talking to God in that particular place—in that little tabernacle in the middle. That I may be communicating. To reach into that little tabernacle and communicate in that little core with the person that's inside there. I want to experience, to achieve that; and I don't seem to be able to do it. The communion. When you went to communion you were supposed to receive God in your soul, your spirit. You could tell him all your pains, your joys. Searching for true communication with another person. It's a spiritual need I have.

"The mystical . . . that comes from my mother because she was always that way. St. Francis of Assisi. The fact that you're not really concerned with superficiality. What is important is the concern of the inner part of the person. That is mystical. I seem to be going more and more in that direction. That the people I have been meeting here, they are more real than what I left in the city. But then, maybe I was not close enough to them. Maybe I was still in the middle-class role of art teacher in Whitefish Bay. So little by little you begin to shed one skin, and another, and another. I've been told that if anyone ever writes a book about the knowledge of God, I should illustrate it.

"For a time, I had a tremendous fascination for death. Passing cemeteries I would think . . . oh, are they lucky. I wished for death. I made one attempt at it. The last two years of Leslie's life were so painful for him, for me. In those times I just kept thinking about it. In my last year's relationship with Scott, I thought it better to end it. But then I think . . . Hell, no! I wouldn't want to be dead.

"I don't think I fear death as much as getting old. I see women, also getting old, and that seems real sad. To find myself sitting in a little old people's home . . . that would be pathetic. I'd rather be dead. I'm all for mercy killing.

"At home in Costa Rica, they really get into death. They throw themselves into the pain. They don't disguise it by politeness, control. If they are crying, they are really weeping. They scream and they cry. They tell the story over and over again. But here . . . here they put their little hats on and go to the funeral parlor. It's all very civilized. I'd rather cry. Do the whole thing. If you're going to dance, you might as well enjoy it. If you're going to make love, really make love."

Being a widow was also something Flora had to live through. "When it first happened, and I said I was a widow, everyone would say, 'Oh, poor thing.' In some respects, it's sad. In other ways it is more respectable than being divorced. But if you had been the kind of woman who always catered to her husband's needs, you now acquire certain freedoms and responsibilities."

For a woman, too, who has known the sun, the tropic landscape of Latin America to suddenly find herself faced with one of the most difficult winters in Door County, which much certainly reflect old feelings of confinement . . . ?

"There is no fear. A certain amount of serenity . . . but also the feeling I would like to get out. The day of the blizzard I was completely alone here, no phone, no way to get out. I was really scared. The wind was howling. But there's a very quiet and peaceful thing about this which you don't have in the tropics, where everywhere you have the feeling that nature is going to overtake the humans. The plants grow big. The flowers are exuberant colors. There's certain something very peaceful about nature here. Everything about the wood seems gentle, nice. But in the tropics I don't have that feeling. The opposite. The jungle. You need a man with a machete to cut your way through."

The subject of ruins, so evident in much of her recent work. What does she see? What is she feeling?

"When I look around me and see a lot of happy, well-adjusted couples, the family, the home . . . barbecues on Sunday . . . and I look back on my life, one chapter after another, I see the ruin of something. When something is abandoned, neglected, not taken care of.

"In my bad days, when I'm really blue, I think . . . what is it? That song, 'What's It All About, Alfie?' Will I ever be able to find that nice little oasis? Sometimes I get so exhausted. I get very drained. And I would like to get there.

"There is one little thing that I have in my desk that says, 'Allow the way to open.'

Many times in my life I thought I was going to go this way, but life opened another way. Sometimes I made the decision, but sometimes it is almost like I didn't. Or if I don't allow the way to open, it doesn't.

"I would like to open some door . . . new doors. My own destiny maker. But once I got here, things began to happen to me where I had no control. Now, again, a reflection of what I'm going through. A transformation of a new Flora which has evolved from all the struggle and pain from my involvement with Scotty. I feel that I'm evolving into something new.

"The Scott that I've been projecting in my new work is a different Scott from before. Not anger, pain, but the transformation of a bird to a woman with hands up. The birds in many of my drawings signify freedom, but I've never made the step. Maybe now . . . from the bird to the woman . . . that freedom . . . I'm finally going to get to it."

*

Flora left Door county and returned to Costa Rica the following spring. Her mother was not well and needed her. And in some ways Flora needed Costa Rica, needed to be home again. A relationship here had ended. Her work—the series of bird/woman drawing reflected that. Though her absence here is felt, I see the artist in her intensely alive in her native landscape, faithfully capturing for us all that make us real and touch our spirit.

A letter from her yesterday calls the essence of this woman and her work back to me again:

Dear Norb,

The tending of mother brings memories of my husband Leslie. The emaciated body, full of sores from bed. She remains sweet, and a s a child, totally depends on me. I moved my smaller drawing table to her bedroom. I sit by a window and have all my paints, etc. conveniently arranged so I can work and watch mother.

I remain calm, have no desire to go out, and when I have done so, I realized how isolated I lived before and now. I have been working mornings, afternoons, and into the night. Since I have so many interrruptions I have to take advantage of every moment. Many ideas come to mind.

The images of my house, woods full of spring flowers. Birds, and me walking, bring a great sadness to my heart. I have to force myself not to think of it . . .

We have upon us the rainy season. The green is so green you can't describe it, and the vegetation so exuberant it is hard to believe it. I am constantly observing birds, moths, insects, small lizards, turtles, snails all within our walled garden. Birds sing to call the rains to the top of their lungs! Incredible.

Sincerely,
Flora
San Jose, Costa Rica

The Summer I Was A Horse
Frances May

There is a myth in America about little old ladies who write poetry. They are everywhere. And their poetry tends to be bad verse of the singsong, greeting card variety, filled with enough platitudes to choke a horse and cause a heart to bleed. Show me a little old lady with a sheaf of poems in hand, and I run a mile in the opposite direction.

My problem with these ladies is that most of them have never truly examined their lives or the lives of others, and consequently, all their ideas, all their language, all their poems wallow in sameness and sentimentality that does none of us any good.

Either a writer listens to what his soul and guts are telling him, finds the words and forms to express this, and affects his and our living, or he's rhyming homilies that leave us all yawning, standing in the dead center of our lives.

I must admit that, without having read her, I figured Frances May, 67, of Sturgeon Bay, Wisconsin to be a member of the Little Old Lady School of Poetry . . . merely because I imagined she was little, I had heard she was old, and I thought she was a "lady." And then I read "Garden of Eden" in her book, Night Letters:

> We went to the fourth floor
> for a snakeskin belt
> in basic black she came at us
> crossed a moss green rug
> flickering   Is there anything
> I can do
> for youse ladies?

And then I read all of Night Letters in a fervor. I am still reading it.

And then two fine poems of hers appeared in the first issue of The Peninsula Review, followed by fourteen more in the second issue, and there wasn't a single "little old lady poem" in the bunch. Instead, there was "Old Pa":

> A stranger to your father's house I came;
> recall that early bird that pecked our honey door,
> a red necked gobbler at the gizzard hour,
> old man wanting young hands to strip a wild heeled cow?
> Broom handle ordered from his ceiling
> under our bed, taps for love in the morning.
> Dream train had been traded for a tractor
> and you'd left all the apples on the tree
> for the hearty comfort of a windfall.
> We had rainy day polkas from the tin roof

to drown bedspring virtuosos.
Sundays after washing sin away, racked up scores,
too spent for feather fellows I scarcely dreamed,
silver fish hatched in lace-edged drawers.
Many a Monday bright-skinned five A.M.
Old Pa rattling all that was dead and dry
I pushed you off with rain checks in my eyes.
Drouth challenged dreamers to sneeze in haymows
but we kept the lock oiled, sometimes held the key
all night for smooth entry in the morning;
there was always some high-heeled heifer in the stall.

Sometime later I called Frances May with the intention of visiting. Would it be all right to phone again another night to confirm our meeting? (I was concerned about calling past her bedtime.)

She laughed. "I learned early in life there are two things that are a waste of time," she said over the phone, "Sleeping and going to the outhouse. I'm like a 10-gallon tank. And I don't sleep if I have to."

And then I walked into her dark house one afternoon and heard the best of soft rock coming from her phonograph. "I like Carly Simon's music," she said.

And then I sat across from her, listened, and slowly fell in love with her . . .

The darkness of the living room gathers about her shoulders like a shawl. She sits with her back to the window, books and manuscripts scattered about her the way some women sit amidst scans of yarn and knitting needles. She speaks of the comfortableness of her home: "I think that's what a house should do after you're in it a while—go away." The two large picture windows behind her frame maple trees that are turning gold against a quiet street of ordinary homes, and the waters of Sturgeon Bay.

Somewhere in the basement sits her ailing husband, Joe, mending fishing nets for friends. She speaks fondly of him, their grandchildren, their son, Joe (affectionately called Johnny), a world champion dog-sled racer who lives in Alaska. Her conversation flies in many directions, but the center is Frances, past and present. Some poets need no more than what they have, where they've been, what they are. Their task is but to render the real and the imagined in a sure way.

She is of this setting, this moment, this place, Door County, yet some distance from it. Seldom does it appear in her poems. Sitting here, storytelling in shadows, she revels in the past, her Michigan childhood and family, coming to Wisconsin alone on the ferry at age 17, her marriage to Joe, kicking around trailer camps, meeting the people, taking it all in, making a life . . . slowly putting it all down in poems.

There are both hard and soft features to her face. She claims bloodlines from Aaron Burr to the Hatfield clan. And there is more than just a touch of Appalachia about her. "I'm more Irish than German," she says. She seems a cross, at times, between Marianne Moore and Marjorie Main—with a touch of Ruth Gordon. And then her laughter (often at the expense of herself) opens her up, taking us (reader or listener) inside. In stories and poems, her secrets become ours to share in a common humanity.

124

Among other things, Frances May will tell you she truly believe she was once a horse in another life. That her main fear is hurting somebody. That women are as liberated as they want to be. That "the thing I would rather be more than anything is a musician. So, if I couldn't be a musician—we couldn't afford to pay a dozen eggs and a quart of berries for piano lessons—I'd have poetry."

She speaks of Michigan now. So many of her poems in *Night Letters* evoke those times that touched the child, shaped the poet, made the woman. She tells of a music teacher, Kitty. "She read to me. We'd sit up there in the attic. She had lots of books. I'd sit there and I'd copy Chaucer, Keats, Shakespeare . . . I thought it was so beautiful. Kitty was just a neighbor lady. A cultured lady who came there." Years later, in a long poem called "Chop Sticks," Frances would recall some of it this way:

>   After Fionna galloped down the gully
> with elbow pivot I rolled afoot,
> crossed the alfalfa patch
> to inform Miss Kitty
> no more piano lessons ever
> Mama said they cost too much
> a dozen eggs,
> but I carried a boxful of berries . . .
>
>   Handicap untouched,
> on a stack of thumbed Etudes
> I took in Liszt and Chopin
> she played away my hour
> her mama and sister Lydia
> whispering summer dresses
> in out do-re-mi screened doors.
>
>   Lesson wrap
> Chop Sticks piano
> rattling three handed.
>
>   Idling cool barefoot
> pokey wicker porch swing
> wet glassed lemonades
> behind purple bloomed clematis.
> Out of our sight
> farm trucks lumbered
> coughing red clay dust
> down township roads.
> Miss Kitty reading
> Tennyson Idylls.

"There were nine kids in our house. There was a willow tree down by the river. I had a box up there and some oil cloth. I didn't want anyone to see I was trying to write. I think the best poem I ever wrote in high school was about a spider. Up until that time I was hiding everything. In the public speaking class in high school I was the class mouse."

A 'Miss Parm' entered her life then, and Frances May, child poet, came of age. Miss Parm was clearly impressed. "She told me to stay after school, and she asked if I had anything else."

Miss Parm

This new girl heard that Public Speaking was a snap class;
guaranteed an easy credit for a shaky diploma,
Miss Ellen Parm had never failed one yet.
That first day I slipped past high-school wheels
where a voluptuous home-coming queen was making a hub
and the best dressed gypsy competing for spokes,
to settle down on an onlooker's bench in the last row.
She gave me no impression of calm, this teacher,
her fluttery feather, goldy-brown hair floated,
escaping a hurry-up knot at the back,
hands mothed up, down, around nests of paper,
tearful voice range like a school bell in a shower,
CHILDREN, CHILDREN, TAKE YOUR SEATS. COME
          TO ORDER, PLEASE.
The blonde who had already been in school too long
undulated to center behind a smooth-haired, classic snob
isolated as an imported cheese under a glass dome.
The gypsy folded next to the queen in the court
of olympiad kings with class wits for jacks,
with messengers and sycophants crowding the boxes.
Surrounded by glamor, I clutched a weaponry of books.
YEATS. YEATS. Miss Parm belled. TURN TO PAGE
          SEVENTY.
AFTER ERNEST READS, MARYBELLE WILL
          EXPLICATE.
Groans rang around the arena, black eyed gypsy flashed,
THEY'LL WRECK IT. LET RAOUL AND ME DO IT
          RAOUL AND I?
YEAH, YEAH. The class rumbled. LET RAOUL AND
          IRENA DO IT.
Miss Parm tapped her desk with a slim gold pencil.
WHO IS IN CHARGE HERE? ERNEST, READING MAY
          AWAKEN YOU,
AND IRENA IVANESCU WILL PARK HER CHEWING
          GUM, PLEASE.
LADIES CHEW GUM ONLY IN THE PRIVACY OF
          THEIR BEDROOMS.
The basket-ball monarch dribbled a dream-skin globe
to the left bank of windows and faced his subjects,
but Yeats took us over. Even stoned by scrabble reading,
the river of his poetry flowed, wetting our feet.
When time clanged, Irena's red butterfly skirt
flirted the crowd out of Irish mist into the halls.
A day came that we turned Longfellowish

and I wheedled a country crick into a babbling brook.
In ankle-deep waters, I did not hear soft footsteps.
SO THIS IS WHAT YOU DO. I felt naked as Godiva
under the breathy voice, hair hanging over my eyes.
I KNEW I'D FIND YOU OUT. YOU MAY READ YOUR
        POEM ALOUD.
All my edges burned, crumbled, flaking off as I followed.
Miss Parm clapped her hands as she settled, hair flying.
BOYS AND GIRLS, HOW DELIGHTFUL TO HAVE OUR
        OWN POET.
PAY ATTENTION. AFTER THE READING, THE CLASS
        WILL EXPLICATE.

The arrow fell short, but it had been dispatched
and I felt a court move to make room for me.
It was more than I knew what I would need
but it was that first rising from the ground.
Looking back, now, at the steep green beginning
I am grateful for a teacher who never failed anyone.

Past and present. From Michigan to Wisconsin. Meeting and marrying Joe. Her life in Sturgeon Bay. Frances May, child poet . . . wife, woman, mother, grandmother. How did the poet in her survive?

"I just did it and stuck it in a drawer. Joe wanted to fish. Joe was a fisherman and a hard-hat diver. He worked for a marine construction company. He was always on the water till he had his heart attack eight years ago. Joe's family . . . they're just very practical people. I wrote my poetry. I had no idea that anyone would have known this about me, but somehow they did. 'Don't get mixed up with her, she's arty,' they said. Well, Joe had his own life, and I had my own life, and we had our life together."

It would be many poems, much writing, and many years together before Frances May saw her first book, *Night Letters*, in print. She was 57 years old at the time. But Frances was never in any hurry. She can't quite explain it, even now, 10 years later, as she contemplates a second collection of her poems. And as for Joe?

Frances smiles. It's the old story of opposites joined in the confusion of matrimony. "If you could just tell me why you do it?" she quotes her husband trying to understand her way as a poet. "Nothing happens to it."

"Well," she told him, "You build bridges. And you want to build something that's going to last longer than you do. I think I want to make something to last longer than I will.

"This happened about 15 years ago. I used to give him poems to read. Now, I'm happy that he doesn't read them, so he doesn't know what I'm talking about. If you're not going to write about the things most important to you, that have done the most to you, you're not going to write anything important.

Accident

With you, I ran after accidents,
        chased firetruck;

127

shuddered away while you soaked
details
I didn't know what laid me low;
breath short, heart staggered.
Tied with a shrinking rope
to a couch, I waxed fat
fed daily with bad news,
face sopping with chill.
Hound eyes followed me,
other women took up the slack
and saved me that chore.
One day
bones struck, jolted off the couch
I saw the green world. Awake,
wanted to celebrate myself.
Why did you run like a hare?
It crossed my mind when
you went down in the good
black suit—
when we were children, you
playing mortician.

"That's as good as a poem as I've written. Maybe my best. I'm telling you the truth in that poem—even though the circumstances didn't happen. Joe is very negative and I am very positive. I was not going to lie there and play dead."

About the writing of poetry and being a housewife . . . "I think it could have been an escape then . . . shopping. It bores me to run around and shop. We had a trailer in the woods. I'd go out for walks. I read a lot. Oh, I read a lot! I had to do something. I also painted once, for a couple of years. I could get lost in painting for hours. But really, it was too late for me to be a painter. I never got lost in writing, though. There was always a part of me doing the poem and yet I could be a better poet than a painter and went back to that.

"Every few years I would go through the poetry I had written and tear a lot of stuff up. I was writing novels all that time too. I've written three novels—this last one I've written three or four times.

"The first poem that I was really thrilled about was in August Derleth's 'Hawk & Whippoorwill.' That was before I knew him. 'The Inescapable' it was called. I wouldn't call a poem that name now. [Retitled "The Watcher" in *Night Letters*.] I sent in others. Every three months I'd send in a batch. On the third batch of poems he wrote: 'I would have accepted this but . . . ' But he didn't say to change. And when he took that poem, 'The Inescapable,' I was so excited! We were camping in the trailer, and I walked three miles to tell Joe. Joe said, 'That's nice.'

" 'The Chain' was my second acceptance, sometime later. 'I liked the idea, but I don't like the style,' Derleth said about that poem. He said of my rewrite, 'It's better than I thought you could do.'

"I wanted quality. It was important for me to be in that magazine. A magazine like that is missed."

Derleth did, however, go on to publish her book, *Night Letters*, Stanton & Lee, 1971. "I was all set . . . another book of poetry . . . then Derleth got sick. [August Derleth died on July 4, 1972.]

"Poetry . . . it's enriched my life so much. Maybe I'm fortunate being a woman. It didn't matter if my poetry made any money or not. Not a bit. And it doesn't bother if people think it's strange. I don't care. They really don't know, do they? They really don't know what's out there."

Perhaps not. Nor do they realize what's 'in there' . . . inside the heart and head of a poet like Frances May. Just how this woman has grown so wise, to write poetry so fine. You go back to the past again. Not the teachers who influenced you, necessarily. Not the books you read. But the setting you grew up in, the scenes you can never quite forget, the people—especially the parents—who one way or another, shaped those forces, awakened those images and caused you to spend most of your life discovering this.

"I do miss my folks . . . they were yarners and storytellers. There were nine of us, brothers and sisters, and we're all living—more or less. I don't know where my brothers are. They disappeared after my mother died.

"My mother was a beautiful woman . . . Junoesque. She had been the belle of the countryside when she was young. She was very unhappy with her second husband. She told me she was married twice and didn't love either one of them. "Total Eclipse" (from *Night Letters*) is almost all true, until you come to the last part where the girl puts out her eyes . . .

NOBODY LOVES ME, NOBODY LOVES ME.
Mama sharpened shears on a pickle crock, sandpapered bones
MOVE BACK FORE YA GIT YOUR HAIR CHOPPED OFF IN
MY PATH
GOTTA FINISH ROSEMARY'S DRESS FOR CHILDREN'S
DAY.
I wailed, MISS LINA WOULDN'T LET ME SING WITH HER.
Mama moaned, YA CAN'T SING AN YA OUGHT TO KNOW IT
BY THIS TIME
IF YA WOULDN'T OF THROWED A CONNIPTION, IT
COULD BE
MISS LINA WOULD A GIVE YOU
A PIECE TO SPEAK.
I croaked through my hair, BUT I WANTED TA SING. NOBODY
LOVES ME.
Mama crowed, NOW, THERE GOES YOUR BOOKS ON THE
FLOOR. READ, READ
THAT'S WHAT MAKES YA SUCH A
FEATHERBRAIN
LOVE STORIES HAHA, HA.

"I don't ever remember my mother so much as patting me on the head; I left home because my stepfather had attacked me. The most terrible day in my life was the day I left, when my mother said, 'If he had been your own father, he couldn't have done more for you.' The terrible thing was to think that your own mother knew and didn't say anything. I took the ferry from Ludington to Kewaunee. I was 17. I remember looking into the water from the boat and thinking, it would be easy to jump off. But no. Never. Never. I had my ticket and 25¢, and I knew I would be all right. Afterwards, mother and I had a great friendship. She even lived and stayed with us later.

"I was only four when my father died. I remember I stood on the floor and I touched his hand. I remember his mackinaw behind the door and how my mother used to cry in it. I remember a pair of glasses that my father wore. They had only one lens. I used to put them on and go around wearing them. I didn't care if the kids laughed or not. Those glasses belonged to my father.

"I never had any bad feelings toward my mother. I realized how terrible her life was. She never worked outside the farm. She had flowers. It was a fruit farm. The women there [Michigan] didn't work outdoors as they do here.

"I couldn't make my family into a nice, genteel-like family. That's not what they were. My mother was a passionate and repressed woman. I think my mother felt betrayed, that this was not the life she wanted. It was my fault. I made trouble. She was afraid of my stepfather, I think. I used to just churn inside. She used to beat me up. I made a few trips to the barn, and she used to horsewhip me there. 'I'll never cry for you anymore!' I told her. And I wouldn't. She would just throw the whip down and scream. She was driven. I was perfectly safe. When she looked at me, I was just like my father. I felt if I didn't hang on, I would be destroyed. I was the oldest. I'd always done more than my share of the work, but I wasn't going to let anyone own me."

Her poetry is rich in narrative. In one form or another, Frances tells stories. There is a richness of language, too, of image, sounds, and certainly, humor.

"I look like six different people writing," she laughs. "Everytime I write a poem it's like as if it chooses its own style. I don't care about traditional style as such, although I have done some sonnets just to keep myself disciplined. Nature poetry . . . I wrote that because I thought that was what I was supposed to write! In high school, when I read 'Richard Cory,' the poem just stunned me, that you could say so much about a person's life. I used to carry it around with me. Now, I want more insight instead of shock value.

"I'm glad I haven't had a book published since *Night Letters*. I still feel a great success even if I have nothing else published. I think my things are better now. I think they can have more value . . . to write a few things people can read after I'm gone. I feel freer . . . yeah . . . I think so. I'll say anything, maybe. My poems and my life . . . it's like it's all so part of each other. Sometimes I tell my friends—I'm not really a person, I'm a book. I'm a gothic. My life is a gothic novel.

"I think I have to say some great friendships have meant much difference to me. Edna Meudt [one of Wisconsin's best known poets] has been a great influence. It's wonderful to be able to write down anything. August [Derleth] too was a great friend. And most of the people in the fellowship of poets I've enjoyed very much.

"Jesse Stuart . . . I knew him too. If I could have ever fallen for any man, it would have been him.

"James Dickey . . . his work . . . there's a passage in his May Day poem that when I read it, I just kept thinking about it. That loosened me up. Oh, God, I can say anything! I'm not trying to be James Dickey, but I can see how he was just getting it all out there, letting it all fly. Paul Blackburn, too.

"What interests me is ideas in poem, power . . . the interaction between people. I have this thing right now. . . . well, it's up here and hasn't taken form yet . . . weak people and strong people. The only way they can deal with strong people is to become martyrs, and then they can be taken care of. This poem, 'Celina,' I had the bones of that poem for about 20 years:

130

Celina

When he came home
from the foundry
every work night
quarter after five
Celina washed his feet
in a big bucket
of sweet soap water,
beer at his elbow.

Women in the mobile park
mostly let her alone.
The four of us
went dancing
at the folk fair.

A little tipsy
we talked
over baklava
when our men
went to the outhouse.

I asked her
why she lowered herself
anyone could see
she had it
all over him.

When I was eight
she told me
I killed my little brother
with Papa's old shotgun.
I chose the meanest
man I knew
to make it up to.
Sometimes I think
I'm gaining on the debt
but I don't know
he's lots nicer
than he used to be.

For Frances, 'bad' poetry, 'little old lady' poetry is "Something that's just sentimental . . . too sentimental. Nostalgic. Something in me says that's not so. I like the truth in a poem. I like strong, true poems. No poem is too hard, too tough for me to read. If it's hard, life is hard."

The phone rings. It's for Joe. Frances calls down the basement to him. He is a continued presence on her mind, it seems, a constant shadow in this room where she sits, reads, writes, types, thinks.

"I learned so much about people through Joe. He's a very physical person, wonderfully kind. I had no experience like that as a child. I may take advantage of

131

him, but it's not that I don't appreciate him. He's said some wonderful things to me, and it's like all the other problems are nothing. And I suppose if I hadn't met Joe, I'd probably be writing about birds rather than people."

Call it tolerance or clarity or care, it continues to errupt in her conversation. The child who suffered an unloving mother, who was victimized by a stepfather, who ran away from home at the age of 17, who married at 19, and who has become this woman, now, this poet who can forgive, understand, love and comfort the very mother who rejected her. This woman, too, who became the wife who could love her husband for what he is, protect her own privacy of poetry, and guide him through his darkest times.

"Joe is not the same . . . ever since his heart operation. He's had four nervous breakdowns. Two years before the operation he attempted to take his own life. He had everything ready down there to do away with himself. I caught him in the act. I just happened to go down there at the right time. I didn't say anything. I went back upstairs. He didn't say anything at first. Later I told him I was going out, and he said, 'When you get back, I won't be here.' 'Then I'm not going,' I said. All his life he placed such value on the physical thing, the outdoors, his work. And after his stroke he said, 'Frances, I'm not good anymore for anything.'

"I should have seen this coming on. Well, I could have called the police or the doctor or something. That's what everyone was telling me to do. But no, I said. I've got to handle this myself. They'll just put him in a hospital or something, and you know what that's like. I didn't say anything for a long time. 'Frances, what are you doing?' I was asked. I'm thinking. And I was. Those people in the hospital, you know, they're not there because they're crazy. They're there because they drive everyone else crazy. No one wants to take care of them.

"Well, it's okay now. It's under control. He still gets depressed once in a while. They've got things like lithium, though, to control these things. I can see when it's coming, and we talk it out now. He'll never be the same, but it's okay. Finally, when I found him that time, when I thought about it enough, I said to him,: 'It's your life, Joe. You can do what you want with it. I'm not going to stop you.' 'I'll never do that again, Frances,' he said. He put all the boxes and stuff away when I went down there the next time, like nothing happened.

"Joe's such a kind person. I like that in him. He believes everybody is good. One of my pet words is 'fair.' You be fair to me, and I'll be fair to you. I think I've been liberated all my life. I think women are as liberated as they want to be. I think Ms. is obsolete. It's silly. What does that have to do with anything? *The Women's Room* I thought was a very narrow viewpoint. What men want to write about, what women want to write about, are two different things. I only use the language where it fits. We invented the words.

"I find that personally what I write, my friends have my work separated from me. They don't say, 'Well, Frances, we wouldn't expect you to write that.' I don't think 25 30 years from now it's going to be any different. Men go out and sit around together and they talk about sex. A group of women getting together for the evening talking . . . it's very different.

"I think I'm lucky Joe doesn't read my poetry. I think it's nice he doesn't understand it or read it.

"Another life for the man . . . that never bothered me at all. Joe had his Charlevoix Helen. I think of my childhood. There's a little person who sits in here in a private room and nobody ever gets in there. I know that Joe loves me very much. Yes, I do care a lot about him, but I can stay cool. If he had friendships, that's okay with me. It didn't take anything away from me. Maybe there's something wrong with me, but I don't think men and women should be possessive of each other. I don't own Joe, and he doesn't own me. Maybe that's not a popular way of looking at it, but that's the way it looked for me. I think a good, long-lasting sexual relationship has to be based upon friendship. When I would go and visit him where he was working . . . I can remember the last good time in Charlevoix, Michigan, just before he got sick. We spent the whole Sunday in bed with the paper, a bucket of the Colonel's chicken, and each other."

First Love

As long ago as we trusted
in love for love's return,
warm and bright as the summer noon
I waded the crick with him
to cool our feet from the dust,
up to my knees in fern;
drank the cold water he poured
into my mouth from his cupped hands,
sinewy, strong as the gourd.
Then, under a Johnny Appleseed limb
to a bob-o-link's three chord tune,
I gave me heart to the hired man
with golden buttered home-made bread,
raspberry jam and a clean tin spoon.

"As for being in love . . . that's the only person I was ever in love with, and I chose not to marry him. Joe I thought was safe. Joe was older. I thought if I married him, the other man, the younger man, I'd have half a life. I'd be fighting all the time. I'm making a difference between 'in love' and 'love.' You can see how I needed the feeling of care and security."

The spirit of this woman seems part of everything she's lived, she's written, she is. "I love to dance. Oh, how I love to dance. I hated my mother, she was so repressed. I was going to dance twice a week, I said. And I said I wouldn't marry a man who couldn't dance. Not the polka—I like waltzes and fox trots. And if I was going to dance now, I'd probably be doing anything the kids do.

"I won't 'pass away.' I'll be dragged away. I'll hold on the bookshelves. It would be hell to haunt the kitchen but heaven to haunt the bookshelves. If Joe should pass away first, I'll sell this place and move to the city. I'll find a room halfway between the ball-park and a dance hall."

As for her religious convictions, "I like to think your poetry or anything that comes out of a caring feeling is all right. I don't know if you can say that's religion. Spiritual sort of sticks. I belong to the Catholic church, but I'm a maverick. Joe believes it just the way he was taught. So I go to church with him whenever he wants.

"Self-righteous people . . . it's like you come up against them and bounce off. It isn't any use. Most of them have given up. My people are people I can really talk to, tell the truth and we can be honest with each other. I'm not a lonely person. I always have people I can talk to. I have a lot of friends that I can't really talk to, but I still enjoy them.

"But I hate gossip. People that know me awhile . . . they save the gossip till I'm gone, because I just say, 'I don't believe it. I don't believe it.' I hate it. It's the worse thing you can do, tear people apart. It's so destructive. I think that's worse than what the people talk about.

"And I don't believe people own each other. I like to give people room, and people to give me room. A privacy. I think that's important. Living in the trailer park, you learned to give each other privacy."

As for the writer's privacy, the woman writer in particular: "You have to do everything else first—kids, the house, etc.—and then if you're strong enough, to take a few hours of time for yourself. You see, I don't drive a car. I saved myself a lot. I saved time. I had time for myself. It was as if I planned it."

"Marriage, you know, I really think it's obsolete. It's the owning. I think we have to learn to stop trying to own each other. It isn't natural. It's something we dreamed up. Women's liberation liberated more men than it did women. I see men and women living together. These women have to be very strong. This doesn't solve the problem either, unless they're just both free. To live by yourself, be friends, have friends, or with somebody if you want to. More freedom. It isn't going to be that way, ever, though. Divorce . . . there's always a lot you can leave and not leave. And you can leave and not leave."

A poet, of course, looks at himself, in himself, and in this way sees and transforms the world around him. In the poetry of Frances May there are frequent glimpses, images, of Frances the child, Frances the woman. There's a persistency of self, evident in the child in the very beginning, a child aware she may not be loved, she may not be the prettiest in the bunch, but she is a force, and there is a beauty out there that she can lay claim to as her own, given the time.

"My sister Rosemary was so pretty, so when I found out I was not pretty, what I decided to do was be good and then they would all love me. But this didn't work. And I remember when I was 16 I put on a hat and I thought, Oh my God, I look good! I had on dangly earrings, and I looked like Greta Garbo, So, I had a sense of what to wear. I remember the time I went to a party and I made myself a gypsy costume—and it was not a costume party—but I was the hit of the party. The boys all loved it. It always astounded me that when I went to dances, I never sat on the bench. I think it was because I always had a good time, and prettier girls than me sat on the bench."

Her prettier sister, Rosemary, is recalled and revealed in a poem:

The Foot-Bathers

You scooped soft water
out of the rain–barrel sweating
under the little pantry window
in a cloud of blood mad mosquitoes,
you laughed while coolness leaked
down dust patched overall
onto your berry brambled toes.
I let you wash your feet first
in the second best blue enamel wash-dish,
sitting on the sagged front steps
hemmed in between mock orange blooms
heavy with nectar and host of insects.
I rummaged the woodshed rag-bag,
lifting a torn blue chambray shirt
to dry our summer-browned legs,
leaving soft white underwear for dish-rags.
You scooted over to make room on the step.

We huddled hip to hip between night
and darkened house, quiet now
with the little ones asleep upstairs,
father and mother in the big bedroom
behind the parlor, time was ours.
The moon rode piggyback over the elm
and dappled the dusty clay hill road.
Crickets chorded under the porch
and tree frogs sawed sweet summer night
into harmony with the gifted sky.
Only you and I, Rosemary, awake
soaking calm through callouses
to carry us across cruel day coals,
buffets and hot sand of berry patches.
With hard muscled brown baseball arm
you pitched a curve through moonlight
waterfall over the spelled rambler rose
and sanded your just washed feet,
tiptoed the ferny border round the rain-barrel,
careful not to stir moss from the bottom
and not too many little black wrigglers,
brought back a scoop of tea-colored balm.
On a warm night in July, Rosemary,
you still bring me a panful of stars.

"I have a closet full of clothes that I like to wear for occasions . . . a closet of
lovely clothes. It is one of the persons I might have been, if I hadn't teamed with a
physical-dominant personality like Joe. My mother was a talented seamstress, great
at making over 'rich peoples's' stuff. When I used to visit Joe on the sites of
construction projects, I 'dressed up.' Joe was very proud and competitive. I enjoyed
it and played it to the hilt. It was good for him. The men liked me better than their
women did. I was never one to hang around with the girls. Our relationship in bed
was that great, too. I did not understand that our friendship was based on bed. I see
now that he was 'wearing me on his arm.' I do think it might have made up some
measure I kept back for the person I kept in the secret room. But unless I am going
somewhere, I am bored by a dressing up process. I don't think clothes. I like to get up
and load my tank with coffee, plan whether to walk, rake, shovel snow or pound the
machine here, put on some appropriate and comfortable stuff and get it going. When
I get with people I remember what they said but hell, no, never what they had on. I've
caught women reading coat labels and that pinned the tail on them. Trying to assess
it all honestly, I was writing the scripts for Joe and me. All tweed and buttons on top,
lacy underwear, reserved for Joe. Youse guys on the crew can look and don't touch.
Sickening, wasn't it? No wonder their women didn't care much for the boss's wife. If
Joe could go back to work, I could do it again? Too late!"

Could she do it again? In a recent poem, Frances takes another look at herself:

Double Image

On an island in the super mart
under a convex mirror
she bent across my grocery cart

fingering glassined macaroons
half whispering at me
these cookies look delicious
what counter shall I look
her peanut shell knuckles
lemon breasts   slat ass
rotten teeth and rabbit chin
gnawed small by things
looking out of her eyes
Take these   I said
settled for frozen bread
and bolted.

"What I saw was the pain and suffering that had made her into what she was. And so I saw myself."

And Frances' 'self,' as she sees it now, nearly 70, in poetry, reality? "I'm a happy person. I like myself. I sound terrible, don't I? I'm doing the best I can with my life. When you are a strong person, other people can be bruised by it.

"One very smart lady said I had a bad beginning, but I rose above it. I'm not hard to get along with, but I'm hard to live with. I'm up all night. I stay up until I can't stand it anymore, reading or writing. I can get along on three or four hours of sleep fine. I can even skip a night once in a while. I've done that since I was a kid. I've read a lot of books that way. I resist thinking about time. I hardly know what day it is, what time it is. I just got away from thinking about clocks and calendars. And this left me room for thinking about other things.

"All my life I've taken care of people. I've been trained to do that . . . relatives, neighbors, kids. I have a thing about children. They see me coming. I have gone and faced parents that were beating up their kids. If a child needs me, I'll be there. No one can stop me.

"I nursed Aunt Lena. It took her 18 hours to die, right there in my bedroom. I promised her she wouldn't have to die in a hospital. She must have heard me say that, and she took my hand and she died with me holding her hand. That was not a bad experience. I learned about the power of life. She was completely different from me. We loved each other. She couldn't change me; I couldn't change her."

The Soapmakers

Aunt Lena gripped my hands across the bed, sweat webbing,
blue agate nailed testimony in our common cross,
stirring of death above our cellar soapmaking room.
I sopped the tallow brow, doctor-consigned to God's agency;
a haze of pardon lingered, ashes to serve the hollow oak.
Gray tendrils, wet bees honeycombing finger bones,
isosceles lips and a crystal tear cornering each eyelid
for the limed trunk staining the lavendered linen.
If tongue unlocked would she thank me this late day
for drying the old cold hands, bathing her marbled loins?
Longer than Rachel's bondage I had served well,
bowed willingly under the lash of her sterility,
sifted coal from ashes for woodburning wisdoms.
I kept the grass green over my father's place,

copied his mouth and hair in a purloined mirror.
Distaff mountain songs were swallowed whole or burned
like my mother's letters crumpled under iron lids.
I spread platitudes over the kernel of greed,
dim golden secret of bank books in a dresser drawer,
scrubbing dark reason clean as our floursack petticoats.
Avarice lit her chipped ice smile, in me was green fire;
she despised who cared little for money and mistrusted her kind.
With the fat of security I took the harsh salt of her justice.
Now, for the first time, I knew the bond of my coherence
with the caustic channeled past the scored flesh.
Counter to rasping breaths, muted clatter from ghost women
skimming rind off the kettle in the soapmaking cellar;
Aunt Lena's uncherished waif steaming out the indolence of poetry
with the virtue of her leach, money and toil.
Over the parched no-man's land came the gentle rain;
forgiveness, ourselves and each other, washing out the wastage
between us there and no last stir but a flowing away.

"What terrifies me about age is not the pain nor the uglies. It's the wheelchair and the pill-food-blanket dispenser. That's why I eschew cake, salt, etc. I do plan to feel good till the time I fall over the edge. Do You hear me up there, or in there, or down there in the Great Whatever? Or maybe swamp lilies or a tree toad. Music there if there is a There. I surely don't give *that* much head space either, outside of a wispy joke about haunting a library.

"I think what we're calling reincarnation may be race memory. We don't know the primitive parts of our minds. Like the thing I have with the kids. This recognition thing. Where is that coming from, this business of communicating on another level? This dream that I get in pieces? Maybe it's like Carl Jung's collective unconscious."

"I was sitting at the table with mother, and I had a picture suddenly . . . this thing about horses. 'Ma,' I said, "I was a horse once in another life.' My mother hit me one and said, 'You go upstairs and pray. That's a wicked thing.' 'Ma,' I said. 'I was a horse!'

"I tried to get acquainted with horses on the farm, but they wouldn't have anything to do with me. Well, I thought they would treat me differently. Then I went to see my friend's Arabian, but he wouldn't recognize me either. So I would just run up and down the hill *being* a horse. I was *sure* I was a horse . . .

The Summer I Was A Horse

Green grass sunny other where
wild horses running
golden manes streaming
follow me follow follow—
on afternoon tea oasis
between Mama and Grampa
she joggled my elbow
"What are you staring at?"
"I was a horse once
in another life."
Mama hammered the slide

137

to the picture wall
with hefty backhand.
"Upstairs at once.
Pray for an hour.
Ask the Lord
to forgive wicked thoughts."

A horse would know
another horse—
balancing belly
on barnyard gate
contemplating equine
country cousins
smiling Uncle George
tobacco teeth
mucked up shoes.
My kind of horse
pulled no plow.

I read Black Beauty
south land aristocrat
miles of fence
barring the fancy
on to Pegasus magic
sprouting wings.

There was Elethea
rich snobby brat
one grade up
in country school
I turned toad
of the month
for a Saturday go
at her Arabian
the gleaming mare
counted me out
nibbled the carrot
turned tail
to fart in my face.

I chomped oatgrass
on the pasture hill
the rose colt
and I
rolling on turf
cut apart by creeks
black snakes stoned
under summer suns
garlanded about
by butter colored cowslips.
Wind stirred my mane

fine and sun dyed
tint of the sorrel
gilded tail.

Green grass sunny otherwhere
follow me follow follow.

"I think it's their movement. I like to see them running. And you don't really own a horse. It doesn't follow you around like a dog. They have a kind of dignity, don't they? Even a farm horse."
Would she be happy to come back again as a horse?
"I guess I don't have any choice. But that would be a promotion, wouldn't it?"

Oh Death Where Is Thy Sting-a-ling-a-ling?
Howard Orr

Howard Orr is one of those rare individuals who can set life itself on its ass at times, then stand back and laugh, his arms encompassing others in the merriment of it all.

Sometimes I think he's a composite of Fritz Perls ("To suffer one's death and to be reborn is not easy"), Jonathan Swift, Martin Buber, Jackson Pollock, Peter Ustinov, Rube Goldberg, Karl Marx, Buddha, and Coyote, the mythical trickster of Indian legend. There is even a touch of Santa Claus to him—whom he has modeled for Marshall Field's in a full-page ad in the Chicago Tribune.

The world is filled with unsung artists, writers, inventors, eccentrics, rebels, and just plain fascinating human beings. And Howard Orr is one of these—and all of them. And more.

A writer lives for the morning mail. I love hearing from people. And a letter from Howard Orr, especially in the depths of a Door County winter, makes a red letter day indeed. His envelopes glow. They are works of art filled with paintings, rubber stamps, obscenities, drawings, and sayings (intricately hand-lettered), wonderful 'Orrisms' like "All men should walk on all the land—with hands outstretched to touch his fellows." His return address might be anything from Orr, Western Ugh! Springs, Ill. to Society for the Prevention of Everything; Lord of the Flies, 1 Motherlode Lane; Howard of the Bare Back Lady's Day; H the O; or Aunt Howard.

He has printed his own postcards too: "Nude . . . Cleaning the Cat-Box" (A figure, looking a lot like Howard, with a vacuum cleaner labeled "Mine" sucking up a cat from a litter box; "Nude At A Wake" (Howard is big on death), the deceased (looking a lot like Howard) stretched out nude in a casket, one arm holding up the lid, the other behind his head, his legs raised and crossed. On the wall, an enema. On the floor, a bedpan and three dumbbells. The message reads: Dear Norb, I miss hearing from you and will write quickly in response to your letter. Yah—I'll be specific about your question re my remark that I feel (know) Santa Fe is not for all souls—it is not. You, on the other hand, would fit anywhere. Keep growing and giving—Howard.

His letters, often filled with insights into others, may at times be quite self-analytical, philosophical, emotional, as well as expansive, poetic, and always humorous:

"Who am I? Who is a raven? Who is a gull? Who is a flower, a stump, butterfly? Who is a gift? Who is a sickness? A wellness? To run from home I learned to creep, walk, and later—I ran. Finer techniques are, to me, mostly developed from within. Cloud-hiding-behind is, of course a magic stunt, known only to all of us. Frequently I do it when I didn't plan it. I guess I've most often walked in the dark when I've yearned to Run, Run, Run. Didn't find a way—I just liked the dark. A few clocks I make—an occasional thermometer thing, and I delight in watching people watch me with the Death Cart. Who changes the light bulb in the small light in the moon? I'm curious. I'm too busy to close my eyes—too alive to die."

And so I delight in this man, as I know others do, though some may find him a bit

much—and even turn and run at the sight of him: an aging Hippie! He makes my day with his written messages, my afternoons and nights with his collect phone calls, Howard-on-the-road (to God knows where), a bit in his cups perhaps, but alive and damn funny.

I look forward to a wise gallery owner someday giving Howard a show of just his envelope art, a publisher who will do a book of his letters, another gallery owner who will exhibit his drawings and paintings, and yet another gallery that will exhibit his clocks and thermometers and death carts . . . and whatever the hell else he comes up with in his good years ahead.

I met him for the first time at Ross and Arlene LewAllen's house in LaGrange, Illinois some years ago. I have pursued this refreshing friendship (often via the mails) ever since. Leaving Door County for Chicago, frequently pressed for time—too many people and places to cover in too little time—Howard Orr is always one of the people I most want to spend an evening with, have a drink with, laugh with, and share stories of who and where we are at this moment in life.

When I am bored with myself, bored with some of the people in Door, I run to . . . to Chicago, most likely, and I look for old friends, people like Howard. I relish his sense of life, I guess, compared to the sameness of my own life in Door which begins to set in and wear me down after a while. I am forever in awe of men like Howard who have quit the straight life of 9 to 5 and struck out on their own to discover just what makes them tick. Sometimes the discovery is less than flattering, but that's all right too. At least a change has been attempted.

141

So maybe I find myself sitting at Harvey's talking to George (one of the world's greatest bartenders) and in comes Howard, and we take a booth, and we talk, and I recall that what I delight in most about his presence is his spontaniety. The conversation of most men is often mundane, while Howard's talk is a creative act. His greatest work of art is Howard Orr, himself.

How do you see yourself, Howard? What do you think others see?

I think others see me as I used to see my father, walking lean-forward, kind of a town bum. Rosie called me the town crazy.

The town crazy?

She is the female version. I'm the male. You know Rosie, don't you? Crazy lady.

You mean James Thurber's daughter, right?

Yeah. But anyway, I look at myself as . . .

Did you always look at yourself that way?

Oh, no. I used to be very seriously Brook Brothers, or Capper and Capper. Everything just right. Not in the sense of following Ivy League. I would do my own selection of clothing and get-up, but it was always very smart and very good.

To please someone . . .

To look good, or better than anyone else.

Because the world you lived in was what?

Was full of industry and I was full of industry. And, I worked in industry. I put myself into every damn thing I do. So, when I was shaving, when I shaved, I did it right. Every hair went.

This would have been your advertising days . . .

Yeah, when I was in advertising. When I was in management.

So what soured you about that world? Caused you to change your costume in a sense?

It happened with the mergers. I went through five mergers in industry and in three cases I prepared the data for the merger and the ballast, so to speak, to make the merger come about, and then got caught in my own web and was always, not always, but most of the time, three times, I was the one to go. But I went—out. Forget it. And when the last one happened, I said I wouldn't do any more industry, just plain fuck it! I couldn't stand it. My body was going nuts, my head was going nuts. I wasn't being . . . I was making money for everybody except me. I started to think about me. How come I'm always in these crazy situations? What do you do? Why am I in this spot, invariably, when a merger takes place? And I started to think, as long as I'm in industry, I'm going to be me and I'm not going to be changing. I'm beyond this business of kowtowing or kissing ass. Following some fool. A good offer came from the Japanese—to take care of their product in this country for a year and a half. They gave me a contract. I thought, by God, this is the time to do it. And so I did. I left. I was gonna be fired anyway, but I left. Had a small separation . . . I think three months. And then went to work for the Japanese. I had a lot of time to travel, a lot of time to think, and I decided I'll never, ever work for anybody again. And I did that.

And your decision was to do what with your life?

I made a list of things I could do, things I did well, and things I liked, and finally decided I would work on the things that I like. I am able to do a lot of things. I have lots of talent. I look at that as something to be proud of. Nothing to brag about. It's just a fact. I know myself. And, so I decided I would work with wood. I love wood. I know something about it. Know something about tools. So, I decided to make clocks. I did some other sculpture and played around with it and it worked. I was happy. I started to let my hair grow and my beard grow. It was in resentment, obviously, and pretty soon, I started to do these shows. Ross [LewAllen] helped me immensely there, just beautiful. I started to get into these shows in a kind of carnival atmosphere and gypsy, damn pleasurable and away I went. I had a good time and even made a little bit of money. A little bit. Ruth had a very good job, still has. The kids were pretty far along, wanted to go to college . . . I was 57 when I said, no more anything. And I did it. I stayed with it. I think a lot of people thought it was crazy. I was certainly not a conforming role that I was playing, or that I was doing—actually living. Whether it's right or wrong. Whether it's good or bad. I don't know. But I lost a lot of personal concern, like clothing. Didn't mean anything. I was very fastidious about cleanliness. I would bathe two or three times per day and always wear clean clothes. But the clothes might be as old as I am. You know, corduroys . . . I'll wash 'em tonight and wear 'em again tomorrow. But I wash them all the time. And, I'll do that and enjoy it. But I don't enjoy going to Capper and Capper anymore. I just got rid of my last shorts from Capper and Capper. They wore out.

You live in suburbia [Western Springs, Illinois], a fairly uptight community. When they saw Howard Orr walking around with a beard, what happened?

They looked at you and you knew very well what they were saying. They use a horrible word: "hippie." I think there were some dirty hippies, but I think most of them were genuine in their feelings. Like Nichols says—is it Nichols that wrote *The Nirvana Blues*—apparently they go through these stages, and that's the way they go. I wasn't going through a damn stage. I was coming into myself is what I was doing, and whatever happened to my outside appearance. You asked me how do I think I looked? I didn't care. The only thing I knew was that CBS called me and wanted me to do a program with them. They wanted me. And when I had a crewcut they didn't want me. The next thing you know, NBC did the same thing. So, *two* TV stations and that was . . .

As a result of "Howard Orr, the clockmaker"?

I think the clocks and the beard and the blue jeans and . . .

Your whole new persona.

Whole new persona. And I was enjoying it thoroughly. And I was deciding then that I want to confirm this, and I was not communicating with Ruth too well. In fact, not well at all. And I was full of anger and so I went up to this encounter marathon at George William's College up at Lake Geneva there, with Ray Roberston, and there were about 65 people that went up there, and there I met this lady and she was so open and clear, I wondered what the hell she was doing there. Was she an observer or something? It made sense, and then that was all there was to that until later on. Then there was a reunion of the group and she just stood out, like I'd say a light in the dark. That much contrast to the other people. And I got to know her very well. I'd say I fell in love with her. That was OK, but I didn't have any compunction. That didn't bother me. A few years ago I'd have had great guilt feeling. The Calvin influences . . . when I grew up, you know, tits were for nursing! And that's all! And so, I found that that wasn't so. What was it then . . . I was 59 by then? Anyway, I had a great relationship, but that now is 10 years ago my God! Withering. I have new vistas . . . I don't know what the hell they are, but they're out there and I see them and I feel it.

And what about suburbia?

Suburbia, rather than a place to live, is a Way of Life, and self-elevated to a blinding condition—live-alikes, look-alikes . . . boxes. Suburbia is painful to me—

143

it is a stand-still way of life. It is easy to get fund-raisers for Red Cross, Community Chest, Cancer, Blood and on and on associations because industry *expects* its employees to participate in local events. The respectful article, with picture of fatasses, always reads, "Hernold R. Squaredork has been named chairman of the gravey vest give-a-pint society for 1982. Mr. Squaredork is 5th assistant vice-president of LOT-OF-GOLD NATIONAL BANK OF CHICAGO, serving happy customers for over 37 years with branches in Western Springs, LaGrange, Hinsdale, Oakbrook, Berwyn and downtown Chicago.

My home turf is almost anywhere and everywhere. Most people don't have a chance to choose their own turf. I do believe this is true. Often it is said, "If he really wanted a place in Arizona, New Mexico, etc. he would set to and get it." Bullshit. There are too many circumstances and conditions disallowing that great Horatio Jackoff myth. My turf is in my mind. I can conjure up a good fun place while pissing in some slum alley. Not quite all so—but close. Had I a pure and honest choice—I would choose Santa Fe, New Mexico . . . and after that, Oregon. Men of sorts have lived and died in Western Springs. Suburbia sucks—in full.

Landscape is big to me. I love it. I it is as fulfilling as bread and water. Fortunately, I can visualize many of my beloved landscapes and therefore can EXIST, not too badly, in my own back yard.

I have been to Door County—a few years ago—with Ruth. Our attitudes were shitty and non-communicative and bitter. We drove up for to get away from provocative "Landscape" and found the grass was no greener. What I saw, I liked. I like barns and water and neat spots I've never seen. I feel I know a lot about Door by reading about the people in *Door Way* by Norbert Blei.

If someone asks, what do you do, Howard?

I tell people, always, that I'm a designer. Because I am a designer. I'm designing some goddam thing all the time. I'm designing or devising, concocting some contrivance, something that is going to be functional for me, or maybe Pat, or maybe my family, my kids, neighbors, or something. And yet, I can't put my finger on a goddam thing! It's full of sound and fury, signifying . . . you know . . . and oh . . . shakey.

I think designing is in every breath we take. Everybody is a designer, not only I. The only thing is that I say that I am designing. Every once in a while, somebody'll pull a fast one and say, "What do you design?" I have to say, well . . . design your home, your life, your drink, pizza, quiche, garden plot.

So it's structure for a way of life?

Sure. It's a structure. And, I have been a designer.

And are you pleased with the design of your life so far?

No, no, no. I'm very sad about it. Not ashamed of it. But, I 'm very sad about it.

What causes a sad design?

Not to be able to give you an answer to your question of what do you design . . . or anybody else. I won't ever lie about it. I always say something that I have done. But, it's surely not very interesting. It looks exciting to some people. I'm sure it is, because I get a lot of feedback. But, in reality, it's a dumb, dull, goddam unproductive way of life for me.

But it starts with you . . . the desire to do it.

The desire is all right. The desire to do something. And I'm waiting for the goddam something, you see. And, ah . . . I enjoy writing. I would like to sit down and write. Sometimes I'm really excited about it. But again, it would have to be tied in with, say you. I have a great warmth for you, you know. I'd love to tell you that I love you. I mean it. Instead of signing a goddam letter, you know, I love Norb Blei. Sure. But, I

NUDE AT A WAKE ...

love him like it's a man's love for man. But I have an apprehension there too, sort of a fear that to say, well, if I do that someone's going to say I'm a homosexual. To me, that is about as far as I could get from anything. If that's one situation, I'd get as far from it as anything. I mean of all things. Snakes wouldn't bother me. A cliff wouldn't bother me. An airplane. But that, I'm apprehensive that if I say something like telling another man I love him . I want to do that and yet I hold back on it. For women it's easy. I can tell them I love them and they know it. I think that should be easy for me. I'm trying to think . . . my one son-in-law, I can tell him that, and he knows it. He's a hell of a good guy. And he understands and we have a good *sympatica,* another horseshit word. We have a good relationship. He lets me know his problems and I let him know mine, and we have a good arrangement. I admire very few people.

Why? What's wrong with the mass of men?

Dishonest. The old story, everybody has his price. And, I probably too, I probably have a price. And I never think of myself having a price, that I can be bought for the right price at the right time. No. There are so few people I can trust, when I want to trust a great many people. And I'm still naive enough that I'm hurt when I find that someone that I might even idolize in a way, lets me down. They're not letting me down, of course. But, I feel they have. I, I let them let me down. You know, I'm the one that is dealing with it. And, I'm hurt by that.

What I'm trying to say I guess, is that I have compassion for many people and all of a sudden I'm aware that I am not having any compassion for myself. I've come to think well of me in lots of ways, but again, back to productivity. *That* is a great thing with me. I learned to work very early. And I think everybody should work. And I find my work is nothing! It's not helping anybody. It makes a few people laugh. I'll make some wisecrack and people will laugh, you know, big deal. Well, I've come beyond that now. And, I want to be beyond that. I want to be apart from that. I want to be something other than Pagliacci. Very seriously, I'd like to get away from that. I'd like to be serious. And I'm not sure that I know how. Maybe . . . it's a maybe again. Maybe I would be able to take enough time to just do something. Do *something.* I feel that everything I do is speculative.

145

You've been into what is called awareness studies . . . consciousness-raising things. You've experienced some of that stuff, Howard. What do you gain from that? Has it helped you? I guess I'm getting at the extent of the Gestalt thing. And what you're talking about now is essentially that you feel like you really don't complete anything, right? And the Gestalt thing would be to complete it, finish something already.

Right.

And then go on to something else?

Yes. And yet, when I discuss that, people, some people have said, you do. You do. You complete a lot of things, and you've done a lot. Well, I know me better than anyone in the world. And, I know that. Maybe Ruth knows me, which I know she does, in another way. But in the real intimate me, no one knows me, and it's nothing profound to say that we are all in that same situation. But I, I'm troubled with what I do know about me. You see? I knew how to do so many things. I'm unable to do it. Or, I won't do it. At least I'm not doing it.

What are the things you think would give you satisfaction? What would you like to do if you don't want to play Pagliacci anymore? What do you think would bring satisfaction to you and others that you might be the instrument of?

A form of love. To share a love and be able to back it up, present myself with, in a way that would be not only loving, but to be loved also. I used to think that it would be nice to have maybe 10 million dollars and give it all away and watch the people smile. A childish type of dream, you know. Childish type. You know, what the hell's wrong with childish? I think children are magnificent. But, it's not a material thing. I have to look at me. What I have right now. A few pencils, a few acrylics, a few tools. Take what I have now . . .

Love. Would you include that? Do you have some of that?

Oh, yeah. I have love. A lot of love. I receive a lot of love. Like from my family, and I receive love from others . . . from this Pat person . . . Arlene . . . Just lots of people. I'm loved by a lot of people. I know that. So where I would like to go is to take one of the things, just one, that I am able to do, and do it for Christ's sake! Just *one*. I don't feel that I am sort of a messiah or anything, that I have the answers at all. I just know that I'm aware that there are a hell of a lot of things that are wrong, and I know that they are wrong, and yet I'm not doing one goddam thing to help make it easier or correct it, or contribute to the correction.

Do you think the artist does this? Is that why you have had some affinity for that? Or have you discovered that that's not quite the answer either? What role does the artist play? You've been associated with this . . .

Yeah. I like that part best . . . the artist. I seem to be able to satisfy myself with more. I think there's no such thing as a good artist or a bad artist. Just art, period. Or the same thing with a writer. A writer becomes an artist. A dancer, a musician, or whatever you want to call it. To say good, it's just an art. If you qualify in that category, then you have certain things that entitle you to be an artist, and that is a good sense of proportion. A good design. Drop the word *design*. Freedom. Untethered. Open. A flow, like projectile vomiting. A real bang! Let it out. See? And I can do those things, but I hold back at times. And I don't want to do that. I want to do it with anybody and everybody. And I can handle someone that looks at me and laughs, or puts their hands up woooo, back off. That's OK. But I don't want to have to qualify what I'm doing. That may sound real strange. But, I think artists have the ability to see the color at night, and to . . . artists make beautiful poetry. There's a symmetry. At the same time there's an imbalance, and yet the imbalance isn't harmful and they . . . there is a discord, and the discord doesn't hurt you either.

146

And there's harmony and . . . these guys . . . I know what I want. I think the artist is loaded with blessings and paradoxes, that he is unable, though, to present himself as effectively as he might if he would. And, he could if he would.

Do you see your own art taking other directions? Let's go back to the clocks, since you've left them and gone on to other things . . .

From there I did some acrylic paintings. One massive thing I told you about. It was "Ordinary Nudes Bearing Crosses," and it's a lot of color and it's an anger thing too. They are all stick people with different faces. Blank faces. Different colors. Five different colors that represent the five races of man. That's archaic, I know that. They don't teach the five races of man anymore. That's when I was a kid. I have a sculpture I want to do on the medical profession, with wild names for doctors, you know, Doctor Belchphlegm or something, different names. The whole thing is to have drawings for these four beautiful offices and one on top of the other with luxurious balconies and these odd names on the doors, and underneath it is the part of the medical group, and that's the emergency room to the hospital and it's closed. There's a big lock on it. Yet it has an emergency room with a light on it that goes off and on. Next to it is a mortuary with caskets in various sizes and prices. Then, a ladder that goes up, a wooden ladder that goes way up—oh, it's about three feet up—to a pawn shop which is connected to the doctor's office and the guy goes up the ladder with one leg shorter than the other and a crutch under the arm, going up to get money to pay his goddam bill, and one leg is shorter than the other and the doctor has just finished operating on him and he has crippled him for life. And, you know you can get any fee you want out of him. There's a very intense bitterness I have for the medical profession.

Tell me something, Howard! You're almost 70 years old, free now, finally, to do anything you want . . .

Yeah, well almost. Almost. And yet I'm still unable to to get it going. Enthusiasm—Jesus, I have so much enthusiasm. When I heard you were coming tonight I was really excited. Ruth said you called. I get excited about certain people, but there's too goddam few people. In other words, I'm wondering if it must be countless people who get that same excitement when maybe just one person comes into their life for a minute or whatever it is, and they get some excitement out of that. It's one of my indictments of this goddam shrink over here. He keeps people going in for 20 years, coming back, doesn't give them a goddam bit of how to continue on your own. How to get on the bike and ride it! No, you don't ride the bike. I'll come out. When he's 29 years old, you're out still helping the poor bastard get on the bike! And that's what he does. And that's one of my gripes about that kind of medicine. They don't help you one fucking bit.

Where does this compassion for the poor, the down-and-out come from? From the early years? From the way you were raised? The Depression? Would you say you have socialistic tendencies or . . .

Yeah. I do, yeah.

How would you describe yourself politically?

Well, I had, first of all, some exposure to Wendell Willkie. I traveled with him on the train when he ran for president against Roosevelt in 1940. I was a very naive young buck and I was a photographer. The UP, but it was called the International News Service. What I would see was Cordell Hull in Memphis, get on the train. Okay. Here's the head of the Republican Party at the time, Wendell Willkie, running for President against Roosevelt. Cordell Hull was Secretary of State for Roosevelt. We got to Dallas, Sam Rayburn gets on the train. Here I am seeing all this stuff, I wasn't involved in, of course. I made no comment at any time. Mrs. Willkie one time

said, "You seem bewildered, Howard." And I laughed it off, as I recall. I didn't want to get in anybody's way. I just wanted to do my job.

But I guess that comes from my dad. He was always doing something for somebody. He liked to help people. My uncle would kick people out of an apartment he owned. My dad would go and give the people their rent money so they could get back in, you see. The same family! Politically, I wouldn't fit in with either party. The nearest one would be the Socialist Party, where everybody has equal health care, because everybody should have. That's the way I feel. Everybody should have the right to work. I'm a real great supporter of ERA. I think women are magnificent and powerful. They're great and I think they should have every right that every male has. Equal . . . whatever . . . though I know it's not going to happen. Not in my lifetime, or maybe a hundred years, maybe never. Nonetheless, I know that I could alleviate it somehow, but I don't make any effort to do it. I'll give lip service. I'll send 20 dollars and wonder if I can do it. What's my balance going to be in the bank, you know? I'll send 20 dollars to the Klan Watch—it's a group of blacks, I think in Georgia. It's convincing literature, you know. Registered letter, you know. Read it, Jesus, yes, I think . . . Kill those fucking Ku Klux Klaners!

And I feel something is coming, Norb, that is going to develop—that the film is in the process now of being developed. We are going to see what kind of an image is on that film, and I'm the film. I'm going to see that pretty soon. I feel it. I'm going to do something, but I can't say what. Whether it's go to Kentucky and work with those poor bastards over in Appalachia, or go up and work at the hardware store where I can be nice to some people, go to a hospital and visit some poor bastard . . . to do something, anything. Anything for a start.

Money. It always gets down to money, doesn't it, Howard?

Money—simple to me. I'll allow that I might, just might, feel otherwise had I an abundance or all I think (at times) I need. In the truth of me methinks I could share it/give it away—certainly not use it to accumulate *more* money. Money is a medium of exchange—of me bartering (a fun game) to get *some* of the livelihood necessities. As is—it is cause for festering, stinking miseries for countless many humans. It doesn't take a very big or bright wick to see and know that our magnificent earth is shuddering and crumbling and falling due to greed, power, hate, murder, and on and on . . . *traced* directly and finally to money.

In my growing up—and I'm still doing it—I managed pretty well to survive by my wits and so-called creativity—gleaning ample shekels to provide food, shelter . . . and some real honest pleasures and treats. After five fucking mergers in industries, I finally awoke to the fact that I was not only causing a firing line for often thousands of people—I was doing *nothing productive*. I was functioning full force contrary to my hearty beliefs. Of course, I have no answer to this shitty dilemma.

Yet, recently, Howard, you've been somewhat drawn back into that world with offers to model. To "sell" Howard Orr's face, his "hippy," kind-old-face, Santa Claus look . . .

Yes. Modeling is, for the most part, a key part of advertising which I have come to disdain. Once I was an art director in an ad agency . . . an account executive and so on. Then, it was a means of $75 a week and on up to $100, $150. The world is bursting—we saved money, we were flush—oy, we misrepresented and lied and I caused art work to be bigger and better and "buy me" look. I was a shithead. Now modeling is fun, and an ego-helper of sorts. A non-profit ego stunt. I do enjoy the people, the gimmick of seeming myself in print or on TV. Contrary to what most people think, the money is *rare*. I get $85 to $100 an hour and do 12 jobs a year, usually from one hour to one and a half hours. This is money? Who gives a shit? Oy! Yeah, sure—the clown in me does come out when I'm modeling. Time and again the sessions are uptight until a few antics are performed or wisecracks. Then off we go and all is well. But I can live with out it, easily. I honestly don't know how I'd conduct me if some account signed me for a long series of ads . . . and TV! It would catch up with me . . . *I am confident.*

You have this great sense of humor in your writing, your work, your very presence. How do you explain this humorous side of you? Is it something you always had? Do you look upon it as maybe a way of avoiding reality? Of what importance is humor?

Great. I'm bewildered when I confront somebody who doesn't have a sense of humor, or seems not to have. Or, they react with a frown instead of a laugh and smile. Or they don't see the humor in something that's so obvious to me.

You don't get your kicks out of laughing at the guy because he doesn't see the laughter in it?

No. I feel that humor is as important to anyone's life as is, oh . . . water to life, food to life, sex. It's all important and . . .

What's funny to you?

Almost anything. I don't like to laugh at someone's misfortune. If someone falls, I never laugh. I know other people who go into hysterics. You know, they see somebody fall on the ice or a door slaps them in the face and they lose their teeth or their nose bleeds . . . it's funny as hell to some people. But that isn't humor. My humor is usually a play on words. And that's fun to me.

To maybe paraphrase a situation . . . like when I used to be very devout in church. there is an expression that Christ is supposed to have said that "Many are called, but few are chosen." I used to like to turn that around to "Many are cold but few are frozen." People, you know, they didn't know whether to laugh. It depends on who they were, how free they were.

What about you own religious background? Where are you now?

Well, early, I was going to be a minister. A preacher, they used to call them. In the Presbyterian Church. And then I went to school on a scholarship, what they call an Eclesiastical Scholarship, and then I had an athletic scholarship also. So I was in pretty good shape in the Depression. Then I broke my leg playing football, and I lost both scholarships! I could never figure that out. Why did I lose both scholarships? So, I had to come home. And I came home and I started to think about it more and more and something was wrong. It just didn't balance. And the more I looked at it . . . oh, as I got to know people . . . I was on the session of the church. That's

what they called the Board of Elders, when I was very young, and I'd see people doing things that I knew were crooked. Bankers. I knew one banker particularly who was as crooked as you could come. He was an elder, and I would see that. I'd hear him talk and it just didn't sit correctly, didn't sit well with me. To a point where I became very bitter about it and then summed it all up one time. Just jumped clear across it.

I was active in a lot of different churches. My daughter, Nancy, qualified for a job. She had all the training and everything that was at the church, and when they found out she was living with a person, they wouldn't let her have the job. So I told them that. One morning in church they had a session called concerns of the people, and I got up, didn't know that I was going to do it. But I got up and I cried, like a child. Like a little hurt child and told them, I think this is unfair, unreasonable and let's take a good look at ourselves right now. How many of you that if ever caught, you'd leave town? And yet, here's a girl who is totally qualified, but out of pure love, she is living with this friend and they do love each other and some day they might marry, I don't know. And I got a big support from that, but I think the church is a phony place. Not religion, but the church. The church is phony. It doesn't matter what church it is, to me. Full of the famous old business called hypocrite.

You've been married how long?

Almost forty.

Forty years? What do you think about that in light of the way your daughter may have been living? Guilt? People living their own lives . . .

I feel again, like a socialistic approach, that each individual can function best when they're as free as possible and a person is free. If I impose any restrictions on on them—except what is good for them like saying, "Don't go near the water because you can't swim—then I would impose that on them, but not from their personal lives. They're all of age, whatever that means. And therefore I'm not going to impose myself on it. First of all, they're not going to pay any or a hell of a lot of attention. If I haven't impressed upon my daughters what I think would be good for them, or given them what I felt they should have had that is good for them, by now, hell, they're not

150

going to do it now. Theyre not going to change. They may, out of respect, but then turn around and do exactly what they want. And, I hope they will. I hope they will be as free to do it. Whatever they do. I wouldn't want them to drink a lot, to a point where it ruins their health or hurts their health. I wouldn't want them to take a lot of drugs, yet I think all of them have been into that. I think marriage is a beautiful thing and very important, but Ruth and I are legally separated, yet we live in the same house, and we're not divorced and probably never will be divorced. "Legal separation"—I'm not sure what that means. We eat together, do a few thing together like movies, a Christmas party or two. No sex. Little discussion. It's a strange way to exist. Why not divorce? Maybe still some turkey sperm Calvinism in me . . . hate the thought, but maybe. Can't put "it" on that either—but maybe. Acutally, a divorce per se would be the *normal-routine-traditional* thing to do. Since I'm none of those three, what's the difference? *If* I were considering getting married I'd need a divorce "they" say. No plans are in my make-up. I am against marriage for me . . . and a lot of other simple souls. This big legal shit separation (whatever the hell it is) serves to make each of us aware that we do not live well together. And that is that— however fucked up it may sound.

How does love fit into this, as far as Ruth and you are concerned? Is there love in a relationship where there is a marriage but not quite a marriage?

Well, in view of our legal arrangement now, there is love, we both have a feeling for each other. We have a great deal of feelings. And, I'm sure a great deal of love. But it's a strange love. To me, it's . . . ah, there are a lot of things we don't do that I would like to do. Little trivial things like taking walks together. We seem to still go out of our way, however slightly as compared to what it used to be, to torment each other in little ways, little things. Just . . . they are distasteful to me. And, yet I do it.

Love and sex?

I think sex is a part of love, but love can survive without it. Without sex. Sex is just a real nice thing to have, but we can all live without it. But, it makes for a happier existence. I think it's sort of a bonding device. I have, I think I used to say I had, a great sex drive. A great deal of sex drive, I'd say. But I don't think I have any more than anyone else. I just am aware of it and also since I'm freer, then I utilize it. And, ah, I have sex relations sometimes three times a week, as simple as that. All right . . . when I was . . . maybe it's just trying to catch up. I don't know. I was one of the virgins when I got married. I wouldn't have made an overture to screw a girl anymore than I would have, you know, slapped her. I mean they were both, you know, out of the question. That doesn't mean I didn't have the drive then, but I didn't do anything about it.

And as for women?

They are considerably more than for poontang. On the other hand, I can't imagine poontang without women/woman. I am a feminist for women's sake, and mankind's sake. I've known a few women. When I come to lie with a woman, for whatever reason, I fall in love with her. Or I detest her. Some women I trust more than any male. Women are to love as any other human. Our potential is boundless. We have not scratched the surface of man's greatness. Males have bungled it. I feel females (women) would do it, in another more growthful and fulfilling way. I'd like to see them really try.

Ross' wife, Arlene [LewAllen] is a good friend, a woman you and I and Ralph [Rausch] and many other friends of Ross love dearly. What makes her so extraordinary in your eyes, Howard?

Why do we all love Lady Arlene? I know only why I love her. It is sexual, sensual, wholesome, honest, refreshing, ALIVE, shimmering, dignified, classical—peasant-like pure Arlene. She *gives* without expecting to *get*. She is the fastest emphathizer I've ever encoutered. She makes me, and I'm sure others, feel *just about perfect* in one's own special setting and set of conditions. She is a natural lover—of people and creatures. Most of all she is undescribable. She is *Arlene*.

Since I've known you, Howard, in much of your work there is this fascination with the death theme, almost always handled with humor. I find it in much of what you do, many of the things you say. Why? Where does it come from? Are you more conscious of it now as you grow older? Though 70 is not an old age. In Door County I know many people in their 80's, very active, a neighbor who is still out there logging everyday. I'm in my 40's, and I'm very aware of the death thing. Perhaps it goes back to the Catholic church for me, where it seemed you lived with death constantly. A heavy trip, you know. And I see you obsessed with it, dealing with it . . . maybe not "completing" it either, but a kind of haunting thing.

Yeah, well when I complete it then it will be really a consummating.

I guess I mean "completing" by maybe not having to mention it anymore.

Okay.

If that's ever possible. I don't know.

I think it's a defiance on my part. I make light of something that I actually may have some fear of. Have I sent you any letters with me in the casket?

No.

Okay. That's a humorous thing, and when I was doing that I thought, "Now I wonder why I'm doing this?" And it didn't satisfy myself, except that I wanted to do it. I have come close to death a few times. I dropped a shotgun one time and it just put a big hole in my leg, but another two or three inches and it would have blown my belly out. I almost drowned one time. The guy I was with did drown, during the war—torpedoes—I floated around for six hours in the North Atlantic. Fortunately I was strong and much younger. But also, I wanted to live. That's a lot of it. Also, I had a heart attack one time and I still survived. So I've had some acquaintance with it, and I was the eternal pallbearer in Kentucky when I lived down there. I was always getting off work. I knew a lot of people, and they died, and they wanted me to be pallbearer, a couple of times a month, you know. The high cost of dying the American Way of Death.

So you don't feel it's necessarily a fear as much as it is a defiance? The feeling of "I'm still surviving after all that." What are you trying to tell other people?

I think I'm trying to make out that I think most people do fear it, or at least hold it in very high regard and with great dignity and any slander of death, or say the

mortician, the singing of hymns and the eulogy are pretty meaningful and are pretty important. The last rites and things like that. I tend to look at them and, maybe tying it with my feeling about the church . . . Invariably somebody of the cloth is making the eulogy, and that's bullshit to me. I've heard so many eulogies which, if I didn't see the character in the casket, I wouldn't know who the hell they were talking about. Really. It's nuts. I don't know. We were laughing at my Dad's service, his wake really. And a lady said, "You shouldn't be doing that!" And my brother said, "Well, if Dad weren't in that casket he'd be out here laughing, doing the same thing we're doing." I never really thought of it until about that time, that Dad was a funny person. He humored us. And he *would* have. He'd have been laughing. It wouldn't matter.

What would he have been laughing at?

Memories maybe. Or incidents that we had encountered. We worked together a lot, my brother and Dad and I. And, we had a lot of funny things happen. And, invariably it was humorous. He told a lot of jokes and a lot of stories, and they were funny. We talk about them and they bring back memories, but they were happy memories, not the kind that bring tears to your eyes. We were glad we experienced that. I'm not going to cry, because I had a fun time.

So you were hearing this rather serious, lofty eulogy and you were thinking, that's not him at all, or . . .

No . . . the person that said you shouldn't be laughing . . . it was just incongruous, it didn't fit with Dad. It didn't fit with us. If Dad weren't strapped in that crazy casket, he'd be out here having a good time.

One of the last, or the most recent things you've been working on—and we kind of share an interest in this, along with the New Mexican landscape—is the Penitentes, that rather early, primitive form of Christianity that still exists out there, in parts of New Mexico today. The death cart. What does all this mean to you? What was your interest in? That concept of death, or . . . ?

Ah, the making it a horrible thing, imposing upon somebody the miseries of putting the rocks in the death cart and putting more in as people were emoting and expressing themselves, really letting their emotions carry them away. Beating the people, flagellation even to the point of death sometimes. Killing them. It's a fascinating . . . To me it holds a fascination like an animal may have for a snake. I've heard of snakes charming animals until they can get them. Capture them. And, ah, sort of hypnotic almost. The first time I saw a death cart, I thought that it was just great! But it's also gruesome, and here's this creature with a bow and arrow, and sometimes a cloth over the head. And then reading about it, the Penitentes, and all the literature you sent me, telling about putting the rocks in and making it heavier and invariably going up hill, making it more difficult, just plain misery upon misery, and just as frequently dying right there . . . .

But you didn't find humor in that necessarily? You didn't tackle that one with the sense of humor.

No, not really. Certainly not specifically. The humor in that only to me would be some expression on the skeleton's face. Or maybe make him dancing. Maybe a flute instead of a bow and arrow . . . you know, adjust it to you own hearing or seeing pleasure. Put maybe a pecker on him, you know, have him reach down, holding it. He's all decomposed except for his tadywacker!

That's for you, Mr. Death!

Right! Here you go! Who said it . . . Death where is thy sting? Who was it that said, Death where is thy sting-a-ling-a-ling?

You've thought about your own death, I'm sure. Would you wish a service something like your father had? Would you consider planning all this ahead of time?

I would consider it, and I do think a lot about it. But I want it to be absolutely cost free. No expense whatsoever.

How would that be done?

Well, it's already done. I belong to an organization where my body goes to the University of Illinois Medical School. My eyes go to the eye bank. I have marvelous eyes for my age. Or for having lived as long as I have. And any other organ that can be a transplant or reused, that's to be used and whatever happens after that, I don't care.

Where does the spirit go?

I don't know. I don't know. I don't believe per se in God. I believe in a power greater than man, whatever that is. I do believe that strongly, some force, whatever it is, and it's mind-boggling to me sometimes when I think of all the wonderous things that are all around us and the unknown. Jesus, the unknown. When you think just over a few years all the things that have happened. The airplane, in my own lifetime. I could go on and on and on. And, yet I can't put my finger on it. There are just so many wonderful things that have happened since I was born, up through my life and yet I look at them as hardly anything for what I believe will come. I don't know what is going to come, but it's untouched.

Do you think you might be part of that in some way?

I don't think so. I think man is too goddam busy doing nothing. Greed. Causing misery to happen. Selfishness. Money . . . so devastating. And then the greed for money and for material possessions. Jesus! And there are so many people and so many needs that are not being met that could be met with just the slightest twist or adjustment in this script or whatever the hell you'd call it, of living, of life. It's almost like tuning a radio or a television. A little twist and it comes in clearer . . . and that could be done so easily with man I think.

And you still want to do that little bit of twisting in your own clockwork?

Yeah, but I would like also to do it without any credit, any recognition. I would like to be a . . . whatever, whatever. But, I'd like to *do* it! I don't care what part of it. A little infinitesimal part. One little cog, one little breath of air on a sail that moves the ship a little closer to drinkable water and food and good things for everybody, instead of the few.

Among Friends
Ralph Rausch

I'm at my desk, here in the coop where I write in Door County. Maybe it's morning, maybe it's the afternoon, but there is a frenzy to my movements. I'm getting out. I'm "cleaning things up," finishing some letters, getting a manuscript ready to mail. I don't like to leave any work hanging while I'm gone, whether I'm gone for only a couple of days to Chicago, or a number of weeks to New Mexico. Ralph is on my mind.

And whether I'm still at my desk, or maybe stopping for a beer at Kurtz's in Two Rivers, or just arrived in Chicago and my old neighborhood, inevitably I pick up a phone and call Ralph Rausch.

He is always there, which I've come to realize through the years is vital, reassuring, important to my own well being. And, I trust, his.

Ralph? Norb.

Where the hell are you?

Here, on my way. See you at Harvey's for a drink about 10. We'll talk.

Great.

I can't think of once he hasn't said "great," wherever, whenever I say we'll meet. The guy never fades. A man needs friends, good friends, and Rausch has saved my ass so many times, in so many ways that I know I'll "owe" him the rest of my life. As a writer, as a friend, I feel I must acknowledge this . . . and explore it even further.

Friendships don't happen overnight. They require years of caretaking, and you've got to realize that you may come to damn near hate the friend at times before you can reap the real value of the relationship . . . what a friend may mean to you, and you to him or her.

It wasn't always this way between us. Not when we first taught together at East High School of Aurora, Illinois, or later at Lyons Township High School in LaGrange and Western Springs, where he was actually my department chairman in English. Or even during the past 15 years while I've been living here in Door, and he back in Western Springs. There have been ups and downs, distrust, anger, resentment, conflicts of all sorts—many of them unexpressed. There have been times, I'm sure, when we've both considered the other a royal pain in the ass. I still dread his criticizing my work, for I can still see the Infallible Teacher coming down on me to set things straight. (I have always hated infallible teachers, and he knows that.) And I know he's wrong—whatever he's going to criticize. And he knows he's right. And his analysis is often brilliant—though I still don't think, at times, he knows exactly where I'm coming from. He moves by reason. I trust instinct.

Quite frankly, I found him an uptight teacher (though a good one) in my first two years of teaching at Aurora—very traditional, a model teacher of detailed lesson plans, specific assignments, excellent delivery, totally responsible. I was fumbling around, wanting to be a writer, trying to figure out if I was a teacher at all . . . sometimes good, sometimes terrible, often irresponsible when it came to administrative directives,

155

faculty meetings, or chaperoning school dances. Just give me the kids and the books and let's go with the ideas.

At Lyons Township High School, we exhibited similar personal characteristics, only more so. He was now my boss, for one thing. I was getting even more improvisational in my teaching techniques (and felt they were working beautifully) while he seemed even more traditional (and that was working for him). In fact, we had both become better teachers; rumor had it we had even become "master" teachers. I like to believe that. We had also become better friends, to a degree.

I felt I peaked at Lyons, the best high school I ever experienced, reached about as far as I could go as a high school teacher. I think Ralph did too, and Ross LewAllen, the third member of our group. There was nothing left except remain good teachers the rest of our lives (risking the inevitable burnout that sets in), or get out of it, make room for other young Turks. And so we all got out of it—for various reasons—though the friendships remain and continue to grow.

Living in Door all these years, I have not developed a single friendship as strong as Ralph Rausch in Western Springs, Illinois, or Ross LewAllen in Santa Fe, New Mexico.

It's difficult to talk with natives because they either aren't listening or don't care to understand. (And why should they?) Outsiders are in the same boat you're in: their heart (and friends) really belongs somewhere else, though they will usually tell you there is nowhere else in the world like Door County.

But Ralph Rausch is there—where I used to be. He hasn't left. I know exactly where to find him. I know he's going through either good times or bad times—as I am. I know he likes my stories of life in the boonies as I love his stories of life in the jungle of textbook editing and publishing. I want to hear about his kids, and he wants to hear about mine. I want to hear what's happening in education, and he may want to hear my feelings about books, movies, restaurants, or people he has met here in Door. We both want to talk about Ross and Arlene in New Mexico, whether he or I have visited there last. We may both want to eventually live there ourselves. I know he likes good brandy and good cigars, and he knows I'll drink any kind of scotch, smoke his good cigars all night long, and drink his good brandy too. He and his wife, JoAnn, will put me up in the spare room any hour of the day or night. And I have my own key to the front door.

More importantly, we have learned to lean on each more the past few years, having both experienced some personal wounds. We play Father Confessor to each other at times.

Maybe that's what real friendship is all about.

We talk into the early hours of morning, in his living room filled with pipe and cigar smoke. Sometimes there's music playing. Two bleary-eyed, mustachioed characters slouched in comfortable chairs, staring at each other out of the shadows in the room, our hands feeling the cold weight of glass tumblers of scotch or brandy trying to make some sense of the language of our lives.

Or we sit at the bar at a place called Harvey's, a brighter, livelier, somewhat crazier scene, eating free cheese and crackers, hollering over other voices, smoking, drinking, laughing . . . and, in this instance, trying to understand our friendship for the first time . . . .

I'm thinking about back in the late 50's, early 60's, Ralph. Do you recall my arrival at East High School of Aurora? Do you have any first impressions?

First impressions? Yeah, when I think about it right off, I visualize you in a big coat with a scarf wrapped around you, a cap pulled down on your head, and a sort of frozen expression on your face. What was that, an MG or a Triumph?

Triumph.

A little Triumph sports car coming in from Berwyn and freezing your ass. Coming in in the winter time. That I remember quite vividly. Why the winter time, I'm not quite sure, but you were an imposing figure then, something out of a Russian novel.

My impressions of you, Ralph, were that you were highly thought of amongst the faculty members. And I remember being invited to sit in one of your classes to observe, because I was a rookie teacher.

I don't remember that. That must have been a hair-raising.

And your being very friendly, and we talked a little bit, you know, during that first year. I think I was probably a little bit intimidated by you at that point. I don't think we socialized much, did we?

No. Because you were in and out like a shot. You were a commuter. We talked occasionally in the faculty lounge with Louie Schaub and the group there, he puffing on his corncob pipe . . . .

Ralph Blackman was our department head, and we'd see him once in a while. He was a good go-between.

Things are coming back to me as we are talking, and I do remember Ralph Blackman encouraging me to encourage you, asking me to help you get used to the routines, to what kind of books were available and what we didn't have, and what the curriculum was like and that kind of thing. I remember even at that time being impressed with the fact that you were obviously well read; even then your interest in writing was very, very obvious. I remember your talking about writing, wanting to write, doing things in your little shed down there on Euclid in Berwyn.

What kind of teachers were we then, Ralph? Were we good?

Shit, no. I think we were fumblers, as most teachers are at that point. I like to think we were good. I like to think that we were a little more humane than some of the others, maybe. Although my impression of your impression of me was that you thought I was kind of a hard-ass.

Yeah. There was an element of that, and I'm still not sure what caused it, whether it was something somebody else had said. I was kind of a loner and played that whole Ensign Pulver game, which I did successfully in a number of schools—trying to stay out of the limelight, just do the work, kind of hide. You had no authority over me at that point. I don't think we established any friendship at that time. That developed later on, but we were aware of one another.

Very much so, and . . . .

I don't think you came to Chicago or anything to see me.

We did come in. I think Jo and I came in once for dinner, and we met Barb for the first time. I remember thinking how pale and fragile she looked, her skin like an eggshell, a very delicate kind of gal. You took me downstairs and showed me your little wood-slatted storage place-work room, with the watercolors on the wall and papers and stuff stacked up there. We did the basement trip.

I don't remember that.

And then, of course, after Christo was born . . . .

Well, the time passed. I went to Mexico and then I went to Europe. And you appeared in the picture once again after I had returned and was working at the City News Bureau in Chicago again, trying to find a teaching job, but still wanting to write. I had started on a Master's at the University of Chicago, but I really wanted to write. I don't know if you called me or what about that teaching job at Lyons Township High School where you were then teaching. And you kind of saved my ass because I needed a job that paid. That's, ah, when I was very indebted to you.

We got a damn good man.

Those were very interesting years at L.T.

Well, those were some of the good years and some of the bad years. As far as teaching is concerned, they were probably the most stimulating times that I can remember, not only because of the kids we were dealing with, but also because of the camaraderie among the faculty, the kind of people there. Sally Thurnau, Ross LewAllen, Burt Krueger, even Frank Bacon in his own way. A very rich mix of sharp minds and different personalities; it was a good time.

We even did a stint of team-teaching at South Campus, and you were department, or assistant department chairman . . . .

Well, you know what they used to say, Aldo (Mungai) was Father Superior and I was Father Inferior.

We taught honor sections and superior sections which were . . .

The *creme de la creme,* supposedly.

What do you remember about that?

Very challenging! Some of the kids had minds that blew you away—extremely well-read kids. You really had to be on your toes. I often wondered about the impact that I (and other teachers, too) had on that kind of kid. You're never quite sure when you are aiding and abetting their growth and when you're truncating it. I always felt, in that particular kind of class with super–intelligent kids, that they are very sensitive to what's going on. Exactly what impact *do* you have with students like that? And what's *really* going on behind the games that people play in the school setting, all the teacher/student roleplaying? How do you cut through that? It was very obvious that that kind of student wanted more from you than just what could happen between teacher and student with 20-25 other kids in a classroom. You had to cope with that kind of thing. How do you give what they need? I always felt slightly—I don't think defensive is the right term—but I always felt that in many ways I didn't measure up, that I was falling short of being able to *really* help that sort of student.

We were different in the way we approached those students.

Yeah, very definitely. I think this even goes back to the Aurora days. I think our whole approaches were different, and perhaps this is where the hard-ass business comes in. Basically, I was a subject-oriented teacher involved with the words, with the art of writers we were studying, with the stories, with the world in microcosm. I think I, sometimes, got carried away by that kind of thing and forgot the humanity in it. I sometimes forgot that students are people with specific needs. Sometimes, I think, that I fought against this. But, the more I matured as a teacher the more I found out that there has to be a balance between the subject matter and the student on the other end of the stick . . . that you can't overemphasize the subject matter and forget about the student, because it's this relationship to the subject matter that's really what teaching's all about anyway. It took me a while to learn that. It's a trap that a lot of teachers, who are really turned on by what they are doing, fall into. They are so immersed in teaching Lawrence or Twain or Dickens or whatever they forget that there is a human being out there who has to relate in some way to what they're teaching.

I remember conflicts because we were both teaching honor sections, but you were doing it one way and I was doing it another. I was not that subject-oriented. I wanted to teach black literature, Russian literature. I was doing it entirely different and maybe I was wrong, or maybe you were wrong, and I was never sure.

But I remember, Norb, we talked about this and we shared ideas. I'd say, I've got this thing that I tried out and it really worked. And you'd say, gee, that's a good idea. Or you'd tell me something you had tried. I think we had an idea exchange going, even though you might have implemented an idea in an entirely different way. We were both interested in getting ideas across to kids even though our techniques were different.

I think my conflict was with your more traditional approach and because I saw Frank Bacon, a real taskmaster, as your father figure . . . that he was behind you, encouraging you, and I didn't have anyone to really feed off except maybe Jerry Bitts. And Jerry, you know, would be kind of off-the-wall, and I could identify with that. I wasn't really certain we were seeing eye-to-eye on this. I remember your liking to teach *Critical Thinking,* where I hated that fucking book. The kids hated it. I hated to put the kids through it. I would rather have taught Russian literature. I thought the other was a waste of time. So part of my conflict with you was being aware of the hard ass thing, plus the fact that you really liked to teach that stuff, and could. Anyway, you left teaching in 1966. It was a tough decision for you because you loved to teach and were damn good at it. But Laidlaw Brothers/Doubleday offered you an editorial position developing a new high school language program with a linguistics base, and you decided to accept the challenge.

Teaching was becoming a dead end, in a way, and you could see yourself heading more and more into the area of administration, and you really preferred to teach. Laidlaw meant more money, more time in the sense of not having to take papers home to grade everynight, and in the long run more security. And you are still there. But a few years prior to leaving Lyons Township, our other close friend, Ross LewAllen, entered the teaching scene. And that is when it all began for the three of us. I met him first at North Campus, and as I recall I kept saying: You gotta meet this guy, this new art teacher . . . what about Ross?

He's the kind of person that, as you know, he walks into a room, he's a stranger but he comes right up to you, shakes your hand, and in 10 seconds it's as if you've known him all of your life. He just makes you feel at ease. And yet, there's something dazzling about him, something sparkling. He's got a lot of energy coming out of him . . . just a thrilling sort of person. Somebody you look at and say, wow!

What kind of a friendship did we have then?

I felt that I was being moved in other directions. We were both teaching together, we had a common bond, common interests, common topics that we could talk about. Okay, but then I'm into publishing, you're still teaching, you're doing other things. And shortly before this time, you really started getting serious about your writing, concentrating on it, trying to resolve, I felt, the conflicting pulls: Do I stay here as a teacher when the real pull is toward writing? I felt that I was becoming an outsider, that you wouldn't loosen up with me, that you were going off in another direction that I wasn't part of. I felt cut off and alienated. Maybe it was part of your really getting immersed in your writing. You've never been one to talk a great deal about your writing. You've never been one to talk a great deal about your writing-in-progress, so there was this wall of silence. I was reluctant to say, Norb, what are you working on? What's happening and where is your head? I didn't want to intrude on your writing. I sensed from your silence that this was something I shouldn't push, I shouldn't talk about. I've always respected the privacy that a writer has to have in order to work on his ideas, and I felt that perhaps you felt you couldn't trust me enough to talk about your writing. I felt very bad because I thought perhaps you felt that I wouldn't understand, that I couldn't relate to what you were doing. This is how I remember our friendship at that particular time.

Yeah, I think that's the problem we had for a long time, which was partially my fault. I was still, am still, a little intimidated by you, by your teaching techniques. You had a kind of austerity about you. And it's true, I never wanted to really share any of my writing because probably I was really afraid of you judging it. I didn't want to show it to you. I was afraid of some remark that might be made in jest, but would be a kind of zinger. And then I'd think, you know: Well, fuck you, Ralph. I think this has been a problem with us for a long while. And Ross comes back into the picture at this time. I think I began to identify with him more and more because there was more freedom about him, more acceptance. I recall, too, kind of alienating you during this period. Not making fun of you or anything of that sort, but just feeling more comfortable with him.

Well, sure. I was Mr. Square, and he was Mr. Loose.

He would invite me into his art class, you know, after hours, and we would do some painting, some jewelry. He would be showing me different ways to handle silver or watercolor. And, yeah, you began to pull into the background. That was before you left teaching entirely. And then just the two of us were left; then it was really gangbusters, really crazy, and I'm surprised we didn't both get fired. We came damn close to it at times.

It's very interesting that in spite of the different directions in which we were all moving, we never really . . . there was never a split. There was never a chasm. We kept in contact. Some kind of polar attraction kept us together. I felt, and I still do (maybe I shouldn't judge him in this way) that Ross always needed acolytes. He likes to be surrounded by people that he feels that he is helping build, contributing something to. And at that time, well . . . I viewed your relationship with Ross as your being another acolyte. Ross has got Norb under his wing, which was not necessarily bad, but I was, I felt, somehow not connected with that kind of thing.

Well, part of the reason was we look upon a writer as an artist, an artist as an artist; we had that between each other. You seemed to be outside this. Ross and I had begun to share a lot of stuff with art. He would do a painting and say, "Write something on it." And I would. He'd say, "Put some writing on here in relation to this or that," and that was a whole new dimension for me. *The Watercolored Word* came out of that whole period and yes, we became . . .

A symbiotic relationship.

A spiritual kind of thing began to develop. And it was always difficult to , not to bring you in so much as . . . I don't know . . . to have you understand that and at the same time not alienate you.

Well, in a way, you see I did understand. I wanted to be a part of it, but I, intellectually, knew why I couldn't be. I understood that and I accepted that. It bothered me because I wanted to be a part of it. Here were two friends of mine doing their little own thing on the side. But I think that part of that too, you see, goes back to the kinds of people we really are, basically, the three of us. I'm very interested both in your perception of me and in Ross' perception of me because my translation from my side of the point is that I'm a very extroverted, aggressive person who comes on very strong, who has strong opinions—an opinionated person, a dominant if not domineering kind of personality. And I'm not. I'm probably the direct opposite of that. I'm a very introspective kind of person.

But you think we had that opinion of you?

I think you had the opinion that I'm a hard driver, that I'm aggressive. That's part of my protective coloration.

That's real close to what Ross and I saw, I think, in the teaching. I've used you in a couple of books so far, you pretty much as you are as in *The Second Novel.* But in the first novel I wrote, *Adventures in an American's Literature,* which deals a lot with teaching, there is a character in there you probably do not like.

The prick of the faculty.

But I just want to explain and apologize at the same time. It *is* fiction. The character's name is Reckelson, and he's a combination of maybe you and a touch of Bacon. Ross and I were in some ways just too loose, what we were doing with kids, how we were conducting classes, our whole not-giving-a-shit attitude. All for the kids and fuck the administration. You were the bad guy because you were part of the administration. That's where you were, with Frank Bacon behind you. Whereas on our side we had not only Ross, but Jerry Bitts, Kim Cusack . . .

Of course, Kim. How could I forget Kim?

And Jerry Bitts had run into a couple of problems with you as well. So you began to take on the bad guy role. We knew, of course, that wasn't the core of you, and it probably wasn't until you got the hell out of teaching that we could talk about these things.

I detested that role: Authoritarian. I'm not authoritarian. If there is anything I do *not* do, it is sit in judgment of people. Yet that was the basic part of that particular job.

It was your facial expression. One could just read your eyebrows and wonder, "What the fuck is going on in his mind?" I was aware of that. That's part of the reason we grew somewhat apart during those years.

Sometimes, perhaps, when we know each other a little better, or when you're in the mood, I'll tell you how I got that way. It's an interesting story.

You know, along the same line of my fear of your judging me, when you were editing . . . I didn't know, I suspected that it might have stemmed from your own desire to write. And you didn't really get a chance or take that option, so I thought, "Maybe Ralph is really envious."

Oh, sure. Of course I was envious. Because . . . it's hard to talk about your writing and my not writing. Yes, I've always wanted to be a writer. I'm one of those people that, and this is the classic cop out of all would-be-writers: I'm a head writer.

You know, it all goes on up here between my ears, but never gets out on paper. But there were always other priorities. You know enough about my background to know that duty, obligation, what one does in relationship to one's family and one's stance as a man and a bread-winner takes priorities over what might seem to be selfish or self-centered or egocentric kind of concerns, which writing certainly the hell is. There's no more selfish or egocentric trait in the world I think than a writer. So, yes, when I saw you with the courage in the first place to say, "I can't teach and be the kind of teacher I want to be and write and be the kind of writer I want to be at the same time . . . one or the other has to go and so I'm opting for writing. I love teaching but I'm giving that up. At that point I felt, God, if I could only make that same kind of commitment. And yet at the same time, as much as I loved you as a friend, I thought what a selfish, terribly selfish thing to do. I couldn't see myself doing that same kind of thing. And I kept saying to myself, 'But I have obligations! I have things, you know, things to do before I sleep, business, and how can Norb do this?'

Did you see evidence in my life of that selfishness?

You're a paradoxical person. You're probably one of the most open and giving people that I know. But when it comes to your writing, other things take a back seat. And it's always amazed me. You see I'm a Depression child. The idea of not having a "steady" job, a paycheck coming in on time, being able to pay one's bills . . . that's almost beyond my conception, because being a Depression baby and hearing all the horror stories and hearing all the stories, and having to live through a lot of the hard times: $1.25 Christmas, my first Christmas, one string of lights, that's what I got, and I heard that story over and over again, and other stories. And I watched my mother go to an early grave and watched my Dad work himself, practically to death with two or three jobs with 7 kids. It's always been how you get that way. There's almost an ascetic . . . well, maybe it's even a perverted sense of putting self last. Writing is what I want to do, but I can't do it until I get all of these other things out of the way. Of course that's self-delusion. Those other things are never out of the way, and I think it takes a great deal of courage to break away from it and do it, and at the same time I felt that when you did that, you're being very, very selfish. And I'm still mystified. How do you pay your bills? How do you do that and still do what you want to do?

I have to rely on friends like Ralph Rausch.

I don't understand how one does that. I've always been somebody . . . you pay the bill on time, in cash if possible. You don't charge things. You pay your house off, which is a stupid thing to do, free and clear. I'm out of debt. This is something that I inherited that I carry with me and it has put me where I am today, which is in a hell of a shape, because I've never really found out, really, who Ralph Rausch is. I have found out who Ralph Rausch had to be, given these times and these circumstances, the role that I had to play. I didn't want that department chairmanship, but I took it because I didn't see any way of going in an opposite direction. It meant $600.00 extra at a time in which $600.00 was a lot. It is this kind of progression where one says OK, I'll defer this because I think it's selfish, and I'll do what I have to do right now and then later on I'll do what I want to do. And I could see you doing what you wanted to do at the time you wanted to do it, and I admired you and was exhilarated by your guts, being able to break away. But at another time I thought, how could he do that? How can he abandon his "responsibilities"? I'm not sure others will understand that I mean "selfish" in a very special sense—a sense applicable almost exclusively to art and artists—a selfishness without which I don't believe there'd be any art or artists. Any artist, but especially a writer, must have an extraordinarily

162

well-developed sense of ME before what he has to write about THEY and We is worth reading. Whether a writer admits it or not, he must love himself *well* in order to feel that his specialness—the view of life he projects through his writing—is worth enough to make public, to say, "Look at it this way, *my* way." And writers don't, can't, shouldn't ever "grow up" completely. They need to be suspended in a certain state that could be called "child-like." Still open to wonder, still unjaded, still curious, still impressionable, still uttering: Gee! Wow! Look at *that!* Still, like children, selfish and wide-open at the same time, still convinced that they are special in this sensitivity and their awareness, "better" in these things than the typical man in the street.

What about your life now, Ralph, with the choices you made?

Well, I think there have been very few times in my life that I have been happy. My people are the lumpiest of the lumpen proletariat. I think the chasm between my father's generation and the generation I started, since I was the oldest of seven, was the leap from my dad who didn't have a chance to finish 6th grade and had to go to work at the age of 13, and my being the first . . . there are a lot of burdens being the first born, the first male child, the first high school graduate, the first college graduate. There were expectations and roles that I was forced to play that got me into the situation we are talking about now. There's always been a set of expectations in the sense we talked of before, about somebody being a self-made man. That doesn't apply to me. I think I'm a self-manufactured man rather than self-made. I don't think I've made it yet. A self-made man is a man who I think is satisfied and happy with where he eventually ended up. I'm manufactured. I am who I am because that's what I had to be, given other people's sets of expectations. That really even applies to my job now and to my transfer from teaching to the editorial field.

In what way?

Ah, in a way that the job itself has all kinds of potential rewards. First of all, it does give me the outlet that I sought for writing. It's not like writing short stories or poetry, yet in its own way it is very creative. And it's very rewarding in the sense that one gets of having turned out a product that probably can affect the lives of students, that can make the learning experience a little bit more pleasurable and even a little bit more relevant. So the potential for reward is very strong. But today's educational publishing world is a kind of a comic atmosphere. It's a collection of cliches and contradictions. Pressure groups constantly looking over your shoulder to make sure that nothing is offensive in your material, and of course if nothing is offensive to anyone, you've got pap, pablem; *bland* material that can't possibly relate to today's student. So that is a constant irritation, a negative to my job. Another negative is that while the people who are working within my own discipline, my own English editors, are tuned in to the subject matter, the student learning about language, becoming excited about words, being able to use words in a creative way, trying to get past the kind of disinterested and . . . how can I characterize this? . . . insensitive kinds of administrators that I am dealing with, the commercial part of it, the people who control the purse strings, the people who make decisions about elements in the textbook content about which they really have no knowledge—it is this constant frustration in trying to convince them that the material is good, is honest, intelligent—that's the tough part of the job.

What else has your job taken out of you, mentally? Spiritually? I've come down from Door, sat in your living room waiting for you to come home from work, watched you enter—ten sheets to the wind, hardly a smile—down a couple of martinis, reach for a cigar. There's something sad to what I experience. We've talked about this a

little. It's got to concern you.

Yes, ah yes, it does. This is hard for me to talk about because it seems to be, at one end of the spectrum, kind of self-congratulatory and at the other end of the spectrum, feeling sorry for myself. But the kind of job, what I'm doing again is supervisory in nature, which I do not like. Which means that I have to work with relatively large groups of people, coordinating them so that, let us say, a nine-book series that involves 26 different people comes off on schedule. I'm responsible for every word in that text, every comma, every picture, every paragraph, design. It's not a job that one person can really handle well because it takes a sort of renaissance man, which I am not, and I'm constantly pushed every day to the limits. I have to read another writer's manuscript and comment on it and change it. Sometimes, very often, I have to rewrite that manuscript myself, in order for it to meet what I consider to be a standard that we have to have in order to publish the material. It is a very high pressure type of job; a lot of tension is involved. You're constantly working with ideas and concepts and the writing itself draws it out of you . . . if you didn't have to worry about all the other tiny administrative details. So it's a job that requires perhaps bits and pieces of six or seven different personalities, some of which I don't have. So I have to substitute for those, divert energies from other parts of my psychic makeup in order to fill those particular gaps. And that's what draws it out of you. When you come home there's not a hell of a lot left. And, reading manuscript every day, words, words, words. I love to read. I used to love to read, but editing spoiled me. Why reading for recreation is practically nil. Weekends I can pick up a book and get it started. Week nights, forget it. You know, to look at another sentence, another line, another paragraph, and not only just the physical act of reading the material, but also the mental set that I've acquired after being a critic all day long, looking at the way words are put together, I can't sit back and let the words speak for themselves. I'm entering into the copy. I'm looking at that paragraph and saying: Jesus Christ, what a great first sentence, but the last three are crap! So I'm reading it as I would read it as if I were at work. Reading for pleasure is something I've had to give up, which is unfortunate. Things right now are getting worse instead of better and I see intellectual freedom, not only at my particular publishing house, but all over the place, being squeezed, condensed, adulterated, whatever you want to call it and I don't see a bright future ahead for people who want to open up the classroom. The whole back-to-the-basics movement scares the hell out of me. I'm not trying to imply here that an older teacher is less creative or less imaginative, or less effective than a younger one, but I think the last statistics we got, were that the average age of the high school teacher in the United States today was 47 years, and this signals an increasing conservatism in the classroom. Back to rote ways of learning, sentence diagraming, objective tests.

That scares me. There are pressure groups like the so–called moral majority who are, as you know, very down on "secular humanism." As far as I'm concerned scratch "secular." It's got nothing to do with "secular." Humanism *per se* is what they're after. You can't even ask the student now what he thinks, or what he feels because that's construed as being invasion of privacy. That's a question that one cannot ask. Anything that asks a student to make a decision, ah, poses a problem, a dilemma, given this would you do this or this . . . you can't put a student in that kind of problem–solving situation because what that implies is that there are no absolutes in the world, there are no exact givens. There are grey areas, ah, which, of course, some of these people deny. I'm very distressed by this direction and these negative things keep combining, and the pressures I feel with the unintelligent administration of the company keep growing.

165

As a friend, I was urging you to dump that goddam job, Ralph, probably the first year you were into it. I saw what it was doing to you and I wanted you to go back to teaching; I was probably thinking about it myself as well. I was trying to write thinking . . . what am I doing this for? I'm a good teacher and I too had an option to come back whenever I want, you know, but I continued to urge you to do that. I still want you to get the hell out of that role, and you always have the feeling well, just a couple of more years and then I can get out of it. And I'm pretty well convinced that you won't get out of it until you're 65. But there was always that kind of devil's advocate and I think Ross joined me in this . . . let's get Ralph the hell out of that job and so on . . . come to New Mexico or come on up to Door County or whatever. Yet you've never been able to do that. We probably think we failed at being able to convince you to do that, yet you've got your own reasons. Are they those very same reasons you got into it in the first place?

You know you two guys remind me of my doctor. My doctor says, "Quit because you're under too much pressure and it's going to kill you." And I look at him and I say, "You quit, because I can tell that you're under a lot of pressure." "I can't do that." "Why can't you do that?" Well for the same reason that I can't. My doctor says, "Get a job as a punch press operator." "Yeah," I said, "you get a job as a punch press operator." This is one of the things that I've kind of joked to my wife about because my two best friends are always trying to tell me to get out of my job. Do something else. But yet, what if I said that to them, "Norb get out of writing: you're starving to death; you're not making a living, you know." You write me a letter and say, "Gee, I can't pay this bill, I can't pay that bill." And I say, "Screw you Norbert! You made your choice. That's your bed, you lie in it. You're going to have to live with it." And yet, how can I take your advice? Well, one thing is that I feel I am a very limited person. There are not many things that I can do well. I'm also a person with a lot of pride. I don't feel I could abonadon something by quiting and backing away because it's tough or because it's drawing a lot out of me. That is against, maybe, this aggressiveness that you see in me, this kind of drive. It would be like saying I can't do it. I quit. I give up. I'm not willing to do that yet. One of the things that keeps me going is that I keep hoping that things will improve as far as the administrative part of my job is concerned. You see, I see what it can be . . . the difference between how the world is and how the world could be. How the world *is* at Laidlaw Brother's is crap; how it *could* be, could be pretty damned wonderful. And I keep hoping that there may be a breakthrough there. But what can I do? What do I know? I'm a very limited person. It frightens me to think of starting over. But I'm not afraid of work. I can go pump gas. That's not it. I'm not a person who's impressed by titles. I'm a project director now, so I become Joe Blow or Ralph the gas pumper. That's gonna bother me? No. That's not it.

This whole business of our friendship growing through the years, through all these different changes in our lives, your going one way, me another, Ross still another . . . I'm considerably indebted to you for our friendship. All of the strong factors that I may have had conflicts with you over in the classroom are yet, in another light, very positive factors insofar as you've always been there, always been someone I could count on. Both Ross and I have talked about this; you've always been *that* friend who was there when we needed him for one reason or another. And I should say, going back to that period of time when we had all left teaching and Ross was in Europe and having problems, that's where I feel, that one time in particular when you really came through, and I failed. I feel very guilty about that time when he was in the hospital, being put back together again, so to speak . . . the breakdown . . . and *you* were the one who was able to come to his aid. And I was not.

166

I think you were frightened about that, weren't you?

Yeah. I went through some bad times about that myself. I think it was great for you to *be* there, to be able to visit him and stuff like that. Later through a friend, George Taucher who lives in Europe, I was able to contact George and ask him to help locate the bus and the paintings in Spain, to ship the paintings back . . . but that was about all I could do. I could not face Ross in the hospital. I could hardly talk to him on the phone because I was at a breaking point myself, and I was scared. I'll always respect you for doing what you did. And I'll always put myself down for not being able to come through under those circumstances. Ross will never forget that. So that's one of the qualities of friendship I'm talking about. A constancy. Something you may not even like in yourself, but it's there, and not to be denied.

Thank you for saying that.

Let's talk a little about Door County . . . what do you think my life is like up there? Just what have you thought, imagined about it since I've been living there?

Well, not entirely idyllic. And yet it has some of those qualities. The ability . . . again, this verges on envy, and perhaps it is truthful . . . the ability to arrange your time, to direct your energies, to be the architect or your own day. That to me is a very enviable position. To be, in a sense, your own man, and to heed the pressure of whatever it is, as a priority at that particular moment. I know I get some letters from you that say, my God, I'm flying off in 15 different directions at once. I got this started, that started, I've got to do this book review, I've got to do that, things are tearing me apart. I've lost my center. I've lost my focus. And, yet, I think the Door County experience for you has been the most salutary thing that could happen to you as a writer. I think Door County really opened you up in many, many ways. When you went up there—your contact with people like Charlie, the natural beauty of the place, your being able to walk on your own land, getting very interested in birds and botany, and being able to identify plants and trees and opening up that kind of thing for you and watching the skies and listening to the sounds, like your telling me about the fantastic sound of the ice when it breaks up . . . like thunder, that kind of thing . . . all of these very sensuous and sensual impressions that bombard you. It's a hell of a place for a writer to be, even a Chicago writer. At one time I thought, "God what a great mistake for Norb, who is a Chicago person, a people person, a city person, to go up there in this God-forsaken place, kind of isolated, alone, yet I think that's become a very important part in your philosophy as a writer and I think it shows through in your writing. A kind of strength. One of the things I like about your writing is your objectivity, being able to pick out detail, minute detail. Going up there gave you some more sights. Like a spider, you got some more eyes. I think it's been great for you. Despite your bitches about being isolated and not having people to talk to, I think it's been a great experience. How wrong am I?

Well, we won't go into that. Back to you . . . I'm repeating myself, but I see you as steadfast, serious, structured, rational, and yet there is a great humor about you, a fine wit. You make a lot of people smile and laugh, which is a very valuable gift. And you're also a very giving person, both you and Jo, and yet some women, some of whom may perhaps work for you, may also see in you a very chauvanistic streak. How do you react to that?

The chauvanistic streak? You loaded me up there. You got at least a double barrel . . .

These other characteristics are for the most part favorable, human attitudes, but this chauvanism thing is a little tied in with the structured attitude . . .

Okay. So we got a paradox. But the whole point is again, you describe my being an inner and outer person. I've always had this feeling that there's a kind of shell here,

167

and I'm trapped inside of it. This is a kind of recurring fantasy that I've had, that if I could somehow unzip this shell or shed it like a crab might, then the real person could emerge. And yet, I think it's again a natural sort of protective coloration that I have to assume.

Do you see any of those same characteristics in me?

No. No, not really. At least not to that extent. You see, I'm very insecure. People see me as aggressive, secure, stable, the old rock, you know. If you need help, go to Ralph. He's there he's on time, he's punctual as hell, he gets pissed off at people who are late . . . all of that kind of thing which is the Prussian part of my German background. But I'm also a *Luxembourger,* the sort of people who cry at the drop of a hat, who can't stand to see a dog go hungry, that kind of thing. I'm extremely unsure of myself. I've suffered from an extreme inferiority complex most of my life. Much to my discredit, in my teenage years, I was ashamed of the kind of house that I lived in, of the kind of people that I came from. I was pretty much a blue-collar person. And so I had . . . that is what I meant by a self-manufactured person . . . I had to try to find a way to bridge the gap between what I was to what I wanted to be. I couldn't see myself spending my life as my father had, working in a factory. And yet, until the very, the 12th hour, there was absolutely no chance of my ever going to college. It was only by the greatest fluke in the world that I ever even got into college. And so, in a sense, I've had to kind of build this shell of dependability in order to make myself achieve the kinds of things I have. And yet I have always felt that I don't belong, that I'm an outsider. I consider myself basically misanthropic . . . that might surprise you. I don't like people, en masse. I like persons. I relate very closely with persons, but I'm uncomfortable with people. I don't know if that makes any sense or not. I don't want to go back into all this early childhood kind of business, but I've always had to struggle, fight, sometimes claw for whatever I had. I've always felt—for instance, my own college experience.—I've always felt cheated because I had to spend so much of my time not doing the things I would have wanted to do, like join the creative writing club, things of that kind. I was digging graves, I was washing and polishing cars, and I'm not saying that I felt sorry for myself, I'm only saying that I felt at that time, that I was the "other." The kind of person who wore chinos and blue jeans, dungarees, not because they were fashionable but that's the only thing I could afford. Other people were wearing dress slacks and sweaters and all that kind of thing, and I didn't belong. So, I got used to being a spectator, a sort of a non-participant. Yet there were certain expectations I had to satisfy. I was the oldest. I had to graduate from college. I became a teacher. I had to be a success as a teacher. I went into editing. I had to be a success as an editor. I had no other choice. My weakness is that I made myself into these expectations so that part of me, yeah, is aggressive because I had to be that way in order to survive. The other part of me is what I really should have been, might have been, could have been and am. I don't know if that makes sense or not but that's how I see it. I look at myself as a mass of contradictions. I really don't know who I am; I'd like to find out. I don't really know what would make me happy and what would satisfy me in this life because I haven't found it yet. Yet people look at me and say, "My God, look this man has: relative financial security, a job with a title and responsibility, he's got a lovely wife, two lovely children, and why isn't he happy?" The answer to that is because that's not who I am.

We both share a tendency to go off the deep end at times, various forms of depression. I don't know how suicidal some of these bouts are . . .

Some are.

Some are, perhaps, and are some of these, for you, in relation to what you were just talking about?

Yeah, yeah. I've been in some very, very serious depths of depression.

You and I talk about this at times, and that's good to be able to do that. Unfortunately, we're never really in the same place at the same time when we're going through these things. I don't know whether that's good or bad. Probably good because one is up when the other is down.

Heaven forbid that we should both be down at the same time.

Mine is related to a lot of things, mostly trying to exist as a writer. I can see now by what you describe in your life, things that must contribute considerably to those feelings. Are you in better control now, do you think? Those bad times?

Well, I think I'm in control in the sense that they seem to be a natural part of my existence. I don't think being depressed is ever going to go away. I think being able to cope with it merely means accepting it and knowing that it too will pass, and that something will happen to give you a little upswing and that it's not the end of the world. I think I was helped by the psychiatrist that I talked to you about before. He told me that a lot of my depression was chemical, and he did help me in that way. See, his view point was—and I subscribe to this now—he said, "You felt that somehow you should be able to pick yourself up by the bootstraps every time you're in a depression. That it was a failing on your part that you were feeling bad. In fact, you were feeling bad about feeling bad." He said, "Now that's ridiculous. In fact, that's bullshit." He said, "Suppose you were diabtic, and you said, 'I'm gonna pull myself up. I'm gonna cure myself of diabetes. There's something wrong with me because I have diabetes'." He said, "that's ridiculous. You've been fighting 5 or 6 years, you're blaming yourself for a depressive mood that you could not possibly have helped yourself out of." And he said that's a classic kind of condition that people get themselves into. The more depressed they get, the more they feel that it is their fault for being depressed, that they are a lesser person because they are depressed. And it's a vicious circle. I can see now that I'm not going to be able to do it by sheer willpower—make myself healthy, happy, by willing it. I hope I don't have to go back to the crutch of chemicals again, but he assured me that I probably will have to sometime.

In the area of friendship again, Ralph, I think a lot of men I know don't have kind of thing that we're talking about. They're just passing acquaintances, but there's no kind of relationship to kids they grew up with, boy friends, for example, that they had in late grammer school or high school. I don't know, if you still have those affiliations with guys you went to school with. So I think about you, Ross, and guys from my neighborhood I still know, guys from high school I still see once in a while . . . I think we're very fortunate when talking to some of these other people, who either because they may have had no tendency to maintain those friendships, just don't have that kind of thing. In our society today, what do you think is to be said about male friendship, camaraderie?

I think there is a great deal of male companionship underground that, being what it is, nobody makes a big deal about it. It's a kind of a natural thing. It happens and people don't talk about it. That's the way it is in my case. But, frankly when I think about my colleagues at work, and their friends, I don't know many of them that really do seem to have "old buddies" now that you mention it. I never really thought about it in the terms that you pose. Perhaps, it's *not* as prevalent as I think, and we might have a situation among the three of us here that is something unique, at least not very prevalent. Certainly I have no close friends at work . . . perhaps one, and I don't trust him. I have not made real friends on the job. I've been there sixteen years.

And ours was generated through teaching. I think that's kind of interesting.

Yeah, I think it is. What if we had met in another profession? Suppose we had all been editors at Laidlaw Brothers? Or suppose we had all been working for the City News Bureau of Chicago, or something like that downtown? Would the same chemistry, would the same thing, have happened? It *is* interesting.

What I don't see in you, Ralph, would be in the area, for want of a better term, shall we say "spirit"? Whether that's a desire to create, tear one's self apart, to risk . . . sometimes I try to provoke it, but it seems we don't quite get into that area. Maybe it's something we both just understand and have no need to express, but maybe it's one of my reasons for feeling closer to Ross at times—we can get into these matters. With you . . . I think it goes back to your attitude, your being steadfast and structured, the Rock of Gibraltar. So we never get a chance to discuss these things. I explore this of course with fiction and stuff like that. And I explore it through, oh . . . I feel more attuned to women who express spirit for me. And I find it very difficult to find that kind of thing in friends or male companionship. Do you have any feelings about that?

Well . . . .

If I even talk about, say, "higher consciousness" with you, or a lot of the things that have been going on in the past years in the areas of psychology and religion, I always feel you're sort of smiling, thinking, "Oh, that's a lot of bullshit." And some of it may be. I think so myself. And yet I seem to run into people interested in these things time and time again, men and women, mostly women, either in my classes or elsewhere. And a lot of the ideas I find certainly in the books I read. And "spirit"— whether it was once expressed for me in religion, the Catholic faith, whatever—has been a part of my background since I can remember. The Zen thing . . . all this. But you and I don't talk about religion or all these other things. I don't know where you stand on some of this stuff or if it even concerns you at all.

Now, specifically, what are you talking about? Are you talking about things like clairvoyance, and things like ESP?

What I'm talking about is the quest, in all its forms. And again I would look upon the artist as of the questing nature. I think we all are "in search" to various degrees, and yet we don't seem to be able to verbalize this, you and I. I've done a lot of this with Ross in the past years, but strangely enough, as he becomes more successful as a jeweler, a designer, a craftsman, the head of his own jewelry company—and financially successful—less and less of this questing nature is evident. So I'm beginning to feel like a voice in the wilderness at this point. Almost as if he is now crossing over to your side. The whole success thing, you know, I see as a very seductive way of dying. The spirit is killed off. I don't think this will ever destroy our friendship, but I'm afraid it will change it. Anyway, I've never been able to discuss a lot of these things with you as I have with Ross, and now I fear I will be losing that with him too as he moves further and further into business.

But you see all of these years I've been waiting. This is part of my natural reticence. I think part of our relationship is that I'm a listener. I'm a good listener, and you're a good storyteller. I love to hear you talk, and I love to hear you express yourself, and very often I don't feel that I have much to offer. What I have to say is kind of mundane or cliched or something that you wouldn't be interested in hearing. So I'm very reticent about expressing myself and I've been hoping that somehow you would be the aggressor in this thing. That you would more or less draw me into it willy-nilly. So I've been for many, many years holding back talking about things of the spirit and the sort of thing that you referred to. But I think you have a blind spot about the success business. I don't think that's necessarily the thing that cuts off sensitive intercourse between people. Ah, and what's success anyhow? Do you see Ross or do you see me as a success? Do you see Ross as a success? How do you interpret success? What does that mean?

A monetary thing. That's the way society measures it, and the writer's especially faced with that. If you don't write a best seller you're not a writer. That's the way America thinks, in a sense, and I have to live with that every day. Even today, in Chicago, talking with some editors, I can see, you know, just talking to these guys, that they're best-seller-minded in a sense. I'm sure they've got a much wider range of it, but it is very difficult for them to accept a short story writer in America. You know: "Why the hell doesn't he write a novel or something?" What we're still talking about is "Why isn't he writing a book to make a lot of money? Why isn't he doing all of these things that he really wants to do?" And I've got the great fear that when one does this, and it happens too often, you know, that the spirit dies and that the work goes nowhere. So you want the money to a certain extent, and you fear it too. At least I do. That's a part of it for me. We talked about this, you and I, where I can't talk about it with Ross. He's virtually getting into business now, which, as you know, 10 years ago we would have never expected to happen. I expected him to be a very fine American painter. And he doesn't even paint now. He designs and manufactures original jewelry which has a great monetary value. Consequently, I don't see him questioning his life or my life or your life, you know. And I'm for the quester, you see, because I think it's what we're here for and I don't like to see that die in my own friends.

Well, some of the answers, I think came out tonight. It's not that it isn't there, it's

171

just that it's been sublimated. It's been encrusted, as it were, another thing that I envy about your work. You're able to husband your psychic energy, your emotional energies are going to be spent, whereas I am at the whim of 26 or 30 people who pull *their* energies from me. I'm like a battery that people are taking juice from, but there's no generator pumping juice back in. I think "spirit" is the generator. You see, you're constantly growing because as you're learning your craft, you are learning. You're reading, you're constantly involved with . . . you're *living* your work. Your work is your life. Ok. You see, my work is *not* my life. My work is a living. There is a difference between work being life and work being a living. So I make a living, but I'm not making a life. See, you're constantly building a life. So I really feel bad when you say, "Have you read?" or "Do you know about?" and "Have you heard?" and I have to say, "No, I don't." I'm cut off from that, but you're constantly immersed in it. You're drawing energy from and projecting energy to the kind of activity that you give your day to. You, you have command over it. Other people have command over my day. I don't, I can't see where my energies go. So again, at the end of a day I'm bankrupt. I come home; I have nothing left for me, or for the spirit. And so, the only thing I can hope to do is recuperate enough, charge my battery enough to face the same maelstrom again the next day, survive that, come home depleted, charge myself up enough to face it again. And that's a terrible way to live. And that's why I envy your life, because your life is kind of self-generating.

We're in our middle years, Ralphie?

You bet your sweet bippy we are.

Your'e 50, and I don't even want to say how old I am. I'm too goddam vain.

I know birthdays wipe you out. Which amuses me.

I hate the thought of old age, of death and dying. Do you think much about all this? About getting old.

Yeah, yeah I do. It's frightening to realize that most of your life is behind you. That you've lived it. Or have not lived it. And you know, three score and ten, I'll be lucky if I make it with the kind of work that I do. But you see, in another sense, I was always convinced somehow—I don't know where I picked up this impression—that I would never live past 40. When I was in my 30's, I really dreaded 40 coming because I *knew* I was going to die. I was *convinced* I was going to die. And so, in one sense, I'm on a bonus. At 50, I'm 10 years over my deadline.

I've had the very same feelings.

But you see mine were exacerbated by the fact that when I was 22 years old, my mother, who was 46, died unexpectedly. And I said, "Now I know for sure. My mother didn't live past her mid-40's, and I'm not going to make 40." Her death confirmed my fear. So in a sense I'm on borrowed time. In another sense, I dread my body growing old and giving up on me. I'm young in my head, but my body doesn't do what my head wants it to do all the time. Death doesn't scare me as an abstraction. Not *being* does scare me.

Where do you think we're headed?

We . . . you and me?

You first.

I don't know. I'm a survivor in a sense. Not unmarked for having survived. Certainly deformed for having survived. Somehow, I think I'm going to be all right.

Are you going to be able to live that kind of life you always wanted to lead, Ralph? In five years? Ten years? Fifteen years? Or do you even know what that life is?

In a sense, I'm like George Blei, your father, in that regard. I mean, from what you've told me about him: the white shirt, the routine, the same train, going into the same job. Getting into that kind of groove. Ah, if I can get up enough guts to break that! The best thing that could happen to me is if somebody would walk into my office tomorrow and say, "You're fired." That would be a decision I wouldn't have to make. That would be made for me. Then I could go on from that particular point.

Where might you go?

Well, one thing that's been playing in the back of my mind, modesty aside—I think I'm a damn good writer when it comes to textbook materials. I've made a lot of contacts in the publishing area, and I think I could have as much freelance work as I could handle, writing books for other publishers. That's something that is very much in the forefront right now. I still would want to try to write some short stories, write some poetry, do something creative. That's a pressure that won't quit. I've got to do it. When? See, that's another thing. The older I get, the more energy becomes crucial, stamina—both mental and physical—becomes crucial. I'm going to have to start being selfish about how I spend it, and how I husband it, and how much I keep for myself for the things that I really have to do. That's a lesson I'm slowly learning.

Where do you think I'm headed?

God, I don't know. I'm worried . . . .

Do you think you and I, we'll both stay in the Midwest the rest of our lives?

No. No, I don't think either one of us will stay here. Not permanently. I think we'll always come back here. I think this will be a way-stop. I can't see myself staying here. From what I can gather from you, I think there is a great, almost irresistible pull to New Mexico. I think you're going to have to resolve that one way or another. Go out. Give it up here for awhile and go out there. Maybe you'll be disappointed. Maybe the enchantment will wear off when that's a more permanent place of residence. Maybe you'll come back here. I don't know. Or, maybe that's where you really belong, and that place is going to capture you and you're going to stay there.

Well, of course, Ross is there, Arlene is there. That landscape, that sun, those mountains, all those people. I identify with all that. Arlene . . . Arlene has played a very interesting role in this relationship of the three of us. In fact, she painted us once—a painting you now own. Who is she? What is she all about to you?

First of all, it takes even a total stranger less than sixty seconds to realize that here is a special kind of person. I've never known anyone who gives you the sense that you are an interesting person, a person worth listening to at length, a person whose company is valued, more than does Arlene. When you talk to Ar, you've got her undivided attention. She absorbs you and seems absorbed by you. She has an uncanny ability to draw you out of yourself, to establish an intensely personal rapport, to allow yourself to reveal more than you ever intended to discuss—all naturally, without design or guile. I've seen her deliberately seek out the wallflower at a gathering and leave him or her feeling like the guest of honor. She has tremendous energy and drive. In the early years of our acquaintance, she was teacher, mother, wife, artist, chief cook and bottle washer at innumerable impromptu parties and eat-overs cavalierly and unexpectedly initiated by Ross to entertain his retinue . . . counselor to students and their parents, loving daughter, concerned sister, understanding sister-in-law, soft shoulder, soft touch, and stable center, anchor, and thus intimidator to a husband who desperately needed some stability and yet was threatened by the strength she represented, the strength he lacked. (I love Ross too much to always tell him the truth.) The list is longer than I can complete or than anyone who doesn't know Ar would believe. In quiet, late-night moments you could sometimes see the tremendous energy-drain of her typical day take its toll and even as she smiled and nodded, trying to let you know that she was

173

still interested and cared, her eyelids would droop, close for seconds at a time and then flicker open to let you know you were still worth the effort of staying awake. I don't buy the ball-buster assessment of Ar popular in some quarters. A strong woman, certainly, but only a ball-buster to a man who can't match her strength or to a woman totally insecure about herself and not confident in her own womanness. Of course, I love Arlene. Who in his right mind doesn't? I have four sisters who know nothing about me. Arlene is the sister who does. And yet as close as I sometimes think we are, I know very little about the Arlene who lives inside her own skull. She always manages to turn your concern and caring for her back upon yourself. There's a shield there, a No Trespassing sign. Many of the high points of our friendship for me have been when she's tusted me enough to let me help her with a problem she'd share only if you deserved her trust. As for her role in our friendship—Ross', yours and mine—I'm afraid that she sees us as we are and tells us diddly about each other when we're alone with her—me about you, you about me, me about Ross, you about Ross, and Ross about the two of us. She knows our weaknesses, our foibles, and also, thank God, the things about us that make us worth keeping as friends. I don't mean she talks behind our backs or says anything she wouldn't tell us to our faces—she simply sees the warts and the blemishes we all bear and is comfortable enough with us all to tell us about ourselves when we're apart. I think she knows and values the love both of us have for Ross and sees in us different but mutually positive influences that may be supportive to the man she loves—and she in turn loves us for those influences. To a large extent, Ar's role in the chemistry of the friendship of "the three musty steers" is something I'm not yet quite certain of. Without doubt she's glue, and equally without doubt she's part buffer *and* partition.

That painting she did of the three of us some years ago . . . .

One thing remarkable about that painting, Norb, is the way she's positioned us, the figures in the painting. Do you remember where we are?

Sure. Ross is in the center, you're on the left, and I'm on the right.

No. Ross is on the left, you're on the right, and I am in the center. I think she saw something about our relationship that we weren't aware of ourselves. I play a role in the triangle—an apex formed by "lines" coming from you toward me and from Ross toward me, and many coming from Ross to you that I'm not included in. But I've got a bifocal vision from my position of the triangle that neither you nor Ross has. Ross talks to me about you. You talk to me about Ross . . . and it's a revelation.

174

Brothers of the Spirit
Ross LewAllen

He is in Sante Fe, New Mexico, just returned from Africa. And I am here in the coop in Ellison Bay, Wisconsin, talking with him over the phone.

That the woods outside my window are green and lush, that the blue lake beckons, that the day is morning crisp and the light soft gold, that the fields are filled with daisies and the roadsides spattered with wildflowers—yellow and orange hawkweed, prairie rose, black-eyed susan—that the fullness of summer in Door breathes a loving sigh of perfect peace "in place," body and soul . . . all this fades in the moment.

I am elsewhere. In New Mexico.

I hear the voice drift above the sunburnt landscape. Know how shadow and light play this hour upon the adobes, the arroyes, the mountains just outside his open door. The silence is tangible.

And then the scene shifts to Africa, and again I am caught up in his stories, joys, dreams, quests. What else? Who else? What more is out there? What do we do with what we bring back alive? How does the artist shape it? Whom do we give it to?

Once again I am reminded of the power of those individuals (some teachers, artists, mystics) to establish their dream, their search, their imperfect lives, as pathways to the human spirit, reenvisioning our own lives in time.

Now it is Africa. Before, it was the whales. And before that, something else. Always something else. A restlessness. A desire to go beyond. A constant craving—new people, new places, new food, new ways of living, new experiences.

Given a traditional upbringing (especially in the heartland), we tend to limit our lives to the acceptable. Perhaps the promise, but seldom the dream. Security is our faith and our bondage.

Some of us live out an adequate life this way, unaware. Some of us break. Still others break out.

Who's to judge the way of anyone's life?

But the joy in the voice at the other end of the line persists, beguiling, contagious, self-reproaching. (What am I doing here? Why haven't I seen Mt. Kilimanjaro? Why haven't I loved the world, the darkness in that way?)

Africa . . . I want to know everything, I tell him.

And though he has barely begun to describe it, though it is not on my immediate list of places I want to go some time, I know I will be going to Africa.

Such a spirit of living and creating abounds in this friendship.

"It's really not that far away," his voice drifts. "I've done some paintings . . . ."

Flashback . . .

Before Africa, before the moment of the phone call, we talked in New Mexico, Ross and I. There were things to be aired between friends.

We have known each other since the mid-60's, and we go back to much of the craziness of those times, politically, philosophically, creatively—Marshall McLuhan's

175

global village, the medium is the message, or the massage. Teaching brought us together, but the spirit of art bonded us in such a way that at times I was convinced Ross LewAllen and I were the same person.

He was the artist. I was the writer. We encouraged each other and even exchanged roles as he opened new ways of art for me, and I revealed watercolored words for him.

He was the brother I never had, and I in turn may have fulfilled the same need in him. Though he was taller than I, built differently, there was enough resemblance in our facial features that during his occasional visits to Door County in the late 60's, natives would often tell me they had seen my brother in town. To this day, when I visit his domain in Santa Fe, people address me on the street as the artist/jeweler, Ross LewAllen.

We are changing, I feel, looking less alike these days we grow older. Yet the identity of spirit, though strained at times, still remains.

Early on I envied, even tried to emulate, the wildness of the artist's life—both what I knew and imagined such a life to be. There is a long, romantic history associated with such a life—wine, women, song . . . decadence, death at an early age. No one knows this better than the writer who, fortunately or unfortunately, seems more destined to imagine and record these experiences than actually live them. A few can do both. But inevitably the work is affected. There is not enough time to both live it and get it all down.

Also, there is fear—fear of a life of total indulgence. Fear of . . . that will take another telling. Another time, perhaps.

Now I wish only to look very closely at a friend who, in turn, may help me see myself better. In Jungian terms, he is the shadow figure perhaps. The alter-ego. The mirror-image. Something of that.

Psychologically, an element of split personality exists here as well—which most artists/writers must deal with if there is to be any power at all. You must be something, someone else, or there is no knowing of the heart's terrain worth writing, painting . . . being.

A time came when these two brothers of spirit, these two figures, these two selves merged, in a way, and the shadow was gone. And though the distance between us at that time was as great as Door County and Spain, we had both, almost simultaneously, crossed what came to be known between us as the thin red line . . . neither knowing the other's reality or reality itself. This was fear. And this was an extraordinary test of friendship. And to this day we are both so marked by a separate acquaintanceship with bizarre images of excess and emptiness on the other side that neither can explain to the other or totally comprehend that state of being except to realize our fear of ever having to experience that again.

He came back with some drawings and paintings, while I retrieved only a few stories and shadows I have yet to explore. He gradually worked his way out through good hospitals, doctors, therapy, a loving wife, family and friends, while I walked around dead for a year on the outside, afraid of writing, afraid of reading, afraid of explaining or seeking help, fearful of confinement, clinging to a daily life of dull routine as the only salvation.

Salvation, too, was here in Door County. I walked and walked and walked the road, the fields, the woods, the beaches. It was here I was to learn the healing powers of nature. And one day, still a mystery and a miracle to me, I was back. A skin had been shed. A new door had been opened. And he, too, was on his return.

That time away as strangers to ourselves (especially to him) had taken its toll. In some ways, the old Ross was gone. And that death, the death of a certain highly tuned spirit, I have never been able to accept—even though I suspect I know the consequences of an artist's way of life. It isn't fair.

I know, too, and accept the fact that it is more important that he is alive, continuing to grow, and on his way to becoming an extraordinary success as a master jeweler in the Southwest and throughout the country. He is the originator of the earcuff, a whole new concept in earring design. And Ross LewAllen EarCuff Inc. now markets his designs throughout the world.

Still, occasionally, I long for the old days, his old ways. I would like to see him drink wine again to excess, smoke boxes of the best cigars, stay out until dawn, laugh and tell stories till he's hoarse, paint beautiful women in a frenzy, pass drawings out to waitresses for tips, hold his environmental happenings all over the country, build incredible merry-go-rounds, teach in a soul-giving way that few teachers can, meet me with a musical band of drunks and deperadoes at the railroad station in Lamy, New Mexico, as he once did, as only an old Ross LewAllen can.

I wish for the fire inside him. To cross the thin red line again—but to come back laughing this time, perhaps shouting, "More fire! More fire!"

What died in Ross was the painter. What almost died in me was the writer.

How I resurrected the writer is another story. Slowly I nurtured that spirit back to life in both Door County and Chicago (where Ross was at the time) and eventually in New Mexico as well, where he finally moved.

He gradually returned to part-time teaching at the College of DuPage and began making jewelry, while I did a little college teaching as well also at DuPage and continued with the "safe" writing. I stayed with the "real" for a long time—people of Chicago and my old neighborhood, people living in the extraordinary landscape of Door County, where I had immigrated.

I slowly found my way into writing again by that kind of storytelling (newspaper and magazine profiles of people and places) which took imagining as well, though not the same kind of imagining as fiction which often scraped the psyche, could be fraught with risk and despair, frequently left scars . . . and just as often released the writer, freed him in a way only art can. And when the time came to enter that realm again—to be the other person, create the unknown place, know the life you may have never actually lived to the ultimate degree—I crossed the thin red line again, still fearful, yet somewhat assured that I could shape what I felt, bring it back alive, and return as I went in: the writer.

The "danger" still exists. The risk-taking grows even greater at times. But so does the reward: living a fuller life, knowing onself better, affecting the quality of life in others.

Santa Fe continues to enter the picture. New Mexico . . . the mountains, the desert Southwest . . . it's all a very difficult attraction to explain. Ross lured me there in the late 60's, and it was there where I wrote a short story, "The Hour of the Sunshine Now." It was as if the setting had been waiting for me, and the story was asking to be written. I'm not sure how it was written or why it possessed me so, but it haunts me even today. There are levels to it that still frighten me. And there are times in my life when I dare not read that story at all.

I know, though, that I have never written one like it in all my years in Door County. And sometimes I wonder about that, and about those landscapes, those people who absorb us and affect us in such different way. And for the writer, the artist who plays with fire . . . those places where we've been burnt, purified, which continue to attract us, pull us in for more. Call it fire, or crossing the thin line . . . New Mexico has that power. Or call it karma. There's a debt to be paid, something to be done there, lived there, and written there yet.

So I return. Always the traveler. Always seeking. Always finding more than I expected. Always knowing that I feel at home there in a way I feel nowhere else. Who knows why, or what all the connections are, what they mean, or where they may lead to?

And now, in the middle of yet another winter of discontent in Door, I am here again, in the bar of the La Fonda Hotel (and later at his home) talking to one of Santa Fe's finest artists and master jewelers, my friend, Ross LewAllen. And we are exploring much about our lives, our friendship, our dreams . . . .

You came into the art department of Lyons Township School about 1964 Ross, while I was in the English department. I recall being told that I had to meet LewAllen in the art department.

The same thing happened to me. Several teachers said, "You've got to meet this person. He's your kind of person." That's what I heard for a long time.

Had you any idea what else you wanted to do with your life at that time? Did you expect to remain a teacher? Did you expect to be a painter?

I expected to be a painter. I never expected to stay at that school very long. Maybe two years, three years . . . which is exactly what happened. I felt real comfortable there, though, because it was very similar to the high school I went to. The other positive thing was, perhaps it was the first time I had done what my parents wanted me to do.

Which was?

To follow in my father's footsteps . . . to go into theater and light and sound, sets . . . which I had done. Then I quit. Went to school. So this was the first time I got a job from what I said *I* wanted to do.

And this was important?

Yeah, right away. I'm not always being an artist . . . now I'm teaching.

What were your feelings about teaching? You said you wanted to be a painter, but were you having any conflicts with this?

It was too soon maybe for the conflict with the painter thing. I enjoyed teaching. I seemed to get some immediate rewards from it. I felt good at it. Confident, because I found myself in an art department of seven instructors where I was the only one who was an artist. So I found that the really exciting students were gravitating towards me. I found that I was losing friends amongst the other instructors because of this. The same thing that happened to you in the English department, I'm sure.

Did you think much at that time about the makeup of a good teacher? Could you stand outside yourself once in a while and say, "This is working, that's working. Goddam, I'm good at this?" You're a born teacher in a sense. What is a born teacher as you see it?

I found it is the energy, my energy and what I was doing outside of the classroom. My own skill. I had a lot to say about what I was teaching because I was doing it myself. My own shows. And all this transferred to the students, I think. And I'd come into class excited. Oh, this happened yesterday! And this! And I'd get a painting in a show and all that. The students picked up on this.

It was pretty much an energy thing for you.

And also, I wasn't afraid to enter into a new area, whether it was pen and ink or watercolor . . . I did it. I demonstrated. I wasn't afraid to let students see how to do it the way I did it, and I found that worked well.

Let's continue about our relationship. What do you recall about our first meeting?

Well, first of all, I started feeling alone over there. You know, like where are the other people like myself? There were fine people, but no one *doing*, so to speak. So you were another person like myself, because people would say, "He's teaching writing and really pursuing a hot career." And again, this is one of the things that comes up, "You've got to meet him, you've got to meet him." That went on for six months, but for some reason I didn't take the energy to . . . I did ask a few people, "What does he look like?" I got the yearbook out and . . .

I don't think I was even in the yearbook.

Well, it was somewhere. I saw you somewhere.

Our first meeting . . . you were coming down the hall, and I said, "Norb Blei." And you said, "Yeah." You had your pipe and you had just lit it, and you were heading out to the parking lot and going to the Log Cabin, I think. I had a camera around my neck. I think I was right in the middle of a photography class. I took a picture of you, I guess. Then I had it processed and gave it to you.

I remember we would go out after class on Fridays and have a drink somewhere . . . that joint on Ogden Avenue. It began then. You were probably one of the few people in my life where this happened. Anyway, this friendship began to develop where each of us began influencing the other. In that period of the 60's we had the whole Marshall McLuhan thing: the world as a global village, the interest in the visual over the linear. That we could talk about it and eventually do it in our own way. Happenings. This was the time I wrote *The Watercolored Word.* I remember you doing a painting and saying: "Here, write something on it." Where the hell are those paintings? You had a tremendous effect on me at that point because, as you know, deep down I'd really like to be able to be a good painter, but I know I'm not and never will be. But you would not stifle that.

That's exactly what happened to me.

I've always been in awe of the artist.

And I've been in awe of the writer, ironically.

And, I in turn would force books on you. "You gotta read this or you should . . . ".You know we talked about Miller, Henry Miller and . . . .

Yeah. You had me read about 10 books. That was another thing. Your knowledge of literature, all through these years. You know like two years ago when I got mono, you just kept shoveling me a book every three or four days. It was almost like you were timing it: "Well, he's through with that one." You've done that at various times and I really appreciated that. You have a *reason* for sending a book—and so in a way, it's caused me to approach that, perhaps, even try to find out why.

How far would we have advance, say the three of us, in the realm of friendship at the point where first Ralph left teaching and then . . . I don't remember if I left before you or you left before me? But anyway, the thing that we had began to break up by the late 60's. What was this friendship based upon at that period?

Well, when I left . . . no, you hadn't gone to Door yet. I noticed my ties to you were stronger than with Ralph.

From my standpoint, the ties between you and me were always stronger. Some of it may have been because Ralph had a kind of authority over me, as my department head . . . the role he had to assume. That's one level. Also, he was never one I could really relate to on the level of what I was all about as a writer. So I always felt much closer to you than I did to him, and that's been a bit of a problem. Not as much anymore, yet it may always exist to a certain degree. I can relate to your feelings.

I find that I'm more at ease with Ralph than I am with you. I find that I can bleed my soul with Ralph, and I have never felt that with you. I felt I could cry in front of

180

Ralph. And he exhibits that . . . you know, he's a really warm person. You are too, but I don't feel you'd open up like that and let a person do that.

Perhaps . . . in writing you're always observing as well as experiencing and I think the artist is doing that as well. There is always a part of me that is kind of holding back, and where I'm putting it out is on paper. And so, you see, my resolution to all that is "Take a look at that book . . . take a look at that story, that poem, that painting . . . and you'll see it there." So I have this fear of pouring it out up front because by doing so I might kill it and won't be able to utilize it in the best way for me—in words for other people to see. I think the thing I feared about Ralph was judgment. A fear of not living up to his standards. I saw that in the way he taught, the way I was expected to teach . . . .

Ralph must have been a really powerful person.

He exhibited that as well. I have always had problems with authority, and he was an authority figure to me in a sense.

I didn't experience that with him.

All right Ross, . . . let's talk about that period of time after teaching at L.T. You did a considerable amount of traveling. You lived in California, you took a Master's degree, you were doing a lot of painting and some jewelry. I had moved to Door County, and we kept in touch a great deal through letters. Then came Europe. You want to talk about the Europe thing at all? This is a very interesting time in regard to this friendship. We were all separated—I was North, Ralph was still living in Western Springs, and you were in Europe. You and I had both kind of lived the fantasy of being there at the same time, though I had already been there once in the early 60's. But, you know . . . to write, to paint, to get the hell out of this country and do the European thing in the way of Henry Miller. You got there—I didn't this time—and you ran into problems in Spain. That was pretty much your last, heavy, intensive period of painting. In 1970?

1969, 1970.

And . . . things got out of control. I don't know how else to put it. Can you recall that period of time when suddenly your life as a painter came to an end? I've always been afraid to go into all of this with you. The life of the artist was such an important . . . call it a fantasy . . . in both our lives. And I know I was experiencing both envy and despair because you had gotten over there finally, and I was hoping to meet you there, and things weren't . . . I remember getting cards from you and from Arlene, getting little drawings on postcards, things that just ate my heart out. As usual, I came up against all kinds of goddam problems, real or unreal, and I just couldn't make the break and get over there. And things began to fall apart for you. I don't know all the details. I suspect some of them. Did you see the artist's life as more than you could handle at that point? Too much involvement with people? Too much involvement with yourself? Which is the thing I kind of thrive on, but I have to admit, too, that I live at times vicariously you know through your art, your work, your life. And when you, in a sense, abandoned that . . . ah, you'll never really know how that devastated me. To the point where I wasn't sure I could handle my own work, my own life. And I think this relationship we talk about, whether it's brotherly or spiritual or what . . . something happened. Almost a transference, one becoming the other. And I was very much aware of the feeling that—goddam, if that happened to him there, him the *artist,* what the hell's going to happen to me there? If he can't . . . if he saw through it all, and there was nothing there, could not make his life whole, it was going to do me in. And so you came back under the worst possible circumstances, a broken person, a broken spirit in a sense, and to this

181

day I feel that whatever you were undergoing in the way of rehabilitation and getting yourself back in one piece, *I* was feeling equally. Even such a severe state of depression that I could never think of visiting you because I was afraid I wouldn't get out of there myself. I remember calling you, and you being a bit spaced out, and god, that spaced me out! I couldn't even pick up the phone again after that, I knew your voice would be so strange, and your talk so bizarre . . . I just, just couldn't handle it. So I used Arlene. Arlene was the ballast for me. I could talk to her and she was always very positive.

You might have been getting the wrong picture, you know, by not dealing with me at that particular time.

I've always felt a bit of a shit that I wasn't able to do that. By the same token, I always felt good about Ralph, grateful that he was able to be there; I think he's a center in many ways. I think both of us lean upon him at times. Maybe me more than you at times because I'm closer to him.

See, I couldn't lean on you at all that time. And I did on him.

I could use, as an excuse . . . and it's not a very good one, you know, his closer proximity to you. He lived just minutes away from you.

But I was angry at you.

I know you were . . . afterwards, more so than . . . .

I remember saying, when . . . where the hell are you? When the hell you gonna come by and say hello?

Could you say anything at all about your feelings on the role of the artist at that time? Did you feel you had to abandon it? Was it too much? That it wasn't a role so much as a burden?

No. Not a burden. Maybe I tried to approach painting the way you approached writing, which could have been a mistake. It buried me. And perhaps the end result of the painting is different than the end result of a book or a short story. This is why one turns the paintings to the wall, you know. Maybe the stark realism of the painting is different than typing it out. You said a little while ago that you go to the typewriter and get this out, and that goes out with the words.

But you did that in painting.

Yeah, I did it in painting and ah . . . you know . . . Christ! It came back to me!

Could you define what it was you were going at in paints?

My passions . . . for people, women, children, Spain.

Why should passion reverse itself that way and be a negative force, rather than something that's joyous and releasing?

I don't know whether it necessarily burst itself, but my work became so personal, ah . . . it's just like Jerry (West). He won't even show anyone the work from that period of time he went to Denver. It's the same thing, but in a different way. It was that type of work that was a retching of your soul, as opposed to, ah . . . still life. I put it all out there on canvas and what happened was it started spiralling on me. And I think just living in Spain was very depressing.

Depressing . . . whereas an artist would think, "Hey, Spain! The sun! The sea!"

Yeah. You hear this frequently. You know I'm not a flag-waver, but boy, I would never leave this country for a year and live somewhere . . . and think *that's* what I'm going to do with my life. But see, my reason then for going there was maybe to spend 5, 6 years in Europe. And I often wonder now how people go over there that many years.

There are people doing it right now. Do you think it was a very personal, or a deeply rooted thing that made the work turn like that?

Well, it's probably a combination of a lot of things. It was a depressing country, a depressing area . . . beautiful, though. The contrast is incredible . . . the Mediterranean and the depression.

Look at all the work that came out of those situations, though, from Picasso, Van Gogh . . . .

Right. Yeah. Maybe that's some of the ingredients.

Or take Grosz in Germany . . . the art of decadence. Talk about depression!

Right. And my work at that time was very similar to some of the German expressionists. Screaming . . . a lot of screaming stuff, people, other people retching. You asked about the ingredients. The other thing is, I think I was afraid my parents were going to die, and I wouldn't see them again. I had a lot of unresolved things with them. You know, they were up in years at that period of time. Ironically, they lived on into their 80's and I did solve those things. But then . . . I kept thinking . . . I did a lot of things, you know, unresolved death things. There was a lot of death in my work.

Also a lot of the very things you were experiencing. And I remember your talking to me later about the painter you met there, Eddy, who was handling a lot of this

183

stuff, and was handling it successfully—reality and unreality. The thin red line you talk about crossing.

Right . . . I did a lot of thin red line painting.

Prior to the jaunt to Europe, you had lived in New Mexico for a while, and I had come to visit you there. This was still a very up period, and you were working on your Master's degree with Harry Leippe at Highlands University. I remember being here at this same time of year, visiting you, I don't know, a couple of weeks or so, leaving Chicago in the midst of a miserable winter and coming out here and thinking, "Jesus Christ, what a life! What a beautiful place this is!"

This was also when you built that fantastic piece of environmental art work, the Merry-Go-Round, with its boxed figures, the faces of your friends as riders—yours truly included—and you, yourself as the man who makes the merry-go-round go, the ringmaster. The circus, the carnival was a theme, a way of living life with a certain excitement that we had talked about back in LaGrange. When you went ahead and designed, built, painted, orchestrated your own merry-go-round, peopling it with yourself and ideas of some of us.

When I look back, the Merry-Go-Round Man or Ringmaster was an extension of myself. Someone I knew about, that was within me, but not ready to be me. I no longer put an extension of myself in my work—nothing is hidden. I deal directly with the materials. The Merry-Go-Round Man helped to make a social comment. Now I would rather not make a social comment, and I have my work be as direct as possible with a strong theme and direction. The Merry-Go-Round Man also represented a shared creative growth with a good friend, Marvin Neibuhr, a silent thank you to him for being who he is. I do not understand his road today, but I often think of our shared creative moments. Today I can drive by a carnival and have no desire to stop. I think "Merry-Go-Rounds" would be a good name for a new Earcuff design.

New Mexico was depressing in a sense too. Las Vegas was that way, austere, but there were always great people around. Art being done. It was fascinating.

I began hearing that story of the painter, Virginia Tibbetts, and you—you were the reason for my coming out here and writing one of the finest stories I ever wrote. But it was some of the same things you were talking about in Spain. You were close to that. You were doing jewelry at the time, very primitive stuff. Haunted. Death images. There was a presence of life about it as well, but I was thinking, during that same period you were over there in Europe, that story had been written and published, and I hadn't seen you and I was going through strange times. After writing that story, and publishing it, I couldn't read it. I couldn't look at it. For the very same reason we are talking about—you know, that thin line of madness and reality and, ah . . . the writer becomes that character and ah, Jesus, I felt such an association with that painter! Then transferring that to what you were undergoing, you know. That story scared the hell out of me. It still scares me.

Yeah.

Again, this is a kind of spiritual bond we have, that we have experienced a lot of these same things. We handled them in some ways in different mediums, but we were undergoing this. There you were in Spain, painting very Jungian, psychologically deep things, influenced at this point by this painter Eddy. Eddy was, in the terminology of the day, "Go for it." You risk everything. You go into that darkness and you come out of it. My feeling was that you went into it and you didn't come out of it. I was handling this in prose, but you were the *reality* of it. And here was an artist who was swallowed by it, you know? And I wasn't getting the reading on it. Why? I wasn't prepared to understand . . . why that was happening, you see, and completely amazed that that could happen. I thought that the artist always stayed outside of it. I mean he lived it, but he got back out to put it together. And then felt both a sense of expansion and joy that it was done and praised perhaps from other people. And then on to the next things. But I found that Jesus, there's Ross, I mean, you know, . . . climbed into a fucking painting and then you stayed in there! I think a writer does this every time he does a story, depending upon the degree of seriousness of involvement. Sometimes it's a very short stay, a short journey. But always a depression after the completion of something like that, because you've lived that other life. Then you've got to come out and find, get another one to live, you know. And, you're constantly doing that.

Right.

You climbed in, stayed in, and in a sense you were shipped home, and you were still in that painting.

That's a good way to put it: I came home a painting and took a couple of years to get out. And literally walked out of them . . . walked on them *physically* on the floor, and walked out of them . . . one particular day in fact, ironically using *the* paintings that came back from Europe four months later, literally using them as stepping stones back out.

I recall you not even being able to look at them. They were crated up back there in LaGrange in the basement and you were almost saying, "Keep those fucking things away from me. I don't want to see them!"

Right.

I had seen one of your notebooks prior to that. I think those notebooks ought to be published someday. They were incredible.

Yeah, they were incredible sketches. I looked at them a while back . . . when my mother passed away. They were at her house, and then they came out here.

You felt you could handle it at that point?

Oh yeah. I look at them sometimes. Incredible.

Almost like somebody else did them?

Yeah, right.

I remember sitting in a bar with Arlene one night, coming into Chicago to talk with her, and you were going to be back soon. She showed me one of the books and all I could think was: Jesus, the amount of art between these black covers!

Yeah, there were about twelve of them. Sketchbooks is what they were. Maybe just four or five paintings would come out of each sketchbook, the most powerful images, feelings. I put *them* into my paintings.

When we talked about that time and what happened . . . was it a loss of innocence or what? This was not all romance then, the south of Spain, the sea, beautiful women, fishermen drinking in the bodegas, or whatever. I remember fantastic letters: "God, I'm sitting here eating fresh shrimp, drinking wine, painting on into the night . . . ." Everything that everyone has ever imagined about an artist's life, you were living. Whether that's reality or not, I'm not sure. When did it cease to exist for you? And why?

It might have been a period when I was forcing it. I wasn't ready for that. Maybe that's what I should have done right after college, instead of going to teach at L.T.

You had a wife and a young child with you.

Right. Maybe there was that pressure. Maybe one needs to do that alone. Really alone. Maybe that's exactly what I made myself over there, alone. Even though I was with Arlene and Laura, I made myself alone every day.

But the artist does that though. You withdraw always . . . .

Really alone, though I mean.

Yeah . . . that's why artists have such a fucked up track record, insecure husbands and that, you know.

Yeah. All those experiences over there, that's a whole other book. There were several times when I got asked to go up to northern Europe, just me, or Yugoslavia, or Germany you know, and maybe I didn't want to be married, I wanted to be alone.

So you were trying to hack that as well?

Right. And in a way, it was really *my* adventure; and Arlene and Laura were along on it.

But art is always a singular adventure. That's the problem with trying to live an ordinary and accepted life. And I think both you and I have tried very hard to do that and at the same time not die. Keep the art and keep the family. It's very difficult . . . more difficult than the people in that family will ever know.

Yeah. I mean I not only lost a family in that situation, I damn near lost myself. Many artists do.

In a way it was death. Kind of a period in my life where one can literally draw a line and say, "There was up to this, and then this, and then I died here." When you go so far down in the bottom of the well that you see yourself just five feet under the water, you're all the way down and you really die then. And you go through some heavy–duty things.

How do you look upon my reaction and perhaps some other people's reaction that . . . well, what died in you was a terrible thing to happen?

Yeah, right. And I've been safe ever since.

That brings us back to the realm of friendship. The problem that to me is what I've always had with you ever since then. I think Ralph has it to a certain degree too. Wanting, certainly wanting no harm to befall you and certainly wanting no death, but wanting the work that was there and that you were capable of doing and the success and whatever. Because we believed in you.

Yeah, your voices run loud. You moreso than Ralph. Ah, I enjoy giving to Ralph, I feel real good about him having my artwork and you, but your voice has run louder than anyone else's. Most people don't even know. I mean most people I've met in the last 10 years, they don't even know that I paint.

I know, and that pisses me off.

I am painting right now again, but I call myself a Sunday painter.

From a serious artist whose whole life was once in the work . . . .

And I'm still drawing. But it's very safe. I'm not doing it the way I was.

Does that ever bother you at all? That you're not doing it the way you were? It bothers me, for example, to be here in the Southwest, in the center of some of the greatest art being done in this country, and knowing that here I'm sitting with Ross LewAllen, one of the best jewelers in Santa Fe . . . but one of the best artists, and these people will *never* know that!

I guess I'm chicken.

You know, whether it's Fritz Scholder or whoever, you can paint and out-paint any one of these guys! I'm saying that from the perspective of, not a great art critic, but just very intuitively. I see all this other stuff around, you know, and compared to you! Or back in Chicago suddenly coming across some of your early paintings: goddam they look good! Just before coming here, I was over at Howard Orr's, and he's in the basement reframing a great watercolor of yours. I don't even have to look at the name, I know it's yours. And I think, Jesus Christ, where did you get this, Howard?

When my mother moved out here, she had a lot of my old paintings, and we hung them on the walls at her place. People would go over there, and JoAnn's got one, and so-and-so.

Does it ever bother you? Do you sometimes think: Shit, who was this T. C. Cannon? Or who is this Fritz Scholder?

Right. I do. Not a lot, but I do. But I'm chicken.

You don't want to go in that deep again?

Who knows? I might sometime.

I know. I have that feeling too. This is what we were talking about earlier this morning back at the house. I had a feeling that you were kind of at a crossroad again.

See, in that drawing I sent you from out at Spanovich's . . . .

You mean up in Chimayo, when we went to the potter's place, Chris's, up there in the mountains, the mesa . . . .

Yeah, and you just zapped on that thing like crazy. Okay . . . there is something where I let go a little bit. So, see, I let go. I did that drawing, and right away you zapped out on it, and it's *true* . . . that is probably the closest thing to something I was doing 15 years ago that I've done in the last four years.

Maybe it's just a process of doing this very slowly. Maybe one a year, or one every couple of years. Who knows?

You see there's only you and a couple of other people in this world, that know this about me. So I would imagine if I ever did get back it would be at, or could be at your tutelage or whatever word you might want. You know what I'm talking about?

On the theme of the death, or the loss of innocence that runs through all our lives, especially the life of the artist—did you just feel that was a part of life that was gone then? It wasn't really that intriguing?

Oh, there's no question about it. It was intriguing. Obviously the highs of painting are so high, that anyone in this world would want to live it. And when one gets so high on painting, there's only one place to go eventually, and that's down. When you're that high, as I was, it's sometimes like someone moving your hand or moving the pen or the brush. Or you step into your paintings and turn around and look at yourself and say, "hello there." That is being very high. And, I'm not talking about drugs or anything else. This is just high on painting. The result is obvious. You're not moving through life. You're not moving, vascillating between the tropic of this and the tropic of that. You're in the poles. You're up in the arctic and the antarctic, and you go down . . . that's a good way to put it.

The interesting thing is, how . . .

How did I get up there?

No, no I think it's obvious how you got up there, Ross. You had the talent to do it. you had the experiences to relate. I guess my question is how do you get back up there? How do you die and live again?

As I have done, is one way. Coming back and hanging around the middle a lot. Hanging around the equator. And that's what I've been doing for the last 12 years.

You don't deny what the art up in the high echelon is?

No, not at all.

There's a lot of romance involved, and innocence, right?

Right. And obviously I think a lot of danger and a lot of great art comes from that area. There's also great art that comes from the middle too. Many people there, and this was just where I chose to live with my art work. In really a dangerous area, there's only one place to go; you can't stay there.

How do others handle that in your estimation or in your experience?

I'm sure there's been every approach, from artists that have committed suicide, gone over the line, to ones that have come back. Ones that have quit, as I have done. Just experience the depth, perhaps, of the work, and not the self. You know, it's still

around here. So, one like myself who's come back around the equator for the last 12 years, sneaks up there, you know, sneaks up a little bit here and there. Because you've been there, and once you've been there and experienced that, one does want to experience it again. But, one does not want to experience the *fall* again.

Something of the element of fear?

Not necessarily fear. Caution. One in my shoes operates under *risk*. Perhaps when you get my age, taking risk of going back there and operating . . . you see, I know exactly how to do it—I go spend $300, $400, $500 dollars on paints, a plane ticket to Borneo, or wherever you want to go, Africa, whatever, and in about a year, start painting. You don't even have to go there. You can do it here . . . start painting.

But you won't risk that?

Right now, no.

Okay . . . that period of time when you were out of therapy, back in LaGrange, on the mend, doing a little teaching, beginning with the jewelry . . . that was an interesting period for me too. I would be coming down from Door County to teach. I actually lived with you and Arlene and Laura at the time. I spent the best part of a winter there that first time, teaching at the College of Dupage, writing for the Chicago newspapers and magazines. It was always exciting to be around you, Arlene . . . that whole phenomemon of old friends, new friends, former students, friends of friends just passing through. You had made a trip with Arlene to Mexico at one point and came back with photographs and tales of the Yaqui Indian tribe. I began to refer to your house as the Yaqui village because the spirit of it seemed to be just that tempo, so alive. The doors were swinging constantly. People in and out, in and out, stopping by for the night to spend hours talking or listening to each other's adventures. This whole place was an education in itself. You organized parties and art shows—right in the house. You had a jewelry studio in the dining room. People were coming in off the street to watch you work, to buy your jewelry. It was crazy. It was a community house, almost a commune. Mecca. You know, all the overtones of the 60's were evident. I never saw any drugs done there . . . you were beyond that.

The communal thing, though. And you were the power of that, the source, the very crux. Ralph was part of the periphery, and he and I were kind of like two anchors for you. We represented a little bit of the past, which many of your students didn't realize at all. So we had, in a sense, this family, and it just blossomed. What did you feel about all that? Arlene was always there. She'd come home from teaching school and start cooking—and anyone and everyone was fed—and there were times when we hardly went to bed at all, and just sat around the kitchen table till 2, 3 in the morning, and Arlene would be working on her own paintings at that time. Maybe Howard Orr would step in, and it would get crazy. Or Judy Cook, Gordon, Gary, Bob Kapoun. Crazy, but very stimulating.

Right. In fact, it was so stimulating, when we went to New Mexico, people were saying, "What are we going to do?" Entire relationships broke up because of this thing you described. You and Ralph, now, survived that, and that was an interesting time dealing with you and Ralph. You did represent that past. You understood me . . .

A big part of this three-way friendship for want of a better term, is charisma. People are instantly attracted to you. That power again. Consequently, you will never be without friends, whether the friendship is based upon the length of the one we share or not. Or whether it's the same thing.

I really doubt that I will ever experience this three-way thing you're talking about again in my life.

Door County—you visited me there in the past, my landscape, so to speak. What are your impressions?

I understand you in your landscape. Why you stay there, I don't understand. But I understand clearly what you are doing, how you relate to it, what it means for you to walk down the road. I know what the road means to you. I know what Charley Root means to you. I know what Darlene means to you. I know what all those people mean to you. At times I've walked up your road. You've learned from your road. That's your school.

What don't you understand?

I don't understand how you can stay there. Because, you see, I understand *why* you're there. I understand that you can write there, that you feel the same way in your coop as I feel upstairs in my studio, my shop on Washington. That's why I'll never leave there. It happens to be on Washington. That's the magic place for me. That's where I invented the EarCuff. That's where all this good jewelry has come out of for the past 8 or 9 years. That's *my* place. It happens to be upstairs in the corner of the plaza in Sante Fe. Your coop is in the North Woods.

But you still don't understand why I'm there, and why you're where you're at . . . .

I understand that, but now you're talking of maybe coming out here, finishing there and moving on. And who am I to say when one is finished with a place? I go through periods with you where I think you should do things much more than other times. You felt that through the mail, I'm sure. You know: Get the hell out of there. And then again, I just leave you alone at other times.

Why do *you* tell me to get the hell out of there? Nobody else does. Why doesn't Ralph tell me to get the hell out of there?

Because I probably am more in touch with you in a creative way. I'm touch with you with your pen going and what's going on. So, I feel that you might be missing something. Like I see no one acting for you in the role of a provider. So when I call you and say, "I've got a house for you for three months!" That's all I can do for you. Maybe you'll come. Maybe you'll come and do whatever the hell you want to do. Or

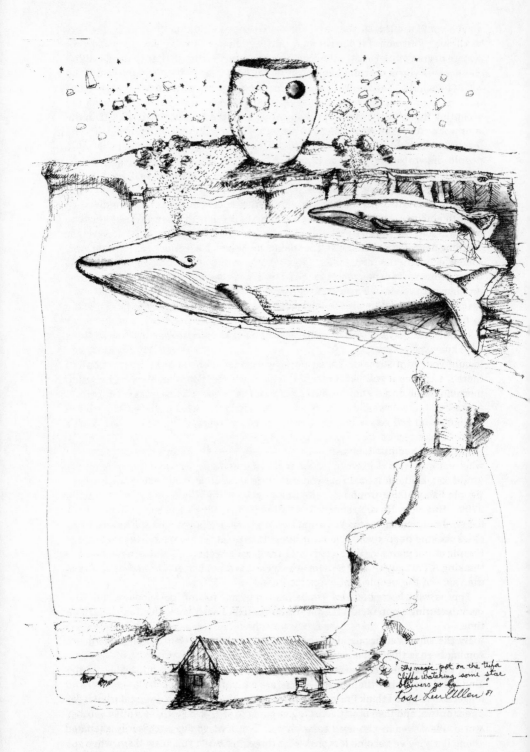

"The magic pot on the tufa
cliffs watching some star
blowers go by"
Ross Lewallen 81

maybe you'll see this in the next four or five years.

All right, I'm gonna hit you with a couple of whamos now. We have all achieved a certain degree of success—not necessarily monetarily, though. But I seem to have a conflict with you concerning such success. My conflict with Ralph is why he puts up with a fucking job like that which is driving him crazy. My conflict with you also goes back to Spain, your not going the route of the painter, not following the dream, not accepting the danger as part of the risk. I do admire you as a jeweler, I do respect your work. But at the same time I see the loss, the terrible loss of Ross LewAllen as a teacher, *that* kind of creativity, *that* kind of spontaneity, *that* kind of charisma, people drawn to you, people feeding off you and the very *necessity* for that to continue because if we are not here for our own development, and that reaching out to others as well, I don't know what the fuck we're doing here! I see you channeling this now, your success, for more money, greater success, more esteem—which is all right to a degree—but denying or refusing to look back on some of those qualities which, in the long run, are probably more important. You have very little respect for teaching anymore, for example. I hated to see Arlene leave teaching, and you were somewhat instrumental in telling her to get out of it, do these other things, don't let those people—students, teachers, parents—feed off you all the time. So, I have this problem with you now. I'm more and more conscious in my own life, my own success, that I am not doing as much for others as I have in the past. I'm going to have to come to terms with that before long.Maybe quit writing for a few years, and maybe go teach for peanuts somewhere where I could be of some help. Maybe a reservation. Who knows? Now I think our friendship can continue in spite of all this, however you handle your own success. Your company hasn't made you a millionaire yet, but there's a chance it will before long. But then what? As we were talking the other morning, what do you do now? I've done it. I've met the challenge. And now I'm fucking bored with my life.

Right. And I'm gonna be glad you're gonna be around.

So I'm concerned with your soul in a sense . . .

Well you have just touched on the chemistry of our relationship. I need to hear what you just said. I need to have people that know all this about me and aren't afraid to talk about it. It does seem that the more "successful" one gets, the fewer people like you are around. Or the harder it is to find them.

2700   But, you, Ross, are instigating that very thing that we were talking about today about management. You want people in management who will get rid of all these fucking people who are not producing in a sense. I can't believe that this is coming out of your mouth. You know? I can't believe that you really think that. I'm thinking, "This guy's lost. He's getting deeper and deeper in this, and he can't see the value of the people that supported him."

This is why I wrestled for probably 1½ years making decisions, about that manufacturing company. At least a year and a half. I wrestled with it for a long, long time.

By the same token, one of the reasons I almost fear making a major move and coming here is that, what's going to happen to me in our relationship is the same thing that's happened to other people who came here. I don't want to alienate the kind of relationship with Kapoun—there are a number of people here—and that no longer exists. And I think I'm gonna come here and we're going to be great friends for a year or two, and then pretty soon you're going to say, "Oh Norb, he's off in another world. He's over in Tesuque somewhere." Not that you've necessarily alienated them, but they've become less that what they were when you knew them, when you were in more soul-searching times. But I come here, Ralph comes here and ah, Ralph has mentioned this any number of times: "What the hell's happened to Jerry? How come Ross doesn't talk to Jerry? What the hell has happened to Kapoun?" and so on down the line. It can't be all their fault, you know.

What you're basically saying is that I'm hard on a friendship.

Yes.

Yeah, I hear ya.

Frankly, I think damn near only Ralph and I have survived that kind of judgment.

Right. I don't know how to respond to that.

Can you understand now, one of my hesitancies about coming here to live? In that I value our friendship so much that I don't want to come here and do what Howard Orr did—in your eyes. And that was to fail. And, if indeed he did fail, he failed you in a sense. He didn't live up to your expectations. And I might come here and spend the rest of my life writing about Door County, or Chicago, and that may seem a real failure to you. "Why the hell isn't he writing a great, bestselling novel about Santa Fe?" or something. "What the hell, he's living here now all these years and he's still writing about Door. Or still writing about his old neighborhood. Or he's teaching Indian kids in a goddam pueblo and starving to death."

But earlier I said I'm not pushing my own thing on people like I used to. And that's the truth.

I think that may be true of all three of us. And I think that may be a very important point to reach—that we don't do that.

Right.

What about Arlene, your wife—what kind of role has she played in all this? What's your view of why so many of your own friends are especially fond of her? She's kind of a center force in many ways. She's played an important role in Ralph's life, and certainly mine, and the lives of hundreds of others as well.

I think, again, I have to go back to that balance. She has the ability, first of all, to really affect people. She also has a fairly clear nature, and people gather around her, I think, to experience what she thinks—almost to the extent of asking her what they should do. I do the same thing too. And I've found, during low periods—say with my business, when maybe things weren't going right—I was really happy that she wasn't involved in it, because she had a good picture from both the center and the periphery. I've always kind of eliminated her from the everyday grind of my life, and used her in this way. And I think other people see that in her. She seens to have time for other people.

And knows how to utilize that time better than some of us maybe?

Yeah. She seems to be able to give 15, 20 people a day, each a little time, you know. Sometimes, I think, at the expense of her own . . . her own job, her own painting, whatever.

How do you think other women look upon this? She's now perhaps a little more of a woman's woman, but she's always been a man's woman. Does that bother you? Do you ever feel any jealously over this? There's an attractiveness, a sexiness about her.

No, not really. I've been angered more by the time that she devotes to these people as opposed to actually being jealous on account of these people. I seem to have always wanted her to get on with some of her own things, you know, her own reading, her own painting, And these things really cut into that, these people. But it is true, she is a man's woman. And they do flock around her. And still, as you say now she's becoming more so a woman's . . .

Well, at least's she's exploring it now.

And that's exciting. I'm almost waiting to meet who she wants to bring around. It's interesting to meet these people and figure out why she has chosen them, what type of person she becomes friends with, as opposed to being friends with a friend of mine's wife, you know. It's hard to tell with her. She'll just be a friend with someone because they are someone's wife, or something like that.

It couldn't be really very deep. I think Arlene will go through life with very, very, very few friends, even though she's friendly to everyone. She's already doing that.

But she will have affected a lot of people?

Yeah, yeah.

Any thoughts about marriage at this point?

It certainly goes through high and low periods. Seeing that movie *On Golden Pond*, or experiencing my parents through a marriage that lasted 58 years has certainly had its effect on me. Sometimes you wonder why you're married.

How important is the woman in your art? In your early work, you painted a lot of women . . .

It's always been important. Painting them was one importance. Now, almost exclusively what I create or make is for women. I enjoy creating things for women. This is a rewarding experience.

Do you find your jewelry designs more in harmony with women?

No. I'm not *designing* for women. I'm doing what I want to do . . . like my whole thing now with the whale, for example. Here I'm using almost a contradictory image, but women *love* it. And here I'm dealing with other, maybe the primitive, the primeval, mammal.

See, that's the thing I always saw in your work—the primitive—that's the thing that excites me. The early jewelry you did was very primitive. That's the kind of thing you suppressed after Spain and has only slowly now worked your way toward that again. I love the kind of thing you were showing me the other day now, this new jewelry of yours based on the Orca, the whale . . . tying ivory and stone to it, the red thread, the darker contrast you've been able to work in the silver, the cut, the incredible design. Jewelry you haven't shown anyone yet. I look at it, you know, . . . shit, it's museum work!

193

See, the connection between that work and the woman is that I'm using the Orca as a departure point for my primitive shapes, primitive feelings, primitive spirits, and then seeing what happened to women when they put this jewelry on, and how it excites them. Those areas of the woman, those primitive areas of the woman—it's amazing.

I see a triangle in animal-woman-metal. The photo of the woman and the horse (Anne "Fred" Jackson and Gypsy) is a first. It seems to capture the essence of what I'm doing. The animal as subject, departure, spirit motion, primitive, primal, giver, toucher. Woman as receiver, wearer, spirit, toucher. Metal as image, malleable, time, object, technique, surface, "my way," language, receiver, toucher. All three—animal, women, metal—are at the tips of my tools when I'm working. When they are in equal balance, a very special thing happens. The woman and the horse photo comes closer to this balance than any other photo of my work. I see myself in the center of this triangle as giver or maker-giver.

Let's look ahead. What do you see for Ralph down the road?

That's a good question. I don't know what to say. I keep kidding Ralph about trout fishing, but I'd like to go trout fishing with Ralph for about six months. He'd probably jump out of his skin after about two months, but that's all right. He would be a great person to do that with. "Ralph, we're going up to Utah, Montana, Colorado, take a few thousand and we're going to go trout fishing. I'm going to paint and draw." Of course, that would be unfair. He wouldn't have his typewriter. So if I jumped out of my skin . . . but he would be a great person to get away from what he's doing, you know, a travel mate. That would be exciting.

Do you think he's got the psychological makeup to do something like that?

Like I said, he'd probably in two months jump out of his skin. If he could live through it . . . but if he could live through Laidlaw without jumping out of his skin, he could do this.

What do you see his life like back there?

Very regulated. Very boring. Maybe at one time it wasn't, you know, in his particular job, but I think he's not real happy. He's happy with Jo Ann, he's happy with his kids, but I don't think he's being reinforced much for Ralph's tremendous skills.

I agree.

And that could be deadly. You, you get good reinforcement. I get it. Where does Ralph get it? And I think that's one of the areas of real difference among you and me and Ralph.

I asked where you thought Ralph was headed down the road. What do you see ahead for me?

I think you're going to become a well-known writer. You're on the road, see, you're on the road. You're laughing.

Yeah.

You have all the ingredients. The first, being talented and being able to, you know, your footsteps through life . . . unique, unique in the way you observe people. You say you have to pull back, and you do that well. You're interviewing me well. Okay, you've got all those ingredients. It's going to grow and grow and grow, because your writing is good. And it's just a matter of more and more people getting a hold of it.

That's why you and I are going to become even better friends, for instance. Because I'm a year ahead of you, and then you'll be a year ahead of me, and we'll be holding onto each other. Yeah, I see that. You and I are going to become much better friends, I mean than we already are, which is interesting to look forward to I think. Because you are going to get frightened.

I'm also at the point where I don't look forward to publishing a book again because of all the shit you have to go through before and after . . . the loss of time, the loss of . . .

But you see, you've got 20 years behind that drive to publish another book. So you will publish another book. And you're working on one right now.

But, I will retreat again. And this is the best part of working on the book, right now, and when I get back to the coop, the privacy to work it out . . .

Yeah, I would imagine.

What about the end of the road? Do you think much about death? You see it a lot in my work. It's been in your work too . . . it was in your work, your early New Mexico work. A lot of the images you used in both your paintings and sculpture, even your jewelry, were death images.

I'm not dealing with it in my work right now, with death. The end of the road. Not necessarily. Not like I did before.

Why has that changed? Why would one have done that earlier in life and not . . . well, with most artists, it haunts them all the while, and they make periodic visits to that domain.

Maybe I'll deal with that internally, as opposed to in my work.

What are your own deepest feelings, conflicts, fears? Death-related or otherwise? Or do these things exist for you anymore?

I don't feel that I'm running.

Do you find yourself, oh . . . risking it once in a while?

Yeah.

You did a little of it last night in the Porsche . . .

Coming home at over 100 miles an hour?

Yeah, coming home at 110 miles an hour.

Yeah, I don't know why I did that. I apologize for that.

It didn't bother me at all. I felt very comfortable.

Good car . . . and a good driver.

Do you find this particular landscape filled with a tradition of death images? Whether it's Spanish, or Indian, or . . .

Yeah, very.

That's one of the fascinations here for me. And one thing certainly I would deal with and have already dealt with in some work. It does fascinate me.

You can hardly drive down a road without a cross, you know, here on the left and two or three of them on a bad turn. Right down the road here are several.

I almost had a cross down the road in Door County before I got here.

Right, right . . . It wouldn't have been honored there or here.

Right. I think that is an interesting honor, or maybe that's the wrong word. I still go back to my parents. I think for some reason that when your parents are both deceased, they have taught you, in a way, how to die. I was not here when my mother died. Just think about that. Maybe she saved me that, who knows? I mean, I was only gone a week and she was doing fine. But, of course, one cannot live it, and can not die through anyone else.

In some ways there are parallels in our lives, our work, Ross. Yet I think writing is so different from what you do, in both the amount of time one has to devote to it and how it affects others. What do you think the writer's life is like? You're reading a novel right now. What do you think all goes into the making of that? Just from the standpoint of a visual person looking at this?

One big difference, of course, is that you just can't go and get hold of a piece of material, you know—silver, gold, stone—and then sit down with that and let that tell you what to do or help you do it. That's an obvious difference. I think that the process of the writer is a different discipline. It's not getting things out of your system, it's living with them for long periods of time. This novel here . . . I think this sustained period of time of living with those characters, and dying with them and loving with them . . .

You know, Ross, going back to that sense of privacy that you kind of miss, not being able to have done some work in the last couple of weeks . . . I miss it, deeply. It's a very hard thing to describe, though we've got room for privacy here, adequate space here and that, there are so many attractions, so many demands, so many things that I want to do, so many things you have to do with your own work, your business, and I get totally wrapped up in all that. We start out early in the morning, we get back late at night, we stay up even later talking, you, me, Arlene. This morning was the first time I awoke really early, and I like to do that, 4:30 in the morning, something like that. It was nice to have those hours. It was beautiful, in fact. God, to see the sky at that time, and that moon . . . and I walked out into it for a little bit, then came back in and began working to the point where the sun was up, and it felt so good to be here again. Tell me something. Do you remember the painting Arlene did of the three of us?

Yeah. Very well.

Who was in the center of that painting?

I was in the center . . . Is that right?

And where was Ralph?

He's on the left and you're on the right. Is that right? You must have looked at it.

Why do you think that's so?

Well, since Arlene painted it, that's obviously a good question for her. But I think I recall I'm lower than you two, if I got that right. I haven't seen the painting in a long time. Very interesting painting, though. I've always like it.

What if I told you that Ralph was in the center.

Okay. I'm wrong. I'm glad you told me. He is in the center, right? Is he lower than us?

No, he's higher than us.

Higher! Well maybe that's good to know. That I'm out of the center.

You're on the left. I'm on the right. And he's in the center.

What have you made of that?

I don't know. All I know is that I also thought you were in the center.

What did Ralph say? Of course, he's living with it. He knew.

Ralph is the one who told me: "No," he said, "I'm in the center." And I said, "That's very interesting."

Did he like being there? Did he comment on that?

He didn't say.

That's probably the way I see him in this relationship, in the center.

Well, we never thought of it at the time. But Arlene must have seen it, or thought about it way back there in LaGrange.

Yeah. She had a definite reason. Any painter who would do that; it would not be just by chance.

Psychologically, taking a reading on it?

Right.

Are you disappointed you're not in the center?

No, not at all. I'm disappointed I don't have the painting.

A Love Story
Arlene LewAllen

It is difficult for men, married or single, to sustain a deep and lasting friendship with another woman—especially the wife of a best friend. Though psychologists now contend that men do need women for friends, we tend to judge such relationships immediately, even vicariously, for their sexual overtones. Yet unless we get beyond this soap opera morality/mentality, we may never discover just what we might need to know about ourselves, the true values that only our other halves sometimes reveal.

As actress Ruth Gordon once said, trying to explain the public's continued acclaim for her movie, Harold and Maude: *"Everyone needs someone to tell it to." Arlene LewAllen, for me and for others, is that someone.*

She is long-haired, slim, with high cheekbones . . . almost Indian looking. I have never seen her look anything less than strikingly attractive whatever the scene, including the kitchen. Her honest enthusiasm for life, work, art, people, family complements her physical presence.

She is the wife of Ross LewAllen. She is an artist, the co-director of an art gallery, the mother of Laura LewAllen, and the favorite teacher of hundreds of kids in school systems as far flung as Illinois, California, and New Mexico. She is also the uncertified counselor to countless adults, a woman's companion, and the best ladyfriend any man could ever have.

The quality this woman brings to almost any relationship is that rarest of human qualities, empathy—which is another form of love. Whatever the nature of feelings inside of you, she becomes them, and the feelings are indeed mutual until some form of release or revelation is achieved. There is that moment in her intense listening, her eyes fastened to your face, her lips imitating yours (is it any wonder she paints gypsies among other subjects?) when she seems to slip into your skin, and a feeling of wholeness and clarity develops, bordering on the mystical. There are no more secrets. No mystery. Only understanding, joy, and love for those qualities, good or bad, which make us all human.

I have known her as long as I have known her husband, my close friend, Ross LewAllen. I came to love her as I witnessed, and at times was part of, their life unfolding in Chicago, LaGrange, Spain, and Santa Fe, New Mexico. And at one point, perhaps upon their return from Spain, when her strength seemed so astounding, I realized for the first time their uniqueness to each other, and yet the separate spirit within each.

Often those, like Arlene, blessed with the ability to listen to stories of others, tend to remain private about themselves. She is no exception. Everyone and almost everything else comes before Arlene. Yet she has never played the martyr. Long ago she seems to have accepted that that's the way things are. Still, she is neither the typical housewife nor a rabid feminist. And who, she might wonder, would really care to listen to her story?

I saw her first back in LaGrange, Illinois, pretty much a stranger, as she saw me. She had been married to Ross only three years and seemed totally occupied in raising their daughter, Laura, then only a year-and-a-half old, and occasional substitute teaching. She was not then the Arlene I know now. What I saw in her more than anything during that period in LaGrange when her husband and I taught together was a silence, a suffering unexpressed bordering on depression. And as for her memory of Ross then, as a young teacher:

"He loved it. He just absolutely loved it. He was with those kids and they were all looking up to him and it was great for his ego. He initiated a lot of things they never had at that school, and he felt real strong and real good about it. Then he used to teach those kids at the Berwyn Institute, you know, on Saturdays and Sundays. He even had summer classes there. I mean, he used to criticize *me* for giving too much! And he'd come home, eat dinner, and leave to have these extracurricular sessions. He was just gone all the time. That was a very hard period for me, because he really wanted to be out of the house. He didn't particularly like the apartment we lived in. I had thought well, maybe I'd clear out an area downstairs and he could have a painting studio in the basement, but he said, no, he'd rather have it elsewhere. Those two years were really hard, because he made it his habit to stay away from home because he was relishing all this glory with the kids. He really hadn't settled down to being married, I don't think. And I was a little envious, because I really enjoyed teaching and here I was with this baby and all, and so I sort of vicariously . . . well, I would grade his papers, set up his grade book, all the things he didn't care to do. I'd write recommendations for the kids. I was thriving on that. I wanted more. But I was hell-bent on keeping a good house and taking care of Laura.

"What I thought was that you had to have the supper ready. And many times he would bring people home from the Berwyn Institute because he knew that no matter what time it was, there would be something there to eat. You know, I'd keep the dinner on forever, and I'd always pick up the toys and Laura would always be clean. That was the whole thing I did. But my own frustration was really great. That's when I did those nude prints. One day I got so frustrated I put up shelving paper all over the house, and I inked my body while Laura was sleeping and I went around the whole house pressing my chest and behind and arms and legs upon all that paper, and when he came home, it really sort of freaked him out.

"I was just so frustrated and I wanted to set up some place to work, and there was Laura and the house—I was constantly cleaning—so I just inked my whole body and just ran around the house pushing myself against all this paper and when he came home, he just couldn't believe it. In fact, he took one of them to the bar where he'd always go after work, and they hung it up. He never told them who it was, or anything about it, but I think he was either so shocked or so impressed . . . I never knew."

I wondered if there was much husband and wife dialogue at that time, the kind of "rapping," "mind-fucking" give-and-take we all experienced later in the 60's after Spain, later at the new apartment in LaGrange.

"No, we never talked about this because he knew he had an easy street. He knew I was so plugged into doing the right thing that he played on that. He came and he went as he chose, and he knew that he could come home. He was very much into his friends. You, as his friend, had a big influence on him with Henry Miller. That's when he did some of those paintings with Miller things on them. He was just trying so hard to grow himself, that he really didn't have any time to worry about me. But he knew that I was like a trusted dog, a trusted person. I would be there, and he just knew that there wasn't too much that I complained about because you weren't supposed to do that. I can't say I was miserable, but I was not achieving for myself.

"One of my beliefs was that in order to keep a man happy at home, you remained in a place where he could bring his friends. I never wanted him to be meeting with his friends elsewhere and not use his home. Until I got to know the different personalities of the people, it was more of a thing where I wanted him to bring the people home, and I wanted him to enjoy the house, and I wanted to meet the people. Why was I doing this housewife bit anyway, if you and other people weren't going to come? Until you became a personality to me, you were just another one of the millions of people that appeared. One of the things that will come up again and again is how I feel about Ross. And it's like I got such a strong love there, such a strong line of me to him that it never crossed my mind that I wouldn't just want to please him. It's hard for me to imagine something that he could do that was bad enough that I could not love him. I mean, this sort of penetrates the whole thing.

"He's not easy to love, but the thing about him is that there is such a kernel of loving. If I didn't believe that . . . I mean, of course, I'd have to just believe that on faith. But I do believe that there is kernel of love in him for me."

And just how does this continue to thrive, a marriage between two creative persons, given the drives that I know Ross has, and given the drive of a creative woman?

"It's more difficult. When you're living with a person like this, you become aware that this person cannot be held down. He needs a lot of room. I used to ask questions about his work, and then I found out that if he talked too much about it, it was as if he had already done it. So I had to remember not to press on certain things. These things I learned early . . . a lot of maybe snide remarks or yelling on his part, 'No, I'm not going to tell you! I don't have to tell you!' You learn that there are certain things that you really don't know and you shouldn't know because they can kill something. Like I'd say, 'Why don't you take me to that little restaurant?' 'That's my secret spot,' he'd say. 'I don't want you to go there.' So you learn that it isn't like being married to Joe the truck driver. It's like these little things, these things are stirring up ideas in his head and once he takes you there, or if he tells you too much, then it limits you in certain things that you can do. Also, living with Ross you find out that he probably isn't very interested in your friends. Ross will go out and meet a lot of people, bring them home, and then I usually saw it as my job, or maybe I just took it on, to kind of cultivate those people and make them want to come back. They would come back for Ross too, but then you also have to learn where to draw the line with friends. If you become too friendly with one of his dear friends, then he does certain things he can't talk about with them anymore. This took me a long time to learn. I was thinking, oh how wonderful, I'm encouraging these people, and then on the other hand he's saying, 'Wow, why doesn't she just let up and let that be my friend.'

"We were married in August of 1962. It doesn't seem that long ago. My mother said she'd give it two years. It does seem a remarkable track record in the fact that Ross has always, you know, been enamored of women. I knew I was in trouble when his college professor told him that in order to draw well, and in order to draw nudes of women well, you had to fuck them. And, for a long time he believed it. And, so he had a long stream of his drawing women that he also had relationships with. I think I always had the suspicion, but I never really chose to believe it. I guess, the real proof would have been Spain, when I knew for sure. But, before that I sort of suspected it. And even then I really didn't ever call him on it. I was really alone a lot during those early years. It was almost a game as to how long he would stay out, night after night. And had I been a little smarter, or if I had known what I know now, I would have just busied myself. But I kept thinking I had to be on hand."

Some of the women Ross painted I met. Most of them, I never knew. One painting of his own and love, 'The Balloon Lady,' I vaguely recall meeting the model once.

"That Balloon Lady . . . I never liked that painting. I mean it was a good painting, but I just couldn't relate to it. There might have been a tad of resentment for you on my part because I felt you knew more about that painting than he ever told me, and that's why you had it."

Which brings up the whole question of this complicated friendship: Ross, Arlene and I. How can a woman, an artist's wife, live with the suspicion that there is possibly more shared between husband and friend, than husband and wife?

"That part is easy for me because I do that with my own friends. I say things to them, my sister or a good friend, that I would not want to share and tell. The only time I might take exception is if there were someone I knew pretty well, a friend of his who knew me, and they would purposely fix him up with a lady. I took it as sort of a slap. I mean if he had found the person himself, that's his business. But most of the time it was the other way around. Ross would find people for other people. But . . . no, I don't feel bad about him sharing things with someone that he wouldn't particularly share with me, because I do that. Everyone needs to do that."

After LaGrange came Las Vegas, New Mexico, where Ross worked on his Master's at Highlands University under Harry Leippe, and eventually California, where I recall Arlene felt . . .

"I was a little apprehensive. But immediately, of course, I plugged into work. I mean, I never really enjoyed the place as I remember. I could have been anywhere. Because as soon as I got somewhere I plugged right into the school system and then my days were taken up. I had to find a job through an agency. And then, there I was, driving up to school. Back in my role. Meanwhile, Ross immediately set out and met a lot of people, and again our house became, really, a halfway station. There were always people staying. And there was no communication because everything was done through other people. I mean, you would just listen to the conversation and you'd hear something you've been wanting to know, but there was not a lot of communication.

"There were so many more people to teach now, and Ross was really a people person, so as soon as he was there and got his footing, I mean locals used to say, 'You know more about the city than we do.' He made it a point to find out. So as far as what we we were talking about before, living with a creative person and all, it's really a wonderful experience. I mean I'm not innately . . . I'm curious,but I'm not curious enough to venture out, and so living with Ross there's always something new coming, a new discovery, a new place, a new person. I really like that. I really enjoyed the fact that he would find new places and then he would share them.

"But there were things about California, things happening there, people doing drugs . . . people I like very much, but they scared me. Because they did a little drugs, and they did this and that and I wasn't always ready to tune into that sort of thing, and I was the only one out of all those people that had to get up in the morning and go to work. I felt a little put upon that I was, again, always with the homework at night and always coming home and cleaning and keeping the things going and then on the other hand he'd tell me how fabulous and wonderful so-and-so was. I had a lot of trouble with myself trying to decide, should I go for it and be wild and, you know, do this thing or that—whatever was happening at that time—or did I have to keep maintaining what was? You see I felt this, what most women feel, that I had always kept the house going. We were living on me in Las Vegas, we were living on me in California. I had the provider's role, which I never brought up, because I knew that would be a very cutting thing to Ross. But he was aware of it. That was why he felt so, I suppose obligated in a way. But then when he sold, of course, he always had money . . . so he always had money in a way. He didn't have to ask me for money or anything.

"But you see, it satisfied this need in me to please him. It might be easy to please him, but you never know that you're pleasing him. I mean, he never gives you enough, so that you're always working towards what is going to please. And, before we were married, he'd say, 'Now someday you're going to be a real woman.' So I was constantly waiting for him to say, 'Ah, you've made it.' There was always this little bait that you'd go along forever. I'm a long distance runner. So I was really merely going along my way, but then the resentment would build up. He'd say, 'I'm off. I see you got a lot of work to do.' I mean, he was delighted that I had a lot of work to do, and then off he'd go. I can't blame him. I mean, he was growing. I don't know whether it's because I'm so scared to really go ahead and commit myself so that I find these things are; they give me a sense of accomplishment, but they also prevent me from charging ahead on my own. Maybe I'm too scared. So I can always say this to myself, never to him. I've never put him in a position where he felt that. So maybe it's a lot of my own fears. Or maybe I fear the two of us together doing the same thing, is just dynamite. But see, a marriage and staying together would be, in my mind, more important than anything. And I don't know exactly why. I mean, when I thought of leaving him, I had it all worked out that I would just, you know, but . . . it's more important somehow for me to maintain the marriage."

After California, they journeyed as a family to Almunecar, Spain, where Ross finally lived the artist's dream of a foreign landscape to absorb and paint. For the woman of his life, it was an adventure of still other dimensions.

"It was a very happy time. I felt we had gotten away from California just in the nick of time because I could see these people were drawing in closer and closer on him. It was like trying to leave before something for him got too heavy. The reason we ended up in Almunecar was because some guy he met at a bar told him about it, and when we got there, it was again, a really good feeling. I was going to be painting. We had this little house. We'd go into town. You know, he'd go in the morning, I'd go and do the shopping of course, and then he found this place to rent and paint in. Laura was in school for the first time. I found myself going out and meeting people. I didn't have to teach. It was remarkable. I had some time during the day. And I could see that he was starting to resent the fact that I would sit and chat with people. 'Who was that guy you were talking with?' Then I started painting and he'd say things like, 'Gee, you've done a lot of painting.' And somehow he was not ready for me to be not working and teaching. I'd tell him I'm going to meet so-and-so, and we are sharing our dreams, and that did not set too well with him.

"He was doing sketches all through our trip through Europe. And I can remember, sort of later in our year there, seeing my shoes. I would take off my shoes and put down my purse on the beach and go into the water, and I can remember looking back and seeing my shoes and purse there and thinking, 'Well, where is Arlene? There's her shoes and purse.' At first it was real good. You know, we'd go for our wine and things, and I was cooking the fish, and he'd be coming home, and Laura was old enough to do things with. Then he got his place and met Eddy, the painter from California. And I liked Eddy a lot, and we'd all do things together. Eddy would spend a lot of time talking to him, and as those talks increased, and he kept telling him that you really had to be a little bit on the line to be a painter, to really feel it . . . he had a big impression, a big input on Ross.

"As for my own painting then, I was painting the market, old ladies sleeping near doorsteps, the shoeshine boy, the fishermen. A whole series of people, people that I had sketched all along. I was probably painting more than Ross at this time because he had a hard time getting started. His first painting still had remnants of California. It wasn't until he got the studio that he started really looking at his sketchbooks and really started to paint, and that's the time he was talking with Eddy, the time he did the locals and the octopus and the local bars, and then when he started doing the pictures with the mirrored image and the line across them. By then, you see, he was already getting depressed. He would spend hours putting me down. We'd sit there, sometimes eating by the fireplace, and he would like criticize or just put me down—

what I was reading, what I was doing, how I was taking care of Laura. And also he wanted to really do things alone. The game began of 'How can I do things alone?'

"He was drinking a lot of wine. He'd stop every day and have his wine, and I remember those long evenings when he would talk and nothing was quite right. And there was this woman, actually I guess it was this woman he rented the studio from, and I think she saw some of his work. I don't know whether she saw it, or whether she just felt he was a good artist. She encouraged him to take that place, because up until then he was painting at home. And then he started in on painting these scenes, and then there was this really bad fight. By now he wasn't eating right. He had to get shots. He complained of stomach aches. Then there were all these different characters who came in and out of our life. And then there was this girl, also, that Eddy suggested to Ross that he get to know a little better. So she became important.

"No, I don't think I ever felt depressed. I liked it there, fine. I had my friends. I had my little stops. I was enjoying it. I felt, though, that something was wrong as far as our relationship again. We were talking, but it was all this sort of negative talk. And then I knew that money was kind of running low. I knew we had to decide what we were going to do. I knew that there was probably something going on with this lady, because she came to me and told me that she was scared of him. He had come on real strong with her due to Eddy's suggestings, I guess, so she talked with me one time. Also I knew that he would ask various people in to see his paintings, and if they didn't give him the right response, he would be upset.

"He would invite me up there too. The first one I remember seeing is the little ringmaster and all the little people on the trapeze and stuff. And then I remember the one that was ah, well then Laura did a little painting with a lot of oranges in it, and he thought she was painting the bloody fight that they saw, and he didn't like it. Meanwhile, my paintings had changed, and I painted him with wings flying above the city. I painted him nude with wings because I could feel that he was leaving, but I wasn't quite smart enough to know the signs. But I felt that he was real spacey. And one time I painted him as the demon, his real face, and then a demon face, and he kept asking me why I did that, what does that mean, and why was I painting him with wings? And I really didn't know why. But I just saw this sort of demon kind of thing.

"But then he painted the ones about Laura. He'd paint Laura with another woman. And then, of course, he painted the line ones, he, Eddy and this woman, and he and this woman. Meanwhile Eddy was drinking very heavily . . . and then the motorcycle ride. The famous motorcycle ride when he took Ross out and said, 'Well, we might as well die.' And he drove so fast he just scared the shit out of Ross. Scared the shit out of him. And he said, 'See, this is what I mean about being on the thin edge.' And I don't know whether Ross thought, 'I'm just not ready for this,' but it really scared him. He was going around all these curves and everything and that really scared him.

"But back to his paintings . . . the first one, I saw it almost like a child's drawing. That he was *the* center. You paint the biggest thing, the thing that's most important to you, you paint the largest, and he was the largest thing and all these people were little people that he was manipulating. Because as he was getting more and more freaked out, he was tuning other things out so he became very perceptive. And I think that was why I had these wings. It was as if he would predict things, and he would tell people things, and then they would turn out to be true. He was like taken with his powers. And so he saw himself as very important. People would ask his opinion. He'd give it to them and he felt that he was really important, that he had the lives of a lot of these people in his hands.

"This woman he painted sort of sensual, kind of wild. But then there were other women, like Muta, who couldn't speak—that became sort of important, because he would say Arlene can understand her, nobody else can understand her. It was like whenever I did achieve something, it was sort of put down. Still to this day. It's like, 'You do everything well.' It's those underhanded sort of compliments.

"The end came, yeah, when he said, 'We're going.' Then, of course, our car was stolen, we had to go to the police station. And all that, that all played a part in his mind where these guys were being interrogated. They made us come in and sign some papers. And I think he felt very bad. These guys said, 'Please, help us, help us.' And we knew they had taken the car. We couldn't help them. Lots of little things you know had heavy meaning. Then one day he said, 'We're going. We're going to leave, and I'm putting a sign on my studio door that says I will be gone by such and such a date. Write home and tell them we're coming.' And that was the sign that he didn't want to deviate from that plan. I mean he knew he had to go home. He was fading and at that point he knew it was time to leave, and he didn't want anything to change, and so he went and put his sign on the studio door that he was leaving and that I was to write and tell them that we were leaving, so that he couldn't back out of it. We went up there to the studio that afternoon and started taking the canvases off the stretchers, and then we went around town telling everyone we were leaving. I can remember people saying, 'Well, what about Arlene? Does she want to leave?' And he'd say, 'We're leaving. We're leaving.'

"By now he really didn't feel good. He really wasn't eating, and he was still complaining of his stomach aches, and he was getting a little wired. We took the paintings off the stretchers, left them all in a pile, brought the canvases to the house and then he said, 'We're leaving tomorrow.' By tomorrow he couldn't do anything. I took him up to the car and he sat in the car and I had to haul all the stuff up there and he just could not do anything.

"It was real scary leaving. All through Europe, every time we would take a vacation, Ross handled all the money. He handled a lot of things, and so when he wasn't able to do anything I was really scared, because I didn't know. I mean I didn't even know if I could find Madrid. I remember this neighbor coming up when I was hauling all the stuff and saying, 'What's wrong? What's happening?' and so I was scared, real scared and I didn't still believe he was as bad as he was, and so I said, 'Well, I'll drive until it gets dark and then you drive. We've got to get to Madrid and to the airport.' So I almost like forced it. I said, 'Now you've got to drive, you've got to get in the car and drive, I mean take over the wheel.' And so he did drive for a while. And then he'd say, 'The cars are coming at me and I can't drive. I'm in the wrong lane . . . .'

"It was difficult, because Laura thought he was drunk. It was hard to get her calmed down and asleep. And then we parked on the side of the road by a building and we stayed there all night. He was very much into wanting me to hug him, and we just sat there all night. And then in the morning, I knew we just had to get going, and by then I was not only scared that I wouldn't know how to get where I was going, but I was also scared that maybe he was a lot worse than I thought. I was also scared that people would think he was on drugs or something. At certain points he would grab the wheel, like at a stop sign or something, swerve the wheel and I'd have to hold onto it and he would be talking, and I can't even remember what it was about. He'd talk and talk and talk and then sometimes we'd stop and he'd grab the wheel or he'd pull out the key and he'd just talk. We had to stop at another little town to spend the night. By then we were real tired. I was exhausted. We got this little room. And sometimes he would go in and out. He signed the thing for us to get this room, and we went up there and he said, 'I'm going to sleep on this side of the bed because I always sleep on this side of the bed.' What he was trying to do was just grab some reality. Then we went out to eat and he said, 'I will order. I will order for all of us.' And he did. But right before we got the room, when we parked the car to go into the room, he said: 'Well, I'm leaving. Good bye,' and he just walked off. And I didn't know what to do. So I just sat there, and after an hour or so he came back and then we got the room.

"He woke up in the middle of the night, then grabbed the passports and wrote real vague, Laura LewAllen and his mother's address on it, so that if anything happened she could get back home. I ran downstairs then and asked if there was a doctor. And I think the doctor came and gave him a shot. Maybe it was vitamin B, I can't remember. We got back in the car then and drove to the town where the airport was. But before we got to this town, we pulled in again, in somebody's courtyard or something, and he sort of fell asleep. Laura and I sat there for a long time drawing pictures. Then finally he woke up and I said, 'Well, now we've got to go on.' And when we got to the airport, of course, he had to sign everything. All the stuff was in his name. We had enough traveler's checks, but when they asked him to sign his name, he wrote 'Friday' or something. And I went, Oh, no! And I said, now you've *got* to sign your name. I can remember asking him to please sign his name. And he did, and we got the tickets. Then we had to spend the night, so I had to get a hotel room. By now he was really very strange, and I just didn't know what to do. I remember walking Laura up and down the corridors, because we had to wait until the next morning. And I wouldn't let him out of the room. I remember I said, 'Now, Laura, you stay here and I'll go get something to eat. I'll bring something back.' And she was scared to stay with him, because by now she was really afraid of him. And then the next morning I had to somehow get rid of the car. And, oh, I forgot, on our drive to the airport he said, 'We can't take all this stuff on the airplane. We can't take all these paintings. We can't take your paintings. We can't take any of this stuff. We've got to get rid of it.' So I pulled over on the road, and I dumped all my paintings, because I didn't want to lose his paintings. His paintings were rolled, and I had all my canvases and I knew we couldn't get on the airplane with them and there wasn't time to take them off the stretchers or anything, so I just pulled over to the side of the road and I just laid them all out in the open embankment there. I often wonder what people must have thought when they came by. I mean, I saw it very plainly that I had to save his paintings, because I somehow felt that this was really important.

"So then it came time to get to the airport the next morning, and what was I going to do with the car and all the stuff? I drove to the airport door and walked him in and Laura and the duffle bags and sat him down. I said, 'Now wait here.' Then I took the car and drove it into the parking lot, to a place where it wasn't too obvious, all the stuff that would identify us, flyers from Eddy's show and stuff like that . . . took that out and kind of went and dumped it in somebody else's car. I just tried to take everything out of it that would identify us and locked it up and then went back into the airport. I couldn't carry the paintings. I left them rolled up under the platform of the car, the van. By then he wouldn't even get up. Like I'd get him up, and he'd fall to

206

the floor of the airport and of course nobody would help me. It was terrible. On the elevator. He wouldn't get out of the elevator. He couldn't stand up in the elevator, and it was real scary, because I just thought, 'How in the hell am I going to get him on the plane?' So then I checked the bags and I just lifted him. I just *lifted* him under his arm and we walked onto the plane, and then of course he was scared to death. That's where his fear of flying comes from. He was never afraid of flying before, but he thought we were going to crash. By the time we were up, though, I was relieved, because I knew I had gotten through the worst. The flight was hard because he was so nervous and so upset. But I was relieved.

"Yeah, the paintings were left behind till your friend, Taucher, in Switzerland got to the van in the parking lot in Madrid and sent them. I had all the sketchbooks in the duffle bags, and a lot of them I had never seen. A lot of them he wouldn't ever show me and I had never looked at them.

"I lived with my Mom in Chicago while he was in the hospital and Laura started kindergarten, because I had to get her back on an even keel. She just did not understand what was going on, so I got her in school. I didn't know whether he was really going to make it. They said he was a very sick man. He wouldn't talk to me sometimes. I'd call and he'd say, 'I don't want to talk'."

The source of Arlene's strength remains somewhat of a mystery. There seems to be no traditional religous base to it. For want of any better explanation, those of us who know and love her, and have seen her faced with other, seemingly insurmountable obstacles, have simply attributed it to 'Well, you know Arlene.' As if that were all the explanation necessary.

"I think it's that I never think that the worst is going to happen. I always say that I'm going to be able to handle it, whether it's the plumbing or whatever. Somehow there is a way to do it, and I find it, whether it's the best way or not . . . and of course I just go from day to day and I just know it's going to be all right. Despite all that was happening to Ross I just knew that tomorrow I was going to be one step closer, and it was going to be all right. And that's how I live my whole life. It's like when things get real bad, I think, OK, there's a way I can do this, and I sit down usually and I think of all my alternatives and then I just go ahead. And I did pray, you know, 'please make him better' and that sort of thing, but basically I just knew that I'd find that something good was going to happen and we'd find a way. And if he knew that I was there and I cared and I loved him, that he was going to be all right. And that's how I think about everything.

"You know, we talk about women and stuff like that, but mainly it isn't really easy to live with a person like me either. Because in my quest to do the right thing and to make everything work for everyone and to keep everything together, it's a terrible strain on the other person, because you put them in a very strange place. 'Well, Arlene will take care of it, I don't have to do it,' the guilt: 'Well, gee, she shoveled 16 shovel loads and I've shoveled 2. I mean, she doesn't know when to stop and I want a break.' It's not easy to live with someone like me. Then he would say, 'She saved my life. I am in debt.' And I'd say, 'I didn't save your life' . . . and for a long time I had to live with that curse. See, this good deed became a bad deed, another heavy duty Arlene pulled through. That became a very, very touchy thing.

"I remember calling you in Door County when we got back, frantically, and you telling Ross, 'Listen to Arlene. Just listen to Arlene.' And then going out for that drink when he was in the hospital and bringing the sketchbooks along. You see, in a way, I was sort of afraid that I was betraying him, because nobody had seen them. I cried and I cried when I first saw them, because it wasn't till he was in the hospital that I dared to look at them. When I first called you I was a little disappointed that you didn't come. I was a little bit hurt. Because somewhere in the back of my mind I figured that if he could talk to you—and I thought of you first—it would do him a lot of good."

I recall one of the drawings in the sketchbook in particular, one of the strangest drawings I had ever seen of his. It was Ross looking at himself from above. And then the line again from Eddy.

"That was Ross walking the line again. I remember the sketch, but I don't think he did a painting of it."

I find it fascinating that Arlene's paintings were so different at that time. That both Arlene and Ross were painting with such power in Spain. Has she thought about that much? Painting with such intensity.

"I think it's because I had the luxury of time, and I didn't feel pressed. I didn't feel like I had to find sort of a working solution or series or anything. I just had the time, and so did he in a way. And he had to, you know, he would turn the paintings to the wall. He wouldn't look at his own paintings."

Back in LaGrange again, the Yaqui Village period, Ross teaching part-time, Arlene teaching, the house constantly filled with people . . . in the midst of all this Arlene began the Indian paintings, then the cowboy paintings; some of these carried over to Santa Fe, New Mexico, the new home. The new series of paintings dealing with the gypsies, yet all of these so different from the gut painting she did there.

"I think it was like I had such strong feelings there. Strong feelings for the people. I would look at them, and I would come home, and the impressions were so strong I didn't need a photograph or anything. I had the time to really get to know them. The artist needs to have time to dig in, time to yourself. You have to have time for real talking and being with people or landscape or whatever it is that you are working with. You can't be on a schedule. You can't have to be home at this hour. You can't have to fight off fatigue and try to paint at night. You have to be living it."

What does she think of autobiographical work? That was very autobiographical work she seemed to be doing in Spain, and she's excluded Arlene, in a sense, from most of her current work. Where is Arlene in her work today?

"I always wanted to do, and I probably still will, a really heavy painting of my mother and Laura. I've done many sketches of it. I also wanted to do Ross and me, and I also wanted to do Ross and Laura. I have sketches of these things, but for some reason I haven't done them. I'm not afraid to do them, but if I were to paint something to do with Ross . . . well, the things I've painted of him, he'd say, 'Why did you do that?' or 'What does that mean?' It's on my mind, but I'm just not ready to do that yet."

That sense of life that Ross possesses, that charisma, the constant challenge to try new things, to bring new people into his life . . . .

"I can't say that I've ever really had a bad time with my life or with Ross. Whenever things got to kind of a stopping point or whatever, then we'd move or we'd change, or our lifestyle would change. Things were always changing, when I'd start feeling kind of depressed or something, then something new would happen and we'd have a fresh start. Nothing ever was humdrum, never. It just feeds into my philosophy that, oh well, tomorrow something is going to happen.

"No, never exhausting. I love it. It is a challenge. I don't want a regular life. In fact it worried me here in Santa Fe that more entertaining, and whatever happens, goes on in his studio . . . but it works out OK. Because now he really does need the quiet time. The house that we live in now becomes a little bit of a sanctuary, where he can do all the entertaining and what have you in town."

Back in LaGrange (and later at Santa Fe Preparatory School) she continued to develop as a teacher, an extraordinary teacher, utilizing some of those same powers she put into her life, her art, her relationships with people.

"I really loved teaching, because I love being able to touch the children and being able to make them feel good about themselves. That seems to be my real talent, I think. Somehow I can encourage people, not in a phony way, to think of themselves as important. In Western Springs I was able not only to do that with the kids, but I was also able to try some new ideas that I had about kids. That they shouldn't be sitting in their seats all day. That they shouldn't have to do this, and they shouldn't have to do that, you know. I was able to really put this into play. I created the whole learning center there. And they broke down the walls and I spent hours with individualized programing, and I really loved it. I was learning a lot myself. And I was seeing how things could be applied to all age levels. And the little ones came into the learning center, and there was something for them to do as well as the older ones. And then I was putting on those plays and musicals and I just loved it. Plus I took a lot of classes.

"I never thought I was pushing too hard. I guess I don't know my own limits. But what was happening in LaGrange was that Ross was spending a lot of time with his own students, he was getting stronger and stronger, and he didn't want me along, and it was almost as if I kept busy and had all my things to do so he wouldn't feel I was helping him too much. He could be more independent. So the busier I kept involved in my own things, the more he could go off and do his things."

The women's movement came into the picture around this period of time. And though Arlene was never into it in a heavy way, it was evident that more and more she was defining herself, and Ross in some ways was encouraging her to make her own friends, go on with her own painting, take the art classes she wanted.

"That was important. Just taking those classes and getting away and realizing that I could actually walk out of that door. I think one of the class nights Ross watched Laura, and two of the class nights I had to get a babysitter. But the point was I was able to release and go ahead and do those things. I took a belly dance class, and yoga class, and a sketching class, and it was wonderful that I could just walk out that door . . . though everything of course had to be just right before I walked out the door. Nonetheless, I could leave.

"Yeah, I was starting to release. See with me, it's like you plug me in and I'll go on forever, if I think it's bringing you happiness and comfort. But then, when I began to realize that maybe I didn't have to do that particular thing, then I very slowly stopped doing it. It was like . . . I'm finished with that thing. And so little by little I learned that I didn't have to iron his jockey shorts, I didn't have to do this or that. And each time I let go, I felt a lot better. And then here in Santa Fe, when it finally came to whether I sould stop teaching and everything, I could release that too."

One of the results of that 70's movement of 'becoming one's own person' was the recognition that Arlene was indeed her own person, and she in turn became our personal friend as well—mine, Ralph's, and others. And that we could now address her privately in such a way.

"Right. I'll start with you. You know that when we started corresponding, that was very, well, not bad, but he would look at the letter and he'd go, 'Here, your name is on this.' And all around him people were doing that. Eventually he got over it and it was OK. But even now, you know, he'll say, 'Well, what did Howard say?' You know, it bothers him. And, so, it's like whether he resents the fact that you could also be *my* friend, even though all of the people around us—the women—were saying, 'you know; I'm keeping my maiden name. Please address letters to me.' So that was a little setback there. And then he'd say, 'Well, you write him. I'm not gonna write him.'

"But I think he feels very close to you. He doesn't understand . . . he worries about you. He sees you as very talented. He believes in your talent and that as you're becoming more successful, he can also believe in it in himself, like you're a link from the very roots. And he can say, 'Yeah, now Norbert's coming into it. Norbert's coming of age. And so am I.' And he loves the more success things. The more things you throw, it gives his more validity.

"Whereas with Ralph, he looks upon Ralph like me. Ross in some ways sees in Ralph this steadfast person he can count on. He sees Ralph as being very vulnerable and successful, but in a whole different way than he wants to go. So when he thinks of Ralph he can think, 'Boy, I'm glad I'm not in his shoes.' Where you might give him courage to continue in art, Ross might say of Ralph, 'Well, Ralph has lived by the book. He's done all the right things. I haven't. And I don't regret it, because I'm not like that. However, I'm glad I know Ralph and I love Ralph,' maybe for the same reason he loves me. I don't know. But you can always count on Ralph. He will always think of you first. Maybe those are some of the same qualities that he sees in me, and maybe that's why he likes him so much.

"I see the friendship of you three as no more remarkable to me than us being married. It's the exact, that is the essence of Ross, and that's what I go by, and that's why I love him, because there is that kernel that I'm talking about. If he commits himself to you and he really cares about you, and you don't let him down, then he'll be with you forever, because he's got so much of his sensitivity tied in with you. So to write you off, or Ralph, it's not a simple thing. Because this goes to his very core. So once you have established that relationship with him, it just doesn't surprise me at all. You'll be friends always. Just like I feel, unless I did something terrible, very unforgiveable, he'd never leave me. That's the way he is. There's certain little . . . I don't know what you even call them, certain kernels in him that he lives by the book in that way."

I've often wondered how she perceives herself in the eyes of other men.

"Well, that's a real interesting question. For years I wondered if I was sexy. I always had this very strange picture of me that I was not sexy. Then, as I opened up to people, and I met men that weren't friends of Ross, that was another curse of my life;never being too friendly, or leading anybody on that was a friend of Ross. I would have to say stop, if you value your friendship with Ross. But I thought to myself, 'Well maybe I am sexy.' But with people now that I have met over the last few years, male friends that I have had, I was never so sure whether it was my looks or my enthusiasm and personality and making them feel good type thing. One fellow said to me, 'I've watched you for four days and I finally had enough nerve to come in and I just wanted to tell you that I love the way you're poured into your blue jeans.' And I thought, 'Well, this guy . . . it can't be so bad. What an interesting way to start.' And so I have found out that other people, I guess, would say that I am attractive, and yet I think I'm so aware of Ross always talking about how pretty other women are, and he always talked of how bad I looked when I was teaching, how much like a pack horse I looked, and nothing ever how pretty I looked. I will say, though, it's funny because when you're here, or other people, I find myself thinking, 'Oh, now when I get up in the morning and I come out in the kitchen and I have something nice on, they're going to think, "Wow!"' But I guess I purposely don't think about it so I stay out of trouble."

As far as her own understanding of how her presence seems to affect others . . .

"Well, when I zero in on someone, I really zero in on them. I mean, you know, I really care about them. Like this one fellow who would come into the gallery and we would go have coffee and finally I just wore him out. He said, 'You have so much energy and you're always so on and you're always so happy, I just can't take it.' I think people know that I sincerely care about them, like Fred. He dearly loves me.

He just can't wait to do something or come and see me. I guess it's because I really do care about him. But I think I'm becoming a little more selective as to who I care about.

"I'm a man's woman. I work better, I communicate better, I can kid better, I can tune into their feelings better. I just have a better rapport with men. With women I tend not to trust them, and yet I don't make them feel . . . unattractive or jealous of me or anything like that. I really try to play it down."

In light of the past, Ross and herself, the women's movement, her own career as a teacher, the manager of a gallery, an artist, just where is Arlene today?

"Well, I've lost a lot of my fear. I have a fear of losing people that I love and I had a fear of losing Ross; maybe some of that drove me on. I had a lot of fears. I had a fear that he would go out, or he would be with another woman—and you know, when those things happen it's not so bad. You really . . . I mean, it's not so bad. So a lot of fears have gone and I wouldn't be afraid to be on my own. I feel that if I were on my own, I would devote far too much time to what I was doing. I feel that in some ways I don't give enough time. I feel like I don't have a good thermometer. Let's say that I took on another gallery job, or that I was alone. I would go right to the top! I would put all my energies into that. But, since I'm not, I don't feel put upon. To me it's like a compromise. I want both. I want to be able to be out of the house and working. I want to be respected for what I do, but it doesn't have to be a real important job, because I make up my own goals.

Her work as an artist? Where is that headed?

"I feel that people are given certain challenges. Everybody has something. I just believe that a lot of people have a lot of talent, but most people have some talent. And I feel that I have this artistic talent and I feel that all through my life, people said, 'Oh, you should be painting, you should be because you're so good.' I find it hard to believe that. But when I do strike out just a little bit, like I got mad two years ago and I said, 'Darn, I'm going to be 40 pretty soon, and here I am living in this art capital and all I've done is teach at the prep school and what do I have to show for it?' I felt that I had wasted too much time and I hadn't done anything, and so I went out and the first thing, I got into this gallery, got into this tile thing. And Ross couldn't believe it. I mean he just said, 'What? You just showed them, and you're in? And they want to do them?' So then I thought to myself, 'God, if it all happens like that, I'm denying this talent. I'm not letting it grow.' And I think that's maybe what I feel the worst about. And yet I fight it, and I don't know why. I don't want to give it too much time, and then again I do. I think I have more things to release before I can get real serious about it. I'm afraid to get real serious because . . . it's the same thing as knowing what my stars say. It's the same thing as what comes out on that canvas. It's like painting Ross with these wings, because I know if someone really hurts me, I can be real mean. I've never done it, but I think I could."

I find it remarkable that both Ross and Arlene are, in a sense, suppressing some kind of artistic release in fear of what they might discover. And though I can understand it in him, and her, I am amazed to learn that husband and wife are both locked in that very same thing.

"Well he has a little better cause because he knows what's on the other side of that line. See I have only touched. When I touched I couldn't help but feel that when I get real strong, in my own right, he fades. I don't know if it's true, though. Maybe I start rising . . . see, I don't know what causes what."

212

Looking back at some of her recent paintings, the Indian paintings . . . what was behind all that?

"The romance and the strength of these people. I guess that goes all the way through. Even in Spain the people I painted were like the strong old lady sweeping her stoop and the woman in the marketplace, and the Englishman, the strongness, and I did one of Ross in a boat as a fisherman, and I did . . . it was always strong, straight is the thing. The cowboy paintings, John Wayne . . . the strength. I don't think I had many childhood heroes, but manliness and strength, and womanliness, but strong! That's what bothers me about some women—fading away—and my first impulse is to go to them, feed them, make them feel good about themselves. But I do that so much, then it gets hard for me if there is not one little inkling of them helping themselves. I think it's like Ross' things are always very mystical and sensitive and floating and fantasy-like, and mine are always like we're going to get through, this person is strong. These women could lift a bus. And I think that's how I feel about myself.

"And the gypsy paintings . . . well, you see, the gypsies really touched me in Spain, I was never able to touch too much on it. I told you the story about the man giving me the medal, and how he would watch me. I was aware of them when I would go into the market. And the Spanish, just the regular Spanish people would watch me. And in the bank, everytime I cashed a check he'd look at my passport and he'd go, 'Oh . . . ah . . . '. And he would say, 'I want you to come and your husband on a picnic with us.' And then I would see the women in the marketplace there. And in Germany I saw a whole bunch of them together. We got to talk to the children right in the encampment, and they'd come up and talk to you. And you see, again, the gypsies represented . . . well, they were strong women. They were strong and they made do. I was thinking the other day how, here we have this beautiful house, and it's all make-do. It's like here we have all this furniture that I never picked out. Not one stick of furniture that I bought, and all these little make-shift things you know, little tacky things. I'm a great make-doer. And I see these women as sort of make-doers. If you don't have meat, you put a carrot in. My mother made-do. If you don't have this, you make-do with that I guess. So the gypsy paintings and the women paintings are, I suppose, my little way of just saying what I feel about women . . . that women are stronger. They have more energy. They are capable of moving mountains. And then men still seem to be . . . well, you nurture them, and you take care of them because they can give you, they can make you see yourself as an attractive, desirable woman. And that's important. You know that song, 'You Make Me Feel Like a Natural Woman'? I think that's very important. You can't get that from a job. You can't get that from another woman. You can't get that from another woman. You can't, no matter how much you try to fill your life, there's nothing like you know, a man laying back and feeling satisfied. And that you played a part in that, and that he thinks that you're really special."

But this is all a very physical thing.

"Yeah, but that's I think because I have not had much that was verbal from men because, number one, I just tried to stay away from it if they were friends of Ross and number two, if they weren't friends of Ross I had to play kind of a cat and mouse game."

Ageing in a woman . . . how will she as a woman grow old?

"I've never going to just give up. Or just say, 'Oh well, now I'm 50, so it's into the

213

housedress, you know.' But I also realize that it's a losing battle. I often sit and wonder how older women see me, because now I look at these younger girls and I say, 'Gee, she's really cute. She's really cute and she's got all this to look forward to.' So, I can imagine how people must look at me. I feel I'm in my prime right now. Probably the best I'm going to be right now. And I think older women look upon all this with, not jealousy . . . oh, regret that time marches on. I look at it as I wish I had been more free at that time, to have had more experiences. I mean, like I would hope that Laura would do more things. Or that this pretty girl would not just be swooped up.

"I feel I've done a very good job with Laura. I feel really good about that, and I know that she will handle things differently and I wish that I had been privy to the same things that she has been. I am really tickled that she is the way she is. She has none of this compromise, none of this 'You must do this.' I mean, she says, 'I'm going to blow that off.' I would never blow anything off. I mean if I was to do it, I had to do it. Or my mother would say, 'When you're out with someone, don't look at anybody else.' I mean right away you were programmed to be faithful and duty-bound, whereas she will not. She won't have that. She's also a man pleaser, which is important. She's also her own person, wheras I've been everybody's person and very seldom my own. And she sees that in me, and she'll tell me, 'Oh, give me a break. Do it for yourself. Go to that movie alone.' She's more aware now why a woman does certain things. She'll make a special trip to bring her boyfriend a treat or something. Or she'll say, 'I can't go out with you because I promised him.' She's more aware now of why, maybe, I would do certain things for Ross.

"I think Ross has provided Laura with a much more realistic picture of a human being. That a human being can be frail, can be mad, can be sad, can be anxious. You know, kind of pick up and say, 'I'm tired and it's time to quit. I'm going to blow this up and I'm going to do something for me.' That has been a vital thing in Laura's life. From me she gets the feeling of really caring for people, doing certain things to make them happy, making herself happy by helping and caring about people, also the stick-to-it-iveness. She's an overachiever because she will stick with it and do it and she's not a quitter. I think she really got the best of both of us. Despite everything, both Ross and I had parents that loved us. He brought with him a lot of the things that were important in his childhood, taking the time to show Laura certain skills, whether photography or art. I really think she also benefits from his spontaneity . . . being able to just pick up and travel. Independent. That has been a real crucial thing, and I think it's been important to him, too. Also the friends, you and Ralph and Harry. These are people that she has known her entire life, and she treats you as an equal. As a friend. She doesn't think of you as any different than she would me or Ross or any of her good friends. When she said, 'I'm glad Norb's coming,' she really meant it."

Her perspective of me, I find particularly necessary, and of great value.

"I feel that in a lot of ways you and I have a lot of similarities, and one of them is this releasing and this feeling of dutifullness and guilt. I feel that when you're in Wisconsin, you're in this kind of closed environment, very duty-bound, and as you were saying the other night, you do the certain required things. By all rights you shouldn't even care what others think or say. I feel when you're at home, you use that structure just like I do, to give you some good warm fuzzies . . . that you have to get yourself, because no one else is going to give them to you. Ross isn't going to give them to me. And so you do what you must, and you say, 'Wow, look at that nice thing

I did. Good for me.' And then, you also realize that this is where we differ. In order to keep up all of this, you also have to have this other sort of separate life and, you know, you can justify it and juggle it back and forth, whereas I've never quite been able to do that. I see you as two different people.

"Well, I see you really as one with that Wisconsin landscape. When you used to walk down that road in your sweater, down to the water and everything, I felt that you really have a kinship to the ruggedness, the coldness. Then again I can see through this; this is a challange, this winter and this water. So, I see you like that. Yet I see you in this landscape, too. That's very evident. That's the easing of you. When you come here it's not that duty-bound business, not that guilt. It's a freeness, and the landscape is more gentle and you're more gentle. You don't talk to me like that when I've heard you at home. You're much more of the tyrant there, much more demanding of those people, much less loose. And when you get here, you release. You're freer with the people. So I see a very different person. I also see that it rattles you here because some of the intrigue is gone. It's easier here. It might be too easy. You don't have to plan as much. Things sort of fall in your lap and nobody gives a care. We could walk right up here and take a room and nobody would care. It's different. And you're different. You're much gentler, I think. And much less harried.

"I always look upon you as a people person when you write, the type of characters that you build, and their strengths and their weaknesses, and it seems to me that this environment here, with its honesty . . . people haven't been burnt like they have up there. Now in Chicago it's a different thing, because there are so many people that it doesn't matter. But when you have picked a place, when it's a relatively small place, and the type of writing that you do, and the sensitivity you reveal about yourself, and even in the earlier works, like the things you glean from people, you have to be in an environment where the people, over a glass of wine, will really pour out things. And even though Santa Fe does tend to talk, it isn't a malicious gossip. People will be open with you. And like you've said, there's great value in the common man. There's great value in a semi-skilled person. You seem to like this, heritage and history, someone who has done something for a long time, or has perfected this skill or maybe learned from an older person. And in Santa Fe there is a lot of that. The tradition of the Chicano people, of the Indian people. The people are more for you than against you. And the earth and the color. Life is simpler. You don't have to fight the elements. You can spend more time doing what you want to do and not having to fight it. It's a whole looser structure somehow, even with the family here. I think it would be looser just by virture of the climate and the mountains, it seems to cuddle you more than your having to fight it."

And what of Arlene's own sense of spirituality? Does she explore it at all? Even between the two of us, it is so rare for her to open up to me on this level.

"With me, I think it's so hard to express those things. At an Indian dance. I get so caught up with the spirit . . . I'm not sure this is what you mean. Or say I'll be driving in to Santa Fe from the house, and I'll look at those mountains and I feel there's like spirits living out there, and there's that whole, the Indians, the tribal Indians are somehow looking down. There's that whole thing I mentioned about the moccasins at the museum, you know. I really believe that an Indian came for his shoes, and a lot of times it's hard for me to express that. I don't have a good outlet to express that. In a way I am very spiritual. I believe, like the kachinas are there and I believe that the spirits are here and they are around. And you can feel them and you can't deny them. You musn't deny them and you musn't stop because that's what preserved them. I love tradition. And there is something about strength for, say, the Pueblo Indians to continue their dances, to continue their rituals. But I also see it in people. That's why I love to look at certain people's faces. It's like sometimes you just look up and see a person's spirit. Sometimes I'm afraid to think about it too much because I feel that I'm so lucky to be where I am. I mean my life is so good. Not that you can be too content, not that. It's just that I feel that here you don't have to be anything. It's so different than California, finding yourself. There may be a lot of people here trying to find themselves or be on a spiritual level, but it's not phony like it is in California. And, so here, I can walk away from somebody and just feel good having talked to them, or walking in the arroyo, or something like that. It's very hard for me to express that."

Does she understand that in my life, in my work, I ask her, where aside from being protective or defensive, that I must also at times retreat to a point where regardless of what she says, or Ross says, or Ralph thinks, I *know* that there is an area inside of me that none of them understand? That none of them can perceive? And that maybe the only way out for me is through writing. And either you see it there in the work, or you don't. Is she willing to accept that, entertain that idea, that I may think all of them are full of shit at times and don't really know Blei at all?

"Yes, because it's not an Alfred Hitchcock situation where you grab him at the end and you say, 'Ha, ha, you fools.' I don't know the whole Zen thing about you, the sensitivity you have for the Japanese, the poems and things. And maybe you also have a hard time verbalizing them, and that's why we haven't talked about them. And when I said 'tyrant' I see that as a protection in certain situations . . . if you weren't more like that, things would probably never get done. It's like there's this little voyeur in you, this observer . . . like from a little boy you were privy to a lot of things which you digested. And I think each person in his own way has a little of that. Like I'm sure Ross has, like he's said, 'I've poured my guts out to Norb for three days.' Like there's a little bit of me . . . someone once told me, 'Don't ever totally get naked and stand really nude because then there's nothing left.' So each one of us feels like there's a little bit of me that I've witheld of my own. I think in relationships it should be that way too. Husbands, wives, friends, you don't tell everything because then it would destroy you. You have to have a certain little part, just like your locked diaries, that nobody is privileged to. But some of it does come out in your writing, the fact that you've laid this whole thing out—and then I can see you put your hands in your pocket with your black sweater, and you go whistling down the road heading toward the water. And I can just see the whole town falling apart and you going, da da da, off to the shore, feeling very smug in a way, and that little kernel could keep you going. I mean, so you're not going to go and blow your brains out, like the guy said. You could leave the whole town there and then you just put your hands in your pocket, and just walk right away.

"See, it's always interesting because when you first meet a writer, first you're aware that everything, everywhere he goes, he's absorbing. Then you say, 'Oh, well if he's absorbing then maybe I should start looking around for things that I think he should write about.' Then you pass all of that and begin reading the things he does write, trying to get a handle on just how much of the things he is absorbing. That's why your story, 'The Hour of the Sunshine Now' interestes me, because here you wrote something that is relative to where I'm living, and that's real interesting to see

what you glean, or your childhood as compared to mine. So then you try to get an understanding about the person through his work, and you really start digging into that instead of trying to find him things to write about. You realize that you better zero in on what he is writing about.

"I see you spending vast, vast amounts of time not writing or typing or anything, but . . . I don't know, you wouldn't call it reminiscing, but recollecting, just sitting there. Even the things in the coop, where you work, lose their identity. I mean they provide a nice safe environment, and you are familiar with them, and you just sit there for long periods of time and just reflect on one person or one thing. I see you just taking a lot of time just doing that. I am beginning to understand a little more, having talked to you on this level, and I think Ross, too. He had never seen you dig, dig, dig. Dig and phrase and work, really work at it . . . much different than a newspaper reporter, you know, giving your name and where you were born and that sort of thing. This is like a real digging process . . . and I was never so much aware of it until I started thinking about myself now: 'What did I really say? What do people really give out? How will he interpret?' No different than a portrait painter, a painter that needs to live and work with the person a while to try to get the essence. And then the whole balance of, 'If he says this, how will it affect people?' I've just become much more aware this visit of the things you do go through mentally.

"And, ah, for what it's worth, I think you have been very good in bridging that gap of whose friend is whose. I feel very much a friend of yours, even though we haven't had a lot of chance to know each other on certain levels. But I feel that you have tried to bridge that gap to make me feel an individual. And I really enjoy seeing the interaction of you and Ross together, because it does have a sort of proof of the pudding what I believe. As much as you can believe in what you think about a person, I see a lot of it coming out in your relationship with Ross. What I believe in him about his fiber, comes out in people that he loves. I can see how he interacts with you, who he loves, and he cares a great deal about and respects and everything. I can see that.

I can bounce off other people he really cares about. And you must understand about me that there is no feeling of being in the way, putting me out, that sort of thing, because I can't emphasize enough that I really like to be around you, so that, at least we've completely reached that level, that there isn't any of that now.

"That painting that I did of the three of you . . . I was thinking about that the other day because in the painting you had on your turtleneck, and Ralph had his tie, and Ross . . . I had seen him come through all this, and I realized that you had made this bond. Most of all, each of you had helped each other. Ross' flipping out was a help to you as much as you were then to him. Ralph, seeing Ross weakened, was something to him too. And to Ralph it was something like, 'Oh, thank God, other people have problems. It just doesn't always come to me.' And for you it was, 'Hey. I better shape up and get myself centered.' And I think I just tried to show that. The technique was kind of splotchy, and it was sort of like, what was going to happen? How would the different people change? And its interesting that since I painted it, the people changed. And now they seem to be back right where I painted them. But you maybe have changed the least. You're still with the turtleneck and the things coming out of your head. And Ralph has changed in that he's grown older, much older than the rest of us in a lot of ways.

"I think maybe I put Ross in the middle and you two flanking him? It's hard to remember. Because I see Ross as most needy of outside support. Ralph has Jo Ann, who is like linked there. And you have support from lots of different people and Ross denies a lot of my support and it seems like he needs the most support. Because he denies it in the people, who, like me, he just can't take it from because that's a weakness. So maybe I would put him in the center. Also, because maybe I see him as in his own way, maybe being a little ahead of both of you, being ahead in sensitivity and truth and honesty about himself. But because of that, needing more support . . . because he's come to a more critical insight into himself."

And if I were to tell the artist she is wrong. That she placed Ralph in the center of her painting?

"Ha! I'll be damned! Yeah, he is in the center. See, what I did was give you the other side of the coin. I gave you what I would see now . . . and then, you know, I can't honestly say that I remember why I put him in the center. Oh, I know what it is! That the opposite of this is that Ralph *is* the center of you two. He *is* the one you can count on. He *is* the one that has, in a lot of ways the one that has patched up differences between you two. So that's that side of it. The other side of it is that, at least the side I gave you, if you two were to be on either end of Ross, not because he is the center as Ralph is on that side, but because he has seen himself from up there, and he has maybe touched more of his own soul, and he's more vulnerable; therefore he needs more support from both of you. So, maybe that's the other side of it. I see Ross as just tremendously talented in all these things that you see in him, and I see him as so extremely sensitive that he needs to be cared for somehow. So that he can continue. Because he gets scared, and then he stops."

As for the future?

"As far as Ralph goes, I think he's a survivor. He'll finish out his time and he may be really strung out afterwards, but I would like to feel that he will get a little place and become, and do something. He'll take up some kind of a hobby to keep him busy. I worry about him. But I also feel that he will be relieved, and he and Jo will take their little trailer or whatever.

"And with you, I see that you will eventually seek a little more space, and I can see you with a little more money so that you can somehow lease the place or have a place of your own to go to for a longer period of time. I see you having something more of your own . . . like, 'I'm paying for this. My talents have bought me this time and this place and I feel good about it because it's my own. I don't have to share it with anybody.' I see you doing more work and loosening up a lot. Like you admitting certain things to us that you may have never said before.

"And with Ross it's hard to say, but I see him letting these people run his things, his business, and him starting something different. You know he talks about a whale center, oh, so many things. I don't see him painting, and I don't see him sitting there making earrings anymore, but I see him starting something new. I'm not quite sure what it would be.

"As for Ross and me, I feel my relationship with Ross has not been based on any kind of sacrifice on my part. I want that to be clear. My life has been filled due to the fact that he is an artist, that he does have these good friends. My life has been enriched. Rather than what I do, a lot of times, it fills my needs to feel equal. To learn from him, rather than disagreeing a lot. And the longevity of our relationship maybe proves this moreso than most people. Rather than lash out at him, rather than show a lot of discontent, a lot of anger and all, I tend to sit back and I learn. And *me*, who appears always the more loving and giving, can really learn from Ross because I think, although maybe he doesn't always show it, this is what has kept your friendships going. Mine is a more showy giving, but his is a giving in a different way and I think the more I've thought about it since the other night, I thought about it since the other night, I thought about maybe he really *knows* the true sense of it. Because he can stop it, or he can be choosey with it. Whereas, someone said to me once, 'Gee, I didn't know Arlene and she hugged and she kissed me. And it made me feel so good. And then I saw her do it to other people, so I guess I'm not so special.' That has always stuck with me because with Ross, if you're special, you're really special and you may not always get it, but no one else is going to get it either. So, I look upon myself as a helpmate. I mean, I *really* bought the marriage vows. I bought them hook, line, and sinker. And, I believe in them.

"About the women, too . . . as you grow older, certain things aren't so important. And, if we've gotten to this good plateau, I don't know if it's the best thing to dwell . . . at certain times when things are happening, it's very sad, very shakey, and then yet you might think to yourself, since there wasn't any love of these people, I really didn't lose in a way. Maybe I lost just a little bit in trust momentarily. But in the long run maybe it was much better that there were certain encounters, so that we have reached *this* plateau, so I really don't want to . . . because I really don't know too much about it, and I don't care to. I don't want to dwell too much on that. Maybe it helped him, and that's what he needed. And maybe it helped now later on to get where we are.

"He has this charisma. Just like last night, you know, he had those people spellbound with his storytelling. He takes a lot of time with people. He doesn't let them tell much about themselves, but he reveals a lot about himself. So people find him, someone who is genuine, sincere, and will talk about himself. He doesn't want to be burdened with their problems or anything, whereas I do just the opposite. I talk very little about myself, and I encourage people to talk about themselves, I try to find solutions for them, and at first it's wonderful, because they just want to dump,

dump, dump and that's fine and I just keep finding creative ideas for them. But after a while, I either wear thin on them, or they feel strong in those areas and then will go elsewhere. But when you leave Ross, you feel like you know him pretty well and people want to, well . . . it's like a serial. He always leaves them with a hanger. He always leaves them with his new plans, and then people will see him years from now and say, 'Well, whatever happened with that dream wheel?' So, it's like once you plug in with him, you've got a continuing saga, and unless you do something really bad or whatever and he loses interest in you, this goes on and on and on."

The Potter of Chimayo
Chris Spanovich

A philosophy which shuts its eyes to
the creative fire in mans nature—to
the Eros or frenzy—cuts man's soul off
from the fresh bodily earthy effects of
life . . . and from the aesthetic and spiritual
of man's nature.
  —Jose Clemente Orozco

I sit here in the early morning, late winter darkness of the coop, just back from New Mexico. The sun has not yet risen. I know what is out there: how the trees hold to the turning earth, how blind white stones rise to the surface, how shadows wait to be released, how horses in the dark distance are huddled against fences.

Our world shapes itself in these dark moments before fire.

Of the people and the land a writer desires to know, it is the spirit of a person or place he truly seeks, and in that way loves again, makes himself whole again, and pulls images from fire to give form to his words, his story, his very life.

The potter, too, touches spirit-earth, spirit-sky, spirit-man in this way. Our bond is the language of hands, releasing visions within us, passing them on to others to see, to touch, to live amidst.

"Power," writes Chris Spanovich, the potter of Chimayo, New Mexico. I hear her voice this morning as I light the pinon incense, inhale the New Mexican desert-mountain air, and watch for the yellow line through the east window of my coop. I hold the roundness of her pot—sun, earth, moon—in my hands, feeling it femininely alive, mysteriously receptive, smelling of mesa and mountain, holding crow feathers, butterfly wings, pebbles, corn, starlight and rain water . . . holding the emptiness of the dreaming mind, which makes it real, seeking my own form in words once again, entreating earth, air, fire and water for extensions of our selves, diminishing the distance between us. "Power," the potter says:

> Under a different set of circumstances
> in another lifetime, I would use
> power for the softening of hardness,
> a lowering of loudness, a silencing of war,
> a spreading of positive energy in exchange
> for negativism, a bringing up of fallen
> spirits, or raising of self-esteem
> and imagery. To accept power and to be able to
> give it away.

221

The tool, the utensil, is an extension
of the fingers. Open, reaching, searching,
giving, receiving. Earth air fire
water: symbolized by tree-roots, wings
pots, ripples.

I step out and head down the road for my morning walk in Door, as I've often described, as friends here and in other places envision me doing. I am in touch with them, with it all, in this way. Wanderer. To be one man in many places at the same time. I left the warmth of spring in New Mexico. The sun. My own shadow in the arroyos, on mountain roads, against adobe walls. It is difficult to summon it here again in Door. I am still there. If there is a way back in, perhaps I will find it. The door is ajar.

The fields are melting. The snowline is retreating along the road's edge. The snow is honeycombed and brittle. The weeds, the wildflowers to come, are all flat and matted from the weight of the winter's snow. I hear soungbirds in distant trees, see meadowlarks gliding into patches of stubble openings in the snowy fields, watch three large ravens in my path, watching me. They ascend in silence so slowly, so sacredly, like black prayers to appease the red god of the coming light.

I walk the hard pavement into the rising fire, sightless, shadowless.

And the road softens, gives to sand and silt. I walk an arroyo, a dusty path. I journey to Chimayo to seek the potter once again, living beneath the mesa where ravens fly high over pottery shards of old Indian tribes.

In the village of Chimayo, with its old world ways, its ties to Spain, its weavers, just off the main road sits the El Santuario de Chimayo church, built in 1813-16, where pilgrims often visit the healing room near the sacristy. From a small hole in the ground, the physically ill, the crippled, the dispossessed reach for the healing powers of the miraculous earth. Along the walls are photographs, crutches, crucifixes, hand-carved crosses, pictures of Christ, notes, handwritten pleas and praises to God. To approach the threshold of the Santuario is to feel the power.

I enter, kneel, and rub the earth into my hands.

On the wall of the healing room a pilgrim left his poem:

I am blind, traveled many miles to Chimayo, a place I love, in its silence and peace I left this gift . . . a poem.

If you are a stranger, if you are weary from the struggles in life, whether you have a handicap, whether you have a broken heart, follow the long mountain road, find a home in Chimayo. It's a small Spanish town settled many years ago by people with a friendly hand, their culture lives today, they will tell stories about miracles in the land, since 1813 Santuario is the key to all good, a church built as graceful as a flower swaying in the summer breeze, nested in a valley protected by wild-berry trees.

In the dusty roads of Chimayo little children with brown faces smile, majestic mountain tops rule over the virgin land, when the day is done the sun falls asleep without regret, sleeping in the twinkle of a stary, stary night, it's that old country feeling in Chimayo I can't forget, in all the places in the world I have been, this must be heaven . . . .

—c. Mendosa
Las Cruces, New Mexico

The healing earth of New Mexico. It never allows a man to forget its powers . . . rising in mountains, resting in mesas, constantly moving in a fine dust touched by the sun . . . magically molded into mud houses . . . the very walls of the house the potter of Chimayo built beneath the mesa . . . the pots that come forth and appear and appear and appear between her muddy hands.

The dirt road to her place is difficult to find at times, almost impossible to maneuver in a heavy rain when the road and even the tiny narrow bridge may disappear in a wash. But then the sun appears and puts everything in place again. Water and fire. Elements of magic to humble a potter's hands.

The setting, the creative act, the woman . . . mysteries of doors touched by sun, other doors to be opened, new ways to be found. "The void is a great feminine secret," said Jung.

The potter reminds the writer of yet another, M.C. Richards, author of Centering *and* The Crossing Point: *"It is the idea of a DOOR . . . a portal, a threshold, a closing, an opening—a secret—and open secret—a sliding door turned into an open secret. This appeals to me, this idea of polarities, that something can be both open and secret; the fusing of opposites is at the very heart of the spirit of poetry. And the fusing of elements; earth, air, water, fire, is at the very heart of alchemy, a spiritual science, the art of nature and man."*

Opposites. The realization and source of all our powers. Day/night, black/white, sun/moon, yin/yang, water/fire, the closeness of Door/the spaciousness of New Mexico, reality/illusion, man/woman . . . the potter would know this. Making things one . . . the artist's work.

Though I visited the potter once before, with Ross LewAllen, though she served us food and drink, shared her work and life, led us up to mesa where Ross sketched canyons and whales, dug up old pot shards, took us to her secret place of birds, up and down new paths, past a field of horses, back to the warm walls of the studio/living quarters she built, walls of mud and straw asking to be touched, through the huge door of old wood and pressed tin . . . though I found her exceedingly kind, overly generous, fiercely independent, wonderfully alive in a Slavic ancestry we both share,

223

strikingly beautiful, amazingly clear . . . though I have kept in contact with her since then, I now approach her place, the dust of the Santuario on my hands, her presence, her very life, alone and with some trepidation. "Man's fear of woman is his fear of death, of darkness, of that chaos he is certain will overwhelm him if he does not hold to the light of his mind, to purity, to reason and the rule of law," says Michael Adam in Womankind: A Celebration.

As a writer of fiction, I have lived through this before and seem about to experience it again. I am reminded of the woman artist, a character I created in the short story "The Hour of the Sunshine Now." I am reminded of the woman in "A Distance of Horses." I knew neither of these women. They came from the dark, creative chaos of the writer . . . to emerge into form, into story. There was a dying and a living to them. But were they real?

> Woman remains close to the body and to the earth; a
> reminder to man of his roots and origin, and so of an essential
> part of his nature. Obeying laws that are not man-made or in
> any way subject to him, woman lives under the sway of the
> moon; red tides flow in her, from her; as a mother she is deep
> in the mire of the world, handling with sublime indifference,
> even with laughter, the piss and shit of her child, all that from
> which man would prefer to avert his eyes, his nose and mind,
> turning from all the dirt and disturbances of earthly life, to
> 'higher things.'
>
> —Michael Adam

The potter has haunted me, as the writer is haunted by any person who expresses something the writer himself needs to express. She is the same stuff those other characters were made of. She is of their very essence, womankind: "Come on . . . don't be afraid . . . I'm moist . . . my necklace is made of mud, my breasts are dissolving, my pelvis is wet. I've got water in my crevasses, I'm sinking down . . . In my belly there are pools, swamps . . . There's moss . . . big flies, cockroaches, sowbugs, toads. Under the wet covers, they make love . . . they're swollen with happiness! . . . My mouth trickles down, my legs trickle, everything trickles down, the stars run, trickle down, trickle . . . "—*Ionesco*

She is all that, and furthermore, she is real. Real in a way a writer of fiction imagines in the making of tales. Real in the way this dust of her dirt road covers my boots, real as the magpies that sweep through her trees, the horses that graze in the field, the shadows on the mesa, the sun glinting off the tin roof of her house. Real as the woman, the potter, Chris Spanovich first stands at the door, then steps out to meet me, her shadow spreading beside her, wandering the Chimayo earth.

The very earth we sit upon and talk . . .

It's actually really hard to find history on Chimayo, she says, because I've done a lot of research. I've tried to find it and there's very little written on it, other than the Santuario being the center, so to speak, of this community, or the draw, or why a lot of people originally settled here. But even so, that church isn't that old, 1812 or something. That's not old for history in New Mexico. The weavers, the Ortega family, have been here quite a while. They advertise as being seven generations of weavers. It is really a cottage industry. There are a lot of people in Chimayo who work for him in their own homes, which makes it very nice, particularly just as a

224

source of income. Otherwise, the distance for jobs is quite large. These people can remain home, work around children, baking bread, making tortillas and so forth. It works out well. But generally it seems as if the men do most of the weaving here. Looking in windows and seeing the looms, generally you will see a man working there. The environment here is right for what I do, but I feel that I can really do my work probably anywhere. I think I can live anywhere. But I'm grateful for being here.

I have only been making pots now for about six years. Prior to that I taught first grade, never for public schools, but only for private schools that somehow gave me permission to use creativity with children. I have always made things, or built things, put things together. I was always interested in doing things, be it sewing, a little bit of weaving, a little bit of painting, a little bit of a lot of things. And once pottery crossed my path, it was just something I felt I needed to pursue so that I would be able to know one thing well, rather than just dabble in lots of different things.

I stopped teaching first grade to take a journey around the world. I stopped teaching in May and left on this trek in September. It would have been, I guess, '75. Maybe '76. I don't remember. I did the trek around the world. That summer, prior to departing, I had saved up enough money to buy a potter's wheel and began to make pots.

I came to New Mexico when my husband was going to graduate school. We had made the decision to leave Southern California. We had gone to Africa . . . I eloped to Africa. We were gone about eight months. Then returned to California to finish school, and then at that point we knew it was time to move on to another location, so came to New Mexico with the excuse of graduate school, which lasted maybe two months . . . the University of New Mexico, though we didn't live in Albuquerque.

Early impressions of New Mexico? The idea of space, in contrast to L.A. The only thing I felt I really left behind in L.A. was a lot of money. The potential of making what's known as "a good income," which is what I was doing when I left. I went at that time from something like—this has been nine years ago, so the figures are distorted—from making $1500 a month to $350 a month. But, what I left was simply money . . . and gained a great deal more by the risk of moving.

The environment in New Mexico is right for any kind of craft. You're surrounded by some of the top people. You're constantly exposed to people who work in various disciplines. You're saturated with it wherever you turn, be it a handmade coffee mug or an Indian pot.

It felt right, making pottery. I needed to continue. I guess the hard part was growing up and believing that in order to exist in this world, you needed to have a job, as opposed to working, and that's something I feel I've learned: that it's the work that has to continue, and the job is for those who haven't found the work.

I now call them my 'killer pot series,' the things I first began to make. Great, thick-bottom mugs that are ugly. My mother has the original collection. Really terrible things, but actually I'm using them because they won't break. You can drop them and they sort of bounce. Making functional ware. That was the beginning. I guess that's what we all interpret clay as. Even now, the students, the first thing they want to do is throw on a potter's wheel. The *machine* seems to be the fascination. Because you can make something, rather than knowing that clay is many other things.

I was in Albuquerque six and a half years. And then from there to here. I was renting a really wonderful place for that time—11 acres, an old adobe with two fireplaces, apple orchards, a beautiful environment to work in. It was out, south of Bernadillo, out in the north valley of Albuquerque. Paying a hundred and forty

dollars a month rent. But then reached a point when I saw that as being endless, and that there were things with the house that needed to be done and because it wasn't mine, I couldn't do them. So I made the decision to become a home owner and spend a year and a half searching three areas that I felt drawn toward—one being in this area, one in Durango, Colorado, and one in northern California. And then set out to find . . . maybe it's a romantic dream . . . a small house that was in need of repair and quite cheap and, of course, really easy to fix up, that wouldn't cost much. And never found that. And I did not intend to build. I didn't think I could do that sort of thing.

I haven't taught school since I took up pottery. Why I'm in Chimayo, I don't know. It's almost like Chimayo has chosen me rather than me finding it. When I bought this piece of land, and the first day I came out to see it, there was a great deal of snow melting from the mountains, and the river was quite high. And the next day I came, the bridge was washed out, so I couldn't even get over here, and stood up by the highway with binoculars looking at this piece of land. And then I managed to get across. The bridge was out until August, so I had to move everything twice. Tons of clay and all the kiln bricks and so forth, because I had the whole setup by then down where I lived. I moved it to a friend's place and then transferred it over here another time.

The combination studio/living quarters sits behind us as peacefully and perfectly in place as the mesa which rises gracefully behind it. The same color as the earth, it *is* the earth shaped now by the hands of the potter into a suitable dwelling where she might live and work in one large room. To see it in sun is to try to imagine it graced by moonlight, firelight, darkened in rain, touched by snow. I recall "A Prayer of the Navajo Night Chant":

> House made of dawn.
> House made of evening light.
> House made of the dark cloud.
> House made of male rain.
> House made of dark mist.
> House made of female rain.
> House made of pollen
> House made of grasshoppers.
> Dark cloud is at the door . . .

I guess I get the credit for building the house. But the reality is that there's literally thousands of people, be it the lady at the post office who hands me a letter from somebody I enjoy hearing from, which gives me renewed energy, and somehow they are part of this. Or the funny little man down at the hardware store who, once I explain what it is I'm trying to do, he'll suggest an alternative way to doing it backwards. And, various people loaning a tool. Mostly what I need to know is the knowledge. I can do the work. I sort of see myself as not terribly bright, but I know how to work. So I rely on other people for the knowledge and don't mind asking questions. And usually ask the same questions of more than one person so at least I get a little clearer perspective of how something should be done.

The physical labor is mine, with the exception of . . . people mean well by their promises. "When you get to a certain point, let me know and I'll help." Then suddenly their mother's dead or their grandmother's sick or something. And that's fine. People give as I, when I can. Sometimes I can't. But things like lifting vigas . . . I of course couldn't do. I sat here for a week not knowing how to start, once the foundation was in. I couldn't figure out, "What do you do now?" And three people came out and showed me how to put up a corner. So, with the exception of the corners, the rest I put up. But that's because I understood what to do. So it was relatively simple.

I had two months, initially two months to get the walls up and sealed in for winter. I came her in the middle of August and in the middle of October I had another commitment, and everything was in a storeroom and put away and I was in a tent and winter was coming. Not liking to be cold, that was an incentive. To just keep going. So I built the studio first, rather than a house. I had to keep working. There's times when I wish I didn't, but I believe not only my work, but I would be different if the reality of it all wasn't there every day.

The development of my pottery . . . these were slow evolutions of meeting myself. The evolutions are really nothing, nothing real specific. I guess learning to believe in yourself. And trusting a feeling that happens inside. Watching and knowing. Learning to know what's right and not right.

I once saw pottery as fragile. I called it attachment, where everything was terribly important. And now none of it's important, but it's very important. I can go in and take on the shelf and pick them all up and throw them out and watch them crash . . . and that's a tremendous point for me to be able to get to. To be able to let all that go. Because, before, every *one* was so owned, and so possessed . . . very precious. But really, nothing's precious. And, every day, I've learned to enjoy the preciousness of the day, and what's going on. Life is magical, needs to be lived to its fullest, everyday.

What do people see in my pottery? I get everything from a lady in New York asking me if it'll go in her dishwasher—why somebody would put a $125 horsehair wrapped pot in a dishwasher for, I haven't quite figured out—to people who really stop and look at colors, at the shape of the color and the shape of the pot, and want to hold them. And some adults even lower themselves to smelling them, which of course is instantly what kids always do. They like the smell and the smoke. Lots of different kinds of feedback. Some don't understand why they should spend $50 on a pot when melmac coffee mugs are only 59¢. You know, they don't see something that you just look at and don't use as valuable in their life. So in many ways, for that kind of work, almost in some dimensions, it's a select audience. But that's okay too.

No, I don't tell people what they don't see, because you can't. You can't tell people these things. You know, you either see it, or you can't. You don't tell people those things.

Sure, it's all a slow evolution. And right now I think, you know, that's the frustration of working with porcelain. I've forgotten the slow evolution, the years that it took to reach the point where the primitive fired work is *right,* and now I'm disappointed, or was disappointed, the first two firings of porcelain being absolutely disastrous, and all the shapes distorted and now what I wanted and the color not right. You know, I've forgotten that those things take time. That everything takes time. I wanted results right away. Because maybe I've gotten spoiled with my own work. I know how to do it and do it well, and I can make lots of them now. And I will continue to do the primitive pots because the colors still give me pleasure. Every one is different, and everyone presents a different set of problem-solving experience. Does it need sticks? Does it need bones? Does it need to be left alone?

The pots are all slab construction. Thin, long, flat pieces of clay that are seamed together or paddled together to form essentially a roundness, a round-shaped pot. There is a bit of texture on them from the paddles that are wrapped in cord, fiber, or burlap and the seam. But the seams are left there. They're not smoothed out. It's a

228

non-smooth uniform pot because it is hand-built. Then they're basically fired in sawdust and a lot of other organic materials added to the sawdust to give shades of pastel from seaweed to eggshell, banana peels. All kinds of shit. I've bags of shit everywhere. Garbage . . . anything that burns gets thrown in and gives different color. There's no glaze, so that any of what you see visually comes from really the surprise of the fire. I guess it's the surprise and the unknown that keeps my interest.

After the firing they're all washed and scrubbed down in the ditch because there's a lot of carbon and residue on them. And then I use various things found in nature, either things I have found here, on the mesas, or from journeys to different parts of the world . . . different things I have picked up: sticks and feathers and beads and bones, grasses, roots, twigs. It must add another dimension to me too. We are related. Yeah, they, that also keeps me going. That's the problem-solving aspect I was talking about. Some pots I think become stronger. I call it almost a collaboration between my pots and what's out there. Combining the two of them into a oneness. And some of them need nothing. Some are strong enough left alone. And some I think benefit by an addition.

The shape of the pottery just felt right. The beginning shapes were . . . I see them as really clumsy, not right. I think right now the work is balanced between the shape and the color and what it represents, what's happening with it. All of those dimensions work. Whereas this new funny porcelain stuff, it's not a one-ness . . . it's all divided. The glaze is right, the shape is right, but somehow its not all right collectively. It's still separate. It's still in little compartments. But I feel that the primitive work is balanced. It's right.

When I'm working with clay, my mind wanders to foreign lands, special people, funny made-up scenes, unreal events. I have no philosophical artistic statement about my work. I hate art talk and people who feel they are "artists." I hope not to limit myself by a label. I'm many things. I make pots not to make a living but rather because I enjoy making them. In order to make a living, I sell my pots.

I'm just a peasant at heart. In all the places I've been in the world, I've been happiest in Africa. Which I guess, according to *National Geographic*, is the primitive

229

continent, though it seems very civilized. That's really civilization. I'm always glad to get back to Chimayo, which I call civilization, after doing an event in Dallas or Los Angeles or San Francisco. It makes much more sense to be here than out there. When I go to a large city, one of the things I know will happen is that I will not get to touch the earth for that week that I am there. I go from hotel room to the sidewalk, to the parking lot, to the van, to the place, to the concrete building, to whatever. And I miss my earth floor, or I feel the absence of it. As dusty, miserable and icky as my place is, it does have its joys.

Things are so simple in the primitive world. They're uncomplicated. They're all right there, if you can see them. I think there's more choices there. It's almost like things aren't defined. You have to define them yourself. Whereas, I'm not picking on Dallas, but things are defined . . . you just make the decision which slot you want to plug into. There's no risk. It's the risk–taking that keeps life interesting. There's not as many choices, say in Dallas, in some ways. I'm very judgemental, so I'm probably way offbase. It's just that the sun's nice. It makes you say funny things. It is a beautiful day.

It's perfectly civilized right there. Well, yes of course, anyone coming here from Dallas would say it's quite primitive . . . no electricity . . . heavens no! Priorities in life: I have a telephone! Running water? Well, sure it's running . . . down there in the ditch. I guess "primitive" is the awareness that it gives me, you know. Every day I am aware of how cold it's been in the morning, of how much water I've used. I, in one day's time, use less water than someone who flushes a toilet once. I've calculated it out. The seasons . . . there are four wonderful, distinct seasons here. Each of them presents different food, different clothes, different chores. I guess just because of living here my awareness of just the day-in and day-out things that are easy to forget, are brought into perspective . . . are there. They're just constantly there. And the idea of building is just a slow evolution too. I miss my juicer and toaster oven and blender. Life is different without those things. And perhaps someday, if it's feasible, there may be electricity. I have the choice, I suppose, of spending my money in the normal way—that you are supposed to build by bringing in power lines and sewage systems and all that. But I'd rather build the house so that I can live and enjoy it, and as time and money happen, then make those additions. That's down the road. Right now the thing I have to handle is straightening out the crooked foundation line for the new house. Yes, the new house. Soon I'll get to go home from work at night, which I look forward to. It's great fun living with your work, but I think, too, it's nice to close the door sometimes and go home and get out of the dust. The dust is hard. Though it's been a great adventure, my long-range plan is to be a bit more civilized. I didn't always live like this, Norbert . . . just slow evolution. I love shag carpets. No, I won't lose this. No, I will get to work here and go home over there to an earth floor, a traditional mud floor. I'll still be on the ground, just not as dusty. Linoleum isn't that bad!

I wake up very early in the morning. Usually by 4:30 or 5. Generally it's too dark to really start working on the pots. I wait until it gets light to do that. But I'll read, or there's always paperwork of one form or another to do. Yes, I'll be doing this under kerosene lamps. How romantic, yes. I'll let you know what my eyes are like in another five years. Oh yeah, I go outdoors at that time. It's wonderful. I have to. Outhouse is up the road. That's first on the list.

I suppose because I'm gone a great deal, I'm on the road a lot, that this time is just very valuable. It's just a real, almost meditative sort of time—or what people call meditation. It's just the beginning of another day. I'm a real morning person, although I think a lot of people wake up and build up through coffee or whatever and reach their peak at noon and then begin perhaps sliding down, and I start at the top and all day long head down. I start full of energy, ready to go, and by 5 in the afternoon, I'm ready to just fall asleep. I'm not much of a night person, though I can stay up if I need to. But generally I'll fall asleep by eight.

The light is everywhere at that time. It comes in everywhere. The light is really, I think, why a great many people who work in arts and crafts are here. The light's always there. There are very few days when there isn't sun. I've gotten quite spoiled by that. I realize that every time I go away . . . where there isn't light.

The colors of the mesa are quite wonderful at that time of day. Yes, and the shadows change. Every time you look up it's a whole new mesa. Up on top, once upon a time, I've never been able to specifically date this, but there was an old pueblo there so that the ground is full of pot shards . . . places where other potters lived.

Morning tea. Then go to work until about . . . I don't know. No electric toaster though. No Pillsbury popovers. It's hard defining the time. Probably about 10 or so I will make a nice, enormous sort of giant breakfast, eggs, a great big thick omelet, and as often as I can, homemade bread baked in the kiln, because I don't have an oven right now, and then work the rest of the day. And then eat again, eat an evening meal sometimes at 4 or 5. I always try to make sure I'm inside between 5 and 7. That's when NPR [National Public Radio] comes on, my link to the news and the great stories and tales of other people. Usually I have music on in the day, tapes of various kinds.

Yes, I can move right from the bed to the stove to the work area. That is an advantage of living with your work. Sometimes from the bed to the work and then remember I forgot to eat. That can happen too. It's an advantage because it is there always, and I can go to sleep and wake up and go finish something because it's dry and ready for me.

Evenings? Haul the water, heat it, have a glorious bath, get cleaned up, because the work is dirty . . . and letter writing to friends. I'm a letter writer, which I enjoy doing. Reading. There's always a pile of books and magazines or something. I try and keep something other than my ceramics books or magazines around to read. Then to bed early. My day starts early.

Sometimes I walk at night, if there's a full moon out. It's quite wonderful to walk because the light's easy. It depends on the season too, how long it's light. I don't know, that all changes. It just depends.

I like privacy. I like coming home, but I also very much enjoy people. I'm not here to hide. It's just a balance. It's a balance for me, going out into the public in cities doing shows or whatever and talking all day and being totally saturated with people, and then coming here and being saturated with myself. I do enjoy the privacy. I like being home.

I think everybody has to balance the commercial aspects, the risks, the changes for themselves, because we all have different goals and different priorities and different fantasies. I'm not supporting a family. I don't have three children that need to go to private school because the school system here is so terrible. I'm just dealing with myself. And so, everyone really, I feel needs to answer that for himself. In terms of the long range, what is it that I really want? I mean, in many ways I hope I never really know; otherwise, what's the point? I'd like to not know. People have it all sorted out. I'm not so sure if they're really on the right road. For me, I wouldn't be on the right road. Everyone needs to decide that for himself.

Money is important. Sure it's important. What it is for me . . . I feel you have to define for yourself and also just to what degree. Money is freedom. I've been poor. I don't like being poor. Money right now buys adobes for the new house. The

Volkswagen is old; it's going to go someday. I enjoy a nice bottle of wine rather than a bad can of beer. It's freedom. Then it depends of course how you choose to use it once you get it. That's for sure.

When did I grow up? After a death in the family . . .

She pauses after this—pauses frequently in her reflections—and I wait expectantly for her to explain the death. The incredible silence—then sounds of magpies in the trees, horses moving in a distant field. The sun merely intensifies the tranquility of the moment, of her own depths of the unspoken, even the unseen. The unseeing. The potter is a teacher of the blind. Since she appears unwilling to pursue this personal death, I approach her feelings about seeing and not seeing . . . how this may have affected her own life, her own work.

I had applied an received an NEA grant to be the artist in residence at the New Mexico School for the Visually Handicapped, which is in Alamogordo, in the southern part of the state, and I had a position there for two months, which meant that two weeks out of the month I was on campus and then two weeks paid essentially to do my own work at home. So it was a tremendous monetary break, and actually that in many ways was part of the beginning of the kind of work I'm doing now. One weekend with blind students from 5 to 21 years of age. We did a primitive

232

fired workshop out in back of the school and did wood firings, bark firings, sawdust firings. All different kinds of various firings. A lot of Indian students there. So many of them were familiar with the traditional dung firing, and I got very excited about the sawdust-fired work, and whenever I could, pursued that a bit more until the point where it totally consumed me and I essentially gave up the stoneware work, though I still will do that because it's a very tradeable thing, piece of merchandise, particularly in a community like this. I trade chili bowls for goat cheese. Stoneware platters I'm trading for vigas for the house . . . and people who trade often-times want to trade for something that's functional. I've traded wood for kitchen tiles and so forth. So, I still enjoy doing it. There's nothing like drinking your tea out of a stoneware mug.

Teaching the blind I realized what a visual world it was and how we are all making value judgments of each other through the initial visual experience. You take that away, you have to rely on other senses to judge people. The kids were very aware that, and I've seen this at different fairs I've done, where Martha and her friend Gertrude come in and point and say, 'Isn't that a pretty coffee mug. I'll buy it." Never trying it on, because it needs to fit you.

The students are, of course, obviously very tactile in pointing out all my flaws. "What's this bump here?" and "Gee this feels like the glaze ran," and of course, you know, it has. They're pretty perceptive. But also, they're just people, and I think one of the reasons why I've been effective there is that I don't see them as blind children. I see them as children, students, kids . . . and that's important. That you don't change just because they have that handicap. We're all handicapped. It just comes in different forms. Theirs is basically visual and that's why they're all here.

I don't know what their perception of me is. I had an interesting experience with one of the blind staff members who I got to know quite well. We'd only talked before. She asked me to her house for dinner one night and explained where her house was, and I drove there and came in and Sandy was cooking in the kitchen and I asked her, "Sandy, what do you know about me?" And she laughed and said, "Oh, this game. Everybody does this to me." She told me that when I talked to her that I look at her eyes. She knew that, that when I speak to somebody, that she knows I had this eye contact. And then she said, "I know you have long hair because the kids always tell me that." They're always touching it and talking about it. And she could, of course, tell by where my voice was coming from, as to the height. And then from conversations we had, she knew some other things about me. But I thought the eye contact was interesting.

The students there and some of the staff who are visually handicapped are perceptive differently than I realized. One night out on campus it was a full moon, and I asked some of the kids could they tell me where the moon was coming from, and they could. They could turn around and feel, sense where it was coming from, and were able to tell me what direction it was. There were some real mind-blowing things that happened there, in terms of being perceptive about color. One of them, she has no vision . . . surgically she's had her eyes removed, she has two glass eyes. And the stars moving made her sick. She had to be taken out of the room because of the motion. They think it was the motion. She was throwing up. A lot of strange things . . . you wonder really what vision is about.

They're acquainted with my pottery. They tell me it costs too much money. I think, in a lot of ways—Oh, look at the hawk!—in a lot of ways it's been good for them to know that pots don't have to be evenly round, that there's merit in things that are distorted and not machine-made. A lot of kids live out in different pueblos and reservations and, you know, generally kitchen dishes and so forth aren't handmade and so their experience with handmade work is limited. It's like a validation of their own crooked, clumsy beginnings.

They like the smell of my things, because they still have that smell in them. They've seen me do a lot of wheel work too, which I'd been working on with them. But I think one of the things, in one sense, I take pride in, though of course, if certain people knew it, they would have me abolished from campus, is that the majority of them don't know how to make pots. They use clay, really as a communication material, as a way of sharing and expressing things that, if they were fired, wouldn't make sense to anyone unless they had been there with us that day. I talk a lot with them about things like dreams. You know, how does someone without vision dream? And we talk about dreams and secrets and I have them make a container for a secret they have. Although sometimes things get fired, they want them fired, but to me teaching and working with clay isn't going in and making a little hanging planter. I mean, you can do that anywhere.

One of the students was about 16 when he lost his vision through some disease. It was very quick. Within two weeks he went totally blind. He told me now that he is blind he dreams in very vivid colors, which he knows he didn't dream before. All his dreams are wild, wild colors. And the one of the students who, of course these things are hard to translate . . . what they are saying may not be, they may be using the same words, but they may be different concepts because we're not starting on the same ground. He has never seen. He said that his dreams are not visual, but he hears . . . the visual image is during the day, which is basically, you know, no light. It's not black. But he dreams in sounds and smells. And the other senses. But again, I don't know whether we are communicating. You know, like to us, a hanging sign that says "exit" with an arrow is giving motion, but it's really not moving, it's really hanging there. And so we've got different references. It's hard to interpret and translate.

Some of them are good storytellers, especialy the Indian kids. It's part of their background. Some of them tell wonderful stories to the dorm parents as to where they've been and why their bed is stuffed with pillows, and why the window's open and they've been missing for five hours. They're delightful! And they steal cars, and they do all those things regular kids do. The last episode was two students caught stealing one of the state cars, and the kid driving was totally blind and the one riding in the passenger seat had some vision, was directing him: slow down, turn right, go left . . . you know. They're delightful. Great kids.

One time I had a conversation with an artist, a painter, and he asked me if someone were to say to you, or to me, "What are you?" my first word would have been a person. That's my gut feeling. I feel I'm a person. His response was that he was an artist and that seems like such a label. One of the best artists I've ever seen or met is the gardener down at the blind school who has the most beautiful rose garden, the most well-tended, elegant rose garden, and for me it's almost like it doesn't matter what you do. It's more an attitude. Be it digging a ditch or having a lumber mill in Truchas. I don't define the arts as I suppose they're usually defined.

An obligation to help others . . . it depends on the person, I suppose. Some people would be disastrous in a sharing kind of position. Some people hide in their work. You know, it becomes an excuse not to deal with other people. I think you get what you give. And I enjoy receiving from the students at the school. I certainly wouldn't want to do it fulltime. I know a lot of the staff members there, and they are different than I because I'm not there all the time. I'm there a few days out of the month and that's it. I just kind of check in on the visiting artists that are there now. It's certainly not fulltime.

Oh probably I'll drift in and out of things. Lots depends on the circumstance. Teaching gives me a tremendous amount. It's all part of that balancing, of keeping all, all what's right . . . all balanced.

I grew up with a mother who was Catholic and went to church just in case there might be a heaven, and a father who went off to the high Sierras fishing because he felt that's the closest to God he would ever get. So, I had a little bit of both, I guess.

It's defining religious—religion and spirit, I suppose. I see myself as a spiritual kind of person. Again, religion almost seems like . . . I don't know. It seems very limited to choose a certain kind of religion when all of the religions in some form or another give you something.

I listen to these people (who have been to India, who speak of having their auras balanced, people on various spiritual quests) because, I suppose that's why they . . . I'm sorry it took that much . . . well, I just think that's an outer directed thing. People are outer-directed, looking for an answer, or you're inner-directed and you find your direction within yourself, I suppose, to obtain what's the inner thing.

Why does there seem to be so much of it here? I think New Mexico attracts people who can live nowhere else in the world or can live anywhere else in the world. It's almost like a refugee camp. Perhaps you just see it more her than, say, Southern California, because there aren't as many people here. Maybe there are still all of the different groups. Where in California there's just a zillion people, so maybe it's just a little more cluttered. But here, without as many people, maybe it surfaces more noticeably. And in Santa Fe, of course, the center of it. And that's where you've been.

Through the huge door, inside the studio/living quarters, the sun pouring through a large window overlooking the mesa, there are shadows everywhere. The smell of earth. Earth walls, earth floor, dust of the earth on the potters hands . . . a radiance of earth everywhere. There is a long table where she works, and shelves stacked with the soft round forms of her pots, seemingly alive and resting there, lurking in shadows, awaiting touch, light, some moment of ceremony. They suggest a feeling of comfort in the night, licked by lamplight, alleviating whatever loneliness may enter the potter's domain.

Near the far end of the room sits a table, a woodstove, shelves filled with kitchen items and clothing, her bed in the corner. A natural orderliness of daily life permeates the premises. She is cooking a pot of black bean soup for lunch. There is bread on the table, wine, brandy, her pottery . . . all the simple essentials for the memorable repast in a potter's mud hut in Chimayo with the door open and the sun blazing and the birds calling and horses neighing and shadows painting the mesa and the dust everywhere and on our hands.

She is an attractive woman, ageless, living a simple, solitary life of work and art and meaning. And I am not the first, now will I be the last man to realize this. Amidst the attraction of such beauty of presence and peace often appears the very human desire to possess. The feeling that by merely having someone, some thing, some of whatever "it" is that speaks to us unconsciously, we might become our selves. . . .

Since we live in a partiarchy, masculine values based on masculine qualities are the prescribed modes of thinking. Women take on the dark side of this; the other side of the coin is the after hours of the "real" world. Women's thinking is non-thinking. Their knowledge is taboo. Only artists and poets, madmen and saints, dare tamper with it, and their products are enjoyed but marvelled at, and their lives are envied, but are suspect and seem cruelly tragic because so much happens in them . . . Men need the qualities they project on women. We believe because of our conditioning that a man is not a man if he has any of the qualities he gets rid of by claiming that they are exclusively female. He knows unconsciously that he needs those qualities, that is why he is drawn to certain women, women who display outwardly the qualities he has hidden within himself, in the dark shadows of his psyche. You see, he doesn't really get rid of these human qualities by projecting them onto women; they are repressed. In order to be manly, a man cannot be himself, he has to repress all femine qualities. This does violence to the psyche. It is no wonder a man wants to possess a woman who is all of those qualities he is missing. She will be an extension of himself, devoid of individuality. She must be receptive to what he projects, she becomes the projection. Her intuition, her peculiar kind of intelligence is geared to this by her conditioning. This is how she fulfills her role as mate to man . . . The tragedy of this situation strikes at both sides. A man may seem to have individuality and dignity . . . the tragedy on the other side is that a woman doesn't even have this false individuality and dignity. She is only part of the man, like Adam's rib. She depends on her man for an appearance of dignity. She has individuality and dignity vicariously. She must repress that part of her psyche that demands these things and project this part onto her man. He opens all doors for her, he blazes a path through the world for both of them. One wonders what men do with their emotions and what women do with their aggressions. What does a man do inside himself when he would weep? What does a woman do inside herself when she would be forceful and take over a situation? There must be murders and imprisionments inside, amputations and other tortures, punishments and deformities . . . Where then do we find men and women who are truly individuals, who are truly themselves? Artists and poets, and other outsiders are escapees from our tragic conditioning. Not that one can escape from it easily but one can at least look at it from the outside, give up the comfort of the herd in hopes of finding the truth. The outsiders experiment with what they have: visions and premonitions, intuitions, hoping to regain the lost paradise of the psyche when it is whole.

—Ruth Hoebel

I seem to attract generally two kinds of men, one being really weak and looking for a place and someone to take care of them, and the other is somebody who is . . . this is hard to explain . . . I've never put it into words. Somebody who seems to see me as aloof and someone to be afraid of. Kind of two extremes. Somebody who sees what I do, they take it personally. They see it as an independence that can't be . . . that can't be . . . I can't get this out . . . and it has nothing to do with our lunch. I think sometimes my independence is a threat to them, yes. These are generalizations, you know, about just a few male crossings in my life.

Sometimes I feel that I'm bait. I don't know, sometimes I can just feel that. And it's very . . . there's a very nice thing about knowing that, in spite of the beginning sagging tits and crow's feet appearing, that I'm still attractive. I mean there's lots of very nice things about that too. But also, it can take from me, it can drain from me, dealing with people's feelings, someone that I want to believe, wants to come by for tea and chat, when really I'm very naive. That's the naive side of me. I like to believe people.

Men have provided many chapters to my life. I'm grateful for all I've learned about myself. Masculinity is an admirable quality. Macho shows the lack of inner evolution. I appreciate masculinity as much as femininity in a man. The key seems to be balance. It's important for me that the man in my life be an addition and not in place of, or a compromise in any form. I sometimes wonder about that "need to feel taken care of" in the majority of women. Responsibility for oneself in all forms is an important dimension. Not many females seem to set that as a priority. Probably males either. Maybe the two are only different in the way they do or don't do it.

I don't see myself as part of the woman's movement at all. It doesn't interest me. That's one of those things where you can sit around and talk about it, you can go to school and study it . . . you can go to school and study pottery, or you can go make pots. You can sit around and talk about it or do it. I guess I'd rather do it than worry about it. There's only 24 hours in a day. Time to me is precious, and it's real hard if I feel like energy is being taken from me. And some of that is sapping!

Just "plain old femimine" is wonderful. Oh, that's great indeed. I like those aspects too. Sometimes even here by myself, after a hard day of working, I'll have this glorious bath and get all dressed up and have a nice meal.

Dressed up and nowhere to go? Oh, but I'm *here*! So I'm somewhere. I dress for myself.

I see myself compromising as far as my work and any relationships. Sacrificing sounds a little one-sided. And lopsided. Sure, compromise sometimes mean sacrifice. Yeah, and that's hard for me because I'm basically real bossy and like my own way. I'm real terrible at that. And ever moreso after living by myself these years, because it's my own routine. I do this for myself. Over Christmas time, having a visitor for two weeks was very interesting. You know, if I put a coffee mug down, I know right where it is and, you know, suddenly here is someone else's coffee mug and a book over there on *my* work table! The old expression of the loving being the easy part and the living being the hard part made good sense. To be married again? If that happens, that would be fine. That would be quite wonderful. There's something special about sharing a life. I guess it would be . . . there would be different rules and different . . . it would be different than the first time, I'm sure, because I'm older now and feel I have more of a direction than when I was 21.

Marriage among artists . . . some of them work and some of them don't, and some of them are . . . I think most people don't want to take the risk of being by themselves. They would rather be with someone than by themselves. It's harder being by yourself in some way. Of learning yourself. It's scary. Why some of them work, I don't know. It's different, different personalities, different situations.

Fears . . . I'm sure there are some. I guess I try not to think about them. I think about living here alone and about what the neighborhood is like. People carry guns, and they don't think. They react and they think later. There's no lock on the door. But, I just try to leave those things open. It sounds very stupid, but I think if I ever worried about what this immediate enviroment really was like, or what it could be like—the unemployment, the drugs, all this business, you know, it's quite terrifying. But I do try to see the beauty of it and take that energy.

I don't know if you can ever be close to these people. I mean, I am who I am. My name isn't Martinez. It's Spanovich. So right away I'm already out. I came here with an appreciation and admiration for what was here, rather than certainly trying to change anything. There's a family bond that's here that's very strong and a real tradition in terms of the family unit. Which is interesting to watch. I sort of poke around and find out about it.

I've had neighbors bring me, on my birthday, a neighbor brought me three T-bone steaks from a cow they had butchered the day before. And I've been given pork chops from a butchered pig and fresh farm eggs if someone's coming to visit . . . a few gifts like that. But basically I'm very low profile and mostly stay by myself here. People will come and check on their animals in the fields, and if I'm out they stop and chat about the weather or farm animals or whatever.

I don't know what they think of me. They know I know how to work hard. They watched me build this place. I'm hoping they respect that. I hope that. Mostly people are very friendly. There are a lot of people that are beginning, well on the highway between here and the post office, to at least wave. I don't know who they are, where they live, but it's a face that seems to know me. And of course I would stand out more than they would stand out to me, just because of driving a Volkswagen bus. That alone.

I identify strongly with my Yugoslavian background. I feel in lots of ways that gives me a certain amount of strength. I can identify this community is one sense with Bovic, where my family is from in Yugoslavia. The idea of just the small little family trying to make a living off their bit of land. There are a lot of similarities . . . though Uncle Vaso doesn't ride around in a lowrider . . . there is some contrast. Yeah, I feel very strongly because of that. I feel a great foundation because of that and somehow I seem, it's probably because of the name, I guess that's part of what I feel, a stronger association with my father's family than my mother's. I don't identify with that near as much as my father's side.

I was back there six years ago, visiting the farm. That particular farm has been in the Spanovich farms for over 200 years, and I'm afraid it's possibly the last of it. Again, as we were talking earlier . . . not that condos are coming in, but there aren't anymore children that choose to stay out on the farm. They've all gone to the city. There's one son that's left there, and he's probably in his early 50's. When he goes, I don't know what will happen. I've often thought of going back and saving it all, but that's a romantic fantasy too.

I can swear in the language, ask for potatoes and 'where's the bathroom?', that's about it. No, I'm sorry for that. My father felt he was doing me a great favor by not using the language because my mother didn't speak it. So I don't know it.

I don't know if my father or relatives understand my life here in Chimayo in relation to the home country. No, we've never talked about it. I know more of Yugoslavia than my father does. Much more. I care more than he, I think. And as far as those people, I don't know . . . the people who are there. I've sent photographs and so forth, but there's always this complication of translation. I have some cousins that speak English that do the translating, but they to be spending their time at the disco and not have enough time to do these tasks.

Dying, death, aging . . . oh yeah, I think about all that. I know it can happen anytime. And so far I'm not really sorry for much of what I have done. I don't know if there's . . . I think you can distort hindsight and say that you would change this or change that, but at the moment, it's the moment. That, if you have made a decision at that moment, that was right for then, then it was right and as you grow older and look back, that's something else. Because you have different knowledge than you had then. And, so far I'm glad for the things I have done. There is always lots to do and more places to go and goals to accomplish. But, it's like when I go away from here I know that I can come back and the windows might be knocked out and everything damaged inside, but for the last, well, since I've been here, it's given me so much pleasure that at least I have that. We have to let go of those things, those attachments. You have to be able to let go of them so that you can really, fully have it. I have neighbors down the road that don't leave their house without a house sitter. They're so afraid to be ripped off. They hide the possessions that are of monetary value that are important to them. Yet they hide them so that no one will see them, so that someone won't steal them. What's the point of having them? What's the point? You know, in order to enjoy them you have to be able to let go of them, otherwise, if you fight it, it's going to be taken. You have to resolve those battles, the attachments.

Growing older . . . I'm going to be an old bitch when I'm old! I'm going to be awful. Crochety and terrible. And if I get sick, it's going to be awful. I'm miserable when I don't feel well. I'm just awful.

I can't wait for my gray hair and I don't have any yet. None. I keep looking . . . where is it? Where is it? No gray hair. Even my younger sister has gray hair!

Let's talk about that death . . .

Those were secrets, I told you!!!

Okay. Let's talk about the death aspect of a relationship . . . You want to cover your mouth, huh?

It depends on the question.

Whether it's a physical death or whether it's a spiritual death . . . can that change one's whole course, one's whole life, one's beliefs?

It can twist your head around to re-evalute your own values. It can make you think, examine the security.

You know, when I come to this area of the country, from very early on, I've always had . . . well, death is one of my favorite things, of course . . . in all its forms. And I see it really "lived" here, in a sense. That's one of the attractions. You know what I mean? Do you relate to that at all? Whether it's the Chicano, Spanish, Indian . . . it seems closer. And it seems more celebrated. I see it in people, in paintings, art work, the Penitentes, and I see it . . . well, just going down the road here, coming into Chimayo, on the edge of the road, the white crosses . . . that kind of thing.

Is death like passion?

It is to me.

I think it's a passion. I think there's a lot of passion here, which is death or life . . . as kind of the extremes.

Even in the local church here, the Santuario, there is something very grim yet . . . .

Mmmm . . . it's very heavy.

But it's very holy, and it's very sacred, and something very living and even joyful about it. I try to visit the Santuario every time I come here. I don't know exactly why. Part of it is perhaps a throwback to my Catholic childhood which remains part of a man's psyche forever. I don't know just what it does to me, but I feel good going in there, and I like to experience the whole scene, the church, the altar, the healing earth . . . the messages of the people . . . the memontos of miracles. It reminds me of Mexico, of Greece, of the old country . . . a primitive grasp of spirit. The Indian. And it is depressing, I guess, to a certain extent, but it doesn't effect me so much that way. I see wild color and gold and fire and extraordinary faces. Worshippers. And I'm so far removed from that where I live. I want to be closer to it.

I think it's energy. People . . . depending on you, the person, you can go in and interpret all that energy as negative or positive. As heavy or as a celebration of joy. It's like two kinds of energy meeting each other. That's why I like to go there and sit sometimes. There's just so much presence of so many people in so many states. And depending on where I am at, whether I am tired or feeling slightly bummed out or feeling very happy, whatever, oftentimes makes a difference on what's received, going in, into that church.

You don't know a hell of a lot about me. We've known each other about a year or so. Just by, perhaps, some of the things I've written and we've talked about in letters . . . can you understand a Midwesterner's attraction to this area?

I can understand anyone's attraction to this area, but it also takes a certain kind of person to be attracted. Sure. Do you think people are like their work? Do you think there's a correlation? Do you think maybe I might know more than what your words say in your books, about you? By what you choose to write about? I just know other dimensions of you, besides what you choose to talk about . . . I mean the things you write about. Whether it's fiction or nonfiction . . . they are dimensions of you.

Inside her adobe there is the primitive, joyful sound of South American flute music, while outside everything appears radiant in the bright afternoon sun. I stand out there looking for the sun above the mesa and momentarily lose my sight. I rub my hand over the warm wall of the adobe till my vision is restored and two shadows appear.

"Would you like to ride horses?" she says. "I can get some horses. Or would you rather save that for next time? It's getting late."

We begin a slow ascent by foot toward the mesa. The earth gives way like powder beneath my steps, releasing small clouds in our pathway. The further we climb, the further the world recedes behind us.

Beneath the mesa I see rows of her large round pots occasionally planted upside down in the earth. Pots that did not fire correctly, she explains, cracks or breaks or pots she simply doesn't like. They of are value to her, though, visually in this way, seen from afar. They appear to be part of the land and land forms, she says. The colors are the same. They seem to belong there. They are also wonderful drums, she says, each with a different sound, some quite beautiful and some a bit flat. Sometimes I come up here to play them, she says.

We reach a place beneath the mesa where the very sky seems within grasp, where her house, a pasture of grazing horses, a distant church, the village of Chimayo, mountains and horizon all seem both too insignificant and too vast to comprehend. To just be there in such silence and light is quite enough.

From behind, the shadows of the mesa stretch toward us, and as we turn she waves to somewhere above where the ravens live. Watching her hand, I lose her in the sun . . .

. . . as I remember her now, this moment in Door, walking this very flat road, the sun having risen well above the line of trees, the lake beyond, and the ravens scattered in the wind.

She was the woman, the fiction, I created in "The House of the Sunshine Now," and she was the woman I imagined in "A Distance of Horses." That woman, that spirit, more importantly. And she had become partly real now, but for the purposes of the writer's spirit, should remain forever unattainable. For possession is a way of dying, be it a person, an object, or a landscape. We live by letting go.

The season is turning to spring in Door . . . as I now turn and head back, down the road, toward the door of the coop. The ice is breaking in the bay, and the woman of clay is standing high on the warm bright earth of Chimayo, shaping the earth again in new ways. And I want to be everywhere and love everyone.

Wandering back down the road I find my shadow in front of me. Light is pouring through the crescent-moon spaces of my arms . . . my shadow arms plugged into my pockets. I am all one. More complete in darkness. All the rough edges shaped smooth. An absence of texture and detail . . . no eyes, no ears, no nose, no mouth, no hands. I am stretching, extending beyond the confines of my body, stepping out into myself . . . as in fiction . . . in the way Ross stepped into his paintings . . . in the way the potter opens emptiness onto form . . . in a way a man might walk right through the final door.

On the road ahead of me, a single raven awaits my shadow, lifting it like a small black cross above the road, across the field into the horizon.

I am moving in a floating way, in shadow and light, in the way I began. And no one can tell whether there is joy or sadness to my face. Not even I.

The Indians refer to it in English as 'wandering'. They say of a certain man, 'He is wandering', or 'He has started to wander.' It would seem that under certain conditions of mental stress an individual finds life in his accustomed surroundings impossible to bear. Such a man starts to wander. He goes about the country, traveling aimlessly. He will stop here and there at the camps of friends or relations, moving on, never stopping at any place any longer than a few days. He will not make any outward show of grief, sorrow or worry. In fact, he will speak of what is on his mind to no one, but anyone can see he is not all right. He is morose, uncommunicative. Without any warning, he will get up and go. People will probably say of such a man: 'He has lost his shadow. He

ought to get to a doctor to get it back for him before it is too late.' . . .
Wandering is something that may unfortunately befall any man or
woman, and it can take many, many forms. It may end up in complete
loss of soul, and lingering death. When an Indian becomes convinced
that he has lost his shadow, he will let himself die out of sheer
hopelessness. Or it may result in temporary madness. The Indian never
courts pain. It would never enter his head to imagine that by making
himself miserable and pitiful in the eyes of the Powers he might gain
their sympathy and aid . . . In order to gain their friendship, in order
to approach them without scaring them away, it is necessary to lose
one's own humanhood and become as wild as possible, as crazy as
possible . . . When you have become quite wild, then perhaps some of
the wild things will come to take a look at you, and one of them may
perhaps take a fancy to you, not because you are suffering and cold, but
simply because he happens to like your looks. When this happens, the
wandering is over, and the Indian becomes a shaman.
                    —Jaime de Angulo

Other Books by Norbert Blei . . .

The Watercolored Word (1969)
" . . . is a fanatastic (no overstatement) have enter the world of poem . . . "
—Small Press Review

The Hour of the Sunshine Now (Story Press, 1978)
"Blei quietly experiments with the Surreal, with poetry, myth, image . . . a man to watch."
—Publisher's Weekly

"A worthwhile addition to collection of modern fiction."
—Library Journal

"One of the best writers in the Midwest."
— Henry Kisor, Chicago *Sun-Times*

"He has all the equipment, skills, discipline, and scope of vision, plus an invaluable element, a fine, deep sense of humor."
— Don Skiles, *American Book Review*

The Second Novel (December Press, 1979)
"One hundred years from now *The Second Novel* will be in print regardless of what else Norbert Blei writes . . . because it is a great book."
— Harold Grutzmacher, Door County
Advocate

" . . . an intriguing revelation of the process as process, or artifice as artifice, often humorous, as directly relating the throes of writing can only be."
—Library Journal

Door Way (Ellis Press, 1981)
"A fascinating assemblage of profiles that adds up to a vivid, feeling portrait of a region."
— Studs Terkel

"I predict that, someday, his Door County will join the great mythical-real landscape that include Salinas, Spoon River and Yoknapatawpha."
— Harry Mark Petrakis

"Blei has a fine ear and a genuine, searching, feeling humanity that is evident in dozens and dozens of observations."
— John D. Callaway, Chicago *Tribune*

"I honestly believe it is a small American classic, and if there were any justice it would be read — and taught — widely."
— Willard Manus

" . . . a necessary option. Blei, who has been widely published, writes of Door County, Wisconsin in a way that brings it and the lives of its people vividly to the imagination. Not to be missed."

—*Library Journal*

" '*Door Way* was so good, I couldn't put it down,' my friend shouted to me across the street."

—Joe Garceau, Door County *Advocate*

"Not a slick brochure for the tourists, it's something more worth having—a sometimes amusing, sometimes poignant, but always honest glimpse of a special region and some of its inhabitants, including a talented writer who chose to live there, at least for a while."

—Robert Wells, Milwaukee *Journal*

"This book on its very simplest level gives us a sort of inside view. Without it, Door is more and no less than what we see on the postcards, in the travel brochures, or on the single dimensional slides Cousin Jim and Agnes took during their summer vacation. Until now, we have not seen the Door with any true sense of depth . . . This book, in fact, puts Blei in line with a few others, for the crown—now shared by Terkel and Norman Mailer—of masters of the most personal kind of journalism, so real, so true, it is almost fiction."

—Chris Halla, *Wisconsin Trails*

"Helped by the photos, the art work, the art objects, the book jacket (all done by the people of the book, the book itself become artifacts), eventually all facets come together. And it's strange: what seems a book of stories about people is really a book about place. Both groups of residents have internalized that outward sea and landscape and both maintain a love affair with it. So that what seems a focus on individuals becomes a focus on landscape and its subtle power."

—Richard Boudreau, *Wisconsin Academy Review*

Adventures in an American's Literature (Ellis Press, 1982)
Blei's novel is a satirical, comical look at the high school English class . . . (It) should prove particularly entertaining to anyone involved in teaching high school English. It would certainly help the general public understand what really goes on in the American High school. This book will provide valuable perspective to any undergraduate considering teaching as a career. *Adventures in an American's Literature* will help provide prospective teachers realize that the high school classroom is not all lesson plans and behavioral objectives."

—*Choice* review service

Door Steps (Ellis Press, 1983)
"In *Door Steps*, Blei turns inward as he records a calendar year's thoughts, impressions and feelings—'little pieces of the day and night that add up to a year in a man's life.' We begin to know Blei more intimately than we did his neighbors in the previous book."

—James Gollata, Mount Senario College

"A pleasant, vicarious journey through the seasons that conveys some of the intensity and immediacy of weather and the natural world that are so much a part of that life."

—Barry Silesky, *Chicago* Magazine

"Blei does what a poet has to do. He shows us a fresh way of looking at things, by milking words of their potential for sound and meaning."

—Ron Grossman, *Chicago Tribune*